P9-CCO-379

THE CARBOHYDRATE ADDICT'S DIET

THE LIFELONG SOLUTION TO YO-YO DIETING

THE CARBOHYDRATE ADDICT'S DIET

by

Rachael F. Heller, M.A., M.Ph., Ph.D.

Assistant Clinical Professor, Mount Sinai School of Medicine, New York, New York; Assistant Professor, Graduate Center of the City University of New York, New York, Biomedical Sciences Program

and

Richard F. Heller, M.S., Ph.D.

Professor, Mount Sinai School of Medicine, New York, New York; Professor, Graduate Center of the City University of New York, Biomedical Sciences Program; Professor, Bronx Community College of the City University of New York, Department of Biology and Medical Laboratory Technology

A DUTTON BOOK

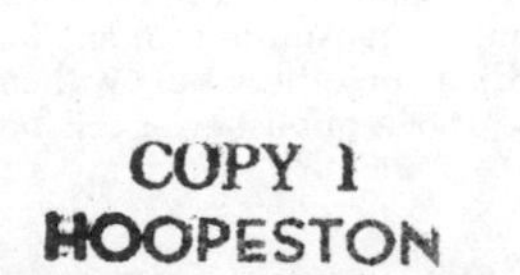

The information in this book reflects the authors' experiences and is not intended to replace medical advice. It is not the intent of the authors to diagnose or prescribe. The intent is only to offer information to help you cooperate with your doctor in your mutual quest for desirable weight levels and health. Only your doctor can determine whether this regimen is appropriate for you. Before embarking on this or any other weight-loss program, you should consult your physician. In addition to regular check-ups and supervision, any questions or symptoms should be addressed to your physician. In the event you use this information without your doctor's approval, you are prescribing for yourself, and the publisher and author assume no responsibility.

The dialogue, quotes, biographical facts, and anecdotes recounted in this book are actual and true-to-life; they come from hundreds of detailed interviews. No individual has been directly quoted nor described unless specific written permission was obtained. All names used in this book have been changed to protect anonymity.

DUTTON
Published by the Penguin Group
Penguin Books USA Inc., 375 Hudson Street, New York, New York 10014, U.S.A.
Penguin Books Ltd, 27 Wrights Lane, London W8 5TZ, England
Penguin Books Australia Ltd, Ringwood, Victoria, Australia
Penguin Books Canada Ltd, 2801 John Street, Markham, Ontario, Canada L3R 1B4
Penguin Books (N.Z.) Ltd, 182–190 Wairau Road, Auckland 10, New Zealand

Penguin Books Ltd, Registered Offices: Harmondsworth, Middlesex, England

First published by Dutton, an imprint of New American Library,
a division of Penguin Books USA Inc.
Distributed in Canada by McClelland & Stewart Inc.

First Printing, March, 1991

10 9 8 7 6 5 4 3 2

REGISTERED TRADEMARK—MARCA REGISTRADA

Library of Congress Cataloging-in-Publication Data

Heller, Rachael F.
The carbohydrate addict's diet : the lifelong solution to yo-yo dieting / Rachael F. Heller and Richard F. Heller.
p. cm.
Includes bibliographical references and index.
ISBN 0-525-24953-2
1. Low-carbohydrate diet. I. Heller, Richard F. (Richard Ferdinand), 1936– . II. Title.
RM237.73.H45 1991
613.2′5—dc20

90-21304
CIP

To the untold numbers of carbohydrate addicts who,
deep down, have always known that it was not their fault

ACKNOWLEDGMENTS

We wish to express our appreciation to the following people:

John Gallagher and Hugh G. Howard (Gallagher/Howard Associates, Inc.)—for their help at every step of the way, from proposal to galley and beyond. Their knowledge and talents were invaluable.

Elizabeth Lawrence—for her expertise and talents in helping to make our meal plan and recipe section interesting and exciting.

Alexia Dorszynski, our editor, whose intelligent comments and hard work have helped to make this book a reality. Thanks to Ms. Dorszynski's assistant, Kristin Olson, and to the other editors, publicists, and staff at New American Library who assisted in the preparation and presentation of this book.

Elaine Koster, our publisher, and Arnold Dolin, Vice President of New American Library—for their integrity, commitment, and belief that good science could also make good copy.

Professor Ronald E. Gordon, Ph.D., Director of Electron Microscopy, Department of Pathology, Mount Sinai School of Medicine; Mr. Norman Katz, Supervising Technologist of Electron Microscopy, Department of Pathology, Mount Sinai Medical Center; and Mrs. Madeline Katz—for their helpful suggestions, comments, and encouragement.

Mr. Norman Katz and Mr. Glenn Maffei, Department of Pathology, Mount Sinai Medical Center—for their fine photographic and technical assistance.

Professor Alan L. Schiller, M.D., Chairman, Department of Pathology, Mount Sinai School of Medicine—for his enthusiasm and support.

Professor Daniel P. Perl, M.D., Professor of Pathology and Psychiatry, Director, Neuropathology Division—for his intelligent suggestions and comments.

Linda Birnback, editor, ARCO Division of Simon and Schuster—for important assistance that helped get this project under way.

Barbara Grossman, then senior editor, Crown Publishers, who believed in this book from the start—for her enthusiastic encouragement and comments.

Larry M. Carlin, Esq., our attorney, counselor, and friend—for advice and suggestions coming from his fine mind and good heart.

Diane Bean—for her enthusiastic encouragement as well as her creative and intelligent suggestions.

The Apple Computer Company—for developing the user-friendly MacIntosh computer that was invaluable in the preparation of all written and graphics materials.

The hundreds of hardworking physicians and scientists—whose research findings contributed to the recognition of carbohydrate addiction as a biologically based problem that can be treated successfully.

The many carbohydrate addicts with whom we have worked over the years—whose stories, experiences, challenges, and triumphs helped pave the way.

CONTENTS

PART III. LIVING THE GOOD LIFE

PART IV. LOW-CARBOHYDRATE MEAL PLANS AND RECIPES

APPENDIXES

Car-bo-hy-drate ad-dic-tion: A compelling hunger, craving, or desire for carbohydrate-rich foods; an escalating or recurring need or drive for starches, snack foods, or sweets.

Carbohydrates may include, but are not limited to: breads, bagels, rice, pasta, potatoes, ice cream, chocolate, pie, cookies, crackers, cake, danish, fruit and fruit juice, potato chips, pretzels, and popcorn.

HEALTH AND DIET RECOMMENDATIONS AND THE CARBOHYDRATE ADDICT'S DIET

A number of well-respected individuals and organizations—such as the Surgeon General of the United States, the American Heart Association, the United States Department of Agriculture, and the Department of Health and Human Services—have issued dietary recommendations to aid in the prevention of cardiovascular diseases, cancer, diabetes, obesity, and osteoporosis, as well as chronic liver and kidney diseases.

Recommendations for low-fat and/or low-cholesterol diets are easily incorporated into, and are completely compatible with the Carbohydrate Addict's Diet.

A detailed list of these recommendations,* and suggestions for incorporating them into the Carbohydrate Addict's Diet, are provided in Chapter 12, Sample Meal Plans, pages 190–192.

* Only your doctor can determine which dietary recommendations are appropriate for you. Before incorporating these organizations' guidelines or any other guidelines into your eating regimen, you should consult your physician.

Introduction

Rachael's Story

By the age of twelve, I weighed more than 200 pounds. The other children in school teased and tormented me, and I had few friends—who wanted to be seen playing with me? I was always the last one picked for the team; someone had to be assigned to me when the buddy system was put to use on class trips.

Even the faculty got into the act, making fun of me and another classmate, the painfully thin Sara Jane. "Now wouldn't it be fun," one of my teachers was fond of saying, "if we could mix Rachael and Sara Jane up together and pull them apart. And then they'd be just right." No doubt you can hear the laugh track in the background.

I saw my first "diet doctor" at age eleven. Every week, he would give me diet pills, pep talks, and lectures about what he called my "disgusting" condition. He took my parents' money but then accused me of "cheating" when I had not. Even then I knew he didn't know how to help me lose weight.

Eventually I refused to continue seeing him. My parents were convinced this was just one more sign of my unwillingness to lose weight. Sadly, this also meant that, for the most part, they lost hope. I was on my own—alone and defenseless in facing my brother's merciless teasing and unrelenting name-calling.

But I didn't give up. I attempted to lose weight on my own, trying every weight-loss method that television and magazines had to offer. Year after year, the results were the same. The diets worked for a week, a month, or occasionally for a couple of months. In the end, though, they all failed.

I weighed well over 300 pounds by the time I was seventeen. Since my doctor's scales didn't go beyond 299, I never knew how much over 300 pounds I weighed.

Isolated by my weight, I was tormented by loneliness. But my life was difficult physically as well as emotionally. My feet, knees, and back hurt most of the time. Walking any distance made my heart race at a terrifying rate.

For the next fifteen years, I tried an unending series of diets. There were pills, prescription and over-the-counter. I tried water pills (doctors call them diuretics), which increase the rate at which the kidneys process liquid waste; the result was many trips to the bathroom, a short-term loss of weight, but an eventual return of the lost pounds. Fasting and a variety of exercise regimens were also on my did-not-work list from those years, as are familiar names like Stillman, Atkins, Weight Watchers, and Pritikin.

The pattern may sound familiar. At first, I would stick to my newest diet scrupulously. Gradually, I would be tempted to begin cheating. In time, staying on the diet would become more and more difficult. I'd suppress the urge to eat, but then I'd slip. It would be occasional at first, then more often. The diet invariably fell by the wayside over a period of weeks, and the weight would gradually return.

Often I would gain back more than I had lost.

I tried some programs several times, reasoning that since they had worked for a while, the results would last if only I tried harder. I did, but they didn't. My weight was the proverbial bouncing ball: twenty-, forty-, even fifty-pound increments came and went, but I never seemed able to get below 250 pounds.

In my late twenties, I saw some members of Overeaters Anonymous on television. With a new feeling of hope, I thought here is a group of people, all of whom know the pain and torment I had experienced. These people had helped each other—and, most important, they had been successful in losing weight.

I was living in Philadelphia at that time. When I learned that OA had no foothold there, I founded an OA group in that city. This required that I travel back and forth to New York City to join a group and learn how to run such an operation. It was an adventure for me, and I reveled in it.

OA was another way to address my continuing desire to lose weight. My efforts to use the lessons I learned in New York were successful, and within eighteen months, my Philadelphia Overeaters Anonymous group had nearly 8,000 members. We held thirty-six meetings a week. And I lost more than ninety pounds.

Yet in the months that followed, many of my fellow Overeaters seemed to lose the power they had temporarily exercised over their compulsion. One by one, most of them regained the weight they had fought so hard to lose.

So did I.

Liquid fasts came next for me, followed by behavior modification training, stomach stapling, Weight Watchers (again), and even hypnotism. My weight went down and up and down and up again.

It was the same pattern over and over. I would find a "cure," follow it, buy it, or submit to it—and sometimes I would lose some weight. Then, within a matter of months, I would begin to gain it back.

I was unable to find a permanent solution, or one that would get me to my target weight for a month or even a minute. And each time another diet failed, *I* felt like a failure.

In 1982, at age thirty-two, I entered a doctoral program in psychology, determined to learn about the psychological causes of overeating. I began to learn that, contrary to popular belief, the research consistently failed to provide any evidence that psychological factors were to blame.

I had to face facts.

First, for me and countless others, diets simply don't work. Oh, some seemed to work for a while, but in the long term, they just weren't effective.

Second, no one knew really what caused overeating—or how to treat it. The bottom line was well known to me already: I was shadow boxing with an as yet unidentified opponent. Diets didn't work, and neither I nor anyone else knew the questions to ask about why they didn't.

This realization brought me back to the starting line again. I was still terribly overweight. I knew that I couldn't blame some unresolved psychological conflict for my outsized outfits. Nor did there seem to be any new, magic solutions for me to pin my hopes on; I'd tried them all without achieving any permanent results.

I did, however, have one asset to draw upon: my twenty years of failures. That sounds like a contradiction, but I had learned my strengths and weaknesses when it came to dieting and food. Every diet program that had left me fatter at its finish had also given me valuable information about myself and the way my body responded.

From fasting diets, for example, I knew I could do without eating for long periods of time. From Overeaters Anonymous, I learned that it was easier for me to do without carbohydrates entirely than to eat small amounts and stop. Behavior modification techniques had shown me that certain places, occasions, and people could act as signals for me to eat.

Eight years ago, I put this hard experience to work for me. I devised a program that made the most of my strengths and placed no impossible demands upon me. It worked and continues to work.

It was the prototype for what today is called the Carbohydrate Addict's Diet. It allowed me to lose over 150 pounds and to reach my target weight—easily, without struggle, and without feeling deprived or hungry—and to stay at that weight for what is now an almost unbelievable *seven* years.

The eating plan I followed was born out of determination and desperation, yet it was an intelligent, logical, and scientifically based approach to weight loss and weight-loss maintenance. It didn't take willpower, exercise, strength of character, or stringent dietary limitations.

It was simple, yet it stopped my food cravings. For the first time in my life, I felt satisfied. It was the first eating program that I could live with. And best of all it worked and continues to work—for me and for many, many other dieters.

Richard's Story

My story is somewhat different. I was a large baby, weighing nine pounds, eight ounces at birth. I was a roly-poly toddler, a hefty kid, then a husky teenager. And I became a big man.

My weight had gone up slowly but steadily. In my twenties, during basic training in the army (and the dietetic emphasis on carbohydrates), I gained fifteen pounds despite torturous physical workouts. In the years that followed, I gained an additional ten pounds, one or two at a time. During most of my twenties and early thirties, I fit the description, "He's a big guy, about six-foot-two and two-fifteen."

I wasn't happy with my 200-plus pounds. Thin was very much in, and there was no pleasure in carrying around twenty-five excess pounds or seeing my belly hanging over my belt. I tried a variety of techniques to trim down. There was calorie counting, an exchange diet, and Weight Watchers (a couple of times). Most of them worked—in the short term. I'd adhere strictly to the program, but one little compromise would lead to another. Pretty soon there were whole days during which I never quite got started on the diet. I became weary of living and eating by the numbers and eventually I would go back to eating whatever I felt like, whenever I felt like it.

At age thirty-six, I decided that if I couldn't consistently decrease my food intake, I would increase my energy output. I turned to running, committed to losing the flabby and paunchy look. Through exercise, if not diet, I pledged that I would lose those extra pounds.

I ran every morning and worked up to a total of forty-two miles a week. I kept it up for more than two years. Every morning for about forty minutes I proudly, even zealously, did my running. I felt wonderful—but I never lost a pound. My 37-inch waist remained unchanged.

What did change after all these frustrations was my fundamental approach to weight control. As a professor of biology, I combined my knowledge of physiology with the latest scientific research in eating disorders. I constructed an eating program that was right for me.

Today, I recognize my problem was what Rachael and I call "carbohydrate addiction." My case was different in degree from Rachael's, but the underlying mechanism was basically the same. So when I put the principles of the Carbohydrate Addict's Diet to work for me, I went easily, almost without effort, down to the weight (168 pounds) and body shape I had sought for years. Best of all, I have remained at this weight ever since.

Rachael's Discovery

Many scientific discoveries are accidental—a unique set of circumstances that provides the observant scientist with the clues necessary to make a discovery. The Carbohydrate Addict's Diet is one such discovery.

Rachael remembers it this way:

One morning, I was scheduled to have an x-ray examination. As instructed, I had not eaten anything the night before. I was still in bed when the phone rang.

A technician from the x-ray lab was calling. "Your appointment has been rescheduled," I was told. "Why don't you come in at four o'clock this afternoon instead?" Still half-asleep, I accepted the rescheduling calmly. No problem, I thought to myself, mentally reviewing my schedule for the day.

"Oh, by the way," the woman on the phone added, "don't forget you can't eat anything between now and then. Liquids like coffee and tea are okay, but nothing to eat."

I hung up the phone. Before I had even had a chance to feel the gentle hunger of the morning, the news sank in. I was to be allowed no food at all until after four in the afternoon. My mind raced ahead. It might be after five by the time they finished with me—or even six if they had a backlog of patients. I panicked.

My mind raced through the alternatives. I considered rescheduling. That seemed like a good idea, but then I realized the same postponement could occur again. I thought of taking the day off from work and staying in bed, but there were too many things that I just had to get done.

Then I considered skipping the x-ray altogether. But that would be just plain foolish, I thought. That thought brought me back under control; I decided that I just had to get on with it.

I felt a bit shaky, but I took a morning shower. Following my usual routine, I dressed and got ready for work. I even weighed myself out of habit.

I weighed 268 pounds.

Then it was off to work, with only a passing glance at my unopened refrigerator. I ticked off the hours in my mind—I would be going without food for nearly twenty hours. I began to regard it as a personal challenge. Other people managed it, I thought. I would, too.

Once at work, I was surprised at how fast the morning passed. I bought a cup of black coffee when the cart came by, but I barely touched it. I was very busy and was only half aware of the comings and goings of the people around me. I worked right through lunch.

At about two o'clock, the coffee cart came to the door again. To my surprise, I realized I wasn't especially hungry; in fact, I felt fewer cravings than I usually did when I had eaten a big breakfast and lunch. At that moment, I shrugged it off, attributing it to my I-can-do-almost-anything-when-I-have-to attitude. But before the cart pulled away, I bought two French crullers—for later. I had them packed in a paper bag, planning to bring them with me to my appointment. As soon as the procedure was finished, I'd eat them in the dressing room.

The afternoon passed, my appointment went smoothly, and I found myself out of the clinic shortly after five o'clock. I didn't feel like having my French crullers at that moment. Since it was dinnertime, however, I went into a nearby diner and, there, *finally*, I got to eat my fill. I had soup, salad, bread with lots of butter, veal parmigiana, pasta, and coffee. I ate my crullers on the way home. They were wonderful.

I remember thinking just before I went to sleep that after a long day of not eating, I had blown my chance of taking off any weight by eating that huge dinner. But a surprise awaited me.

The next morning, I got on the scale and saw I was two pounds lighter than the day before. It was unbelievable.

This doesn't make sense, I thought.

Water weight, I decided. It'll be back in a day or two. But my training as scientist served me well. Instead of just accepting the easy explanation as the correct one, I found myself designing an experiment.

One part of me thought, Why not try eating the same way again? There was no apparent reason why it should work. But what do I have to lose? I asked myself.

I could skip breakfast and lunch again, I thought. I also knew I could treat myself to another guilt-free dinner, just like the previous day. It didn't sound bad—just unusual.

Skipping breakfast presented no problems. In fact, I had the experience, like the day before, of being less hungry by late morning than I was on a usual day after having eaten a full breakfast.

Lunch was more difficult; everyone was going out to eat or bringing food into the office. It took some negotiating with myself to skip the midday meal. But the promise of the whatever-I-wanted dinner won out over the luncheon urge.

In the afternoon I made another little deal with myself, and bought a treat from the coffee cart. For later, I promised myself as I ordered two tasty-looking crullers for my after-dinner treat.

When dinnertime came I was ready. I had been planning it all afternoon. At the pizza parlor, I ordered half a long sandwich, a giant slice of pizza with pepperoni and anchovies, and a Greek salad. I polished the meal off at home, then turned to my crullers. By then I wasn't very hungry, so one was enough.

It was tough, but it was worth it, I thought to myself as I sat back from the table. I also felt more satisfied than I ever remembered feeling before.

The moment of judgment arrived the next morning when I stepped on the scale: my weight had dropped another pound. I remember thinking, Another pound, and the house still smells of pizza!

In the weeks that followed, I kept to the same basic plan. My rate of weight loss slowed to between two and three pounds a week, but it remained fairly steady.

I lost 150 pounds, and for the first time in my life reached my ideal weight.

I will always be grateful for that particular arrangement of circumstances—the postponed x-ray exam and the forced fast. Together, they made possible the experiences that produced the Carbohydrate Addict's Diet. (The diet doesn't require that you skip lunch and breakfast, by the way, only that you adjust your selection of foods during two of your daily meals.) We all come across similar opportunities in our lives. Sometimes we are fortunate enough to recognize and take advantage of them, sometimes not. This time I did. I believe it saved my life.

The Diet Develops

We are successful dieters, but professionally we are scientists. We both have doctorates in our respective fields of expertise; through the use of systematic and prescribed methods, we labor to discover underlying principles and their appropriate application for optimal medical treatment.

Richard's doctorate is in research biology. Over the years, he has been awarded more than $4 million in research funds by the National Institutes of Health and has written a great many scholarly articles and books in the area of biological research.

Rachael's doctoral degree is in research psychology. She's an expert in experimental and research design. As an educator and researcher, she has specialized in studying both the biological and psychological aspects of eating disorders and weight control.

We have pooled our skills, education, and experience to create the Carbohydrate Addict's Diet. More than 6,000 personal stories helped us formulate the diet. Some 5,000 members of Overeaters Anonymous recounted their experiences; in excess of 800 members of Weight Watchers and four other groups have been evaluated. After experimenting for several years with a range of individual treatment plans, we developed a diet program that has proved uniquely successful in treating a set of common eating and weight conditions that our dieters themselves describe as "carbohydrate addiction."

Several points worked in our favor:

- Rachael's training as psychologist coupled with her personal experience proved essential in the development of this diet. People saw her losing weight; some of them began to ask how she did it. So she told them exactly what she was doing and how it felt—and then it worked for them, too.

  She still didn't trust the results. Maybe it's a placebo effect, she remembers thinking. If I tell people they won't feel hungry, then they don't. When two co-workers approached her, she decided to tell them nothing about her own decrease in hunger cravings. Soon both of them returned with independent stories of how much less hungry they felt—and how happy they were with their continuing weight loss. She began to realize that she had stumbled onto something that was very important.

  Rachael's informal control group ruled out the placebo effect.

- As word of the diet spread, more people wanted to try it. Friends of friends began calling, at work and at home.

  Rachael started setting up informal groups, working with three, four, or five people at a time. Not everybody reported the same results. As more and more people heard about and tried the diet, a few of them found that they were still hungry. For most, the diet worked extraordinarily well—and calls kept coming in; for a few, it didn't seem to work at all.

  Rachael was well into her doctoral education by then and was learning how to design experiments. She devised a way to distinguish the dieters who described the diet as "a breeze," "a delight," and "the answer to my prayers," from those who found it to be just another dietary disappointment. What emerged from the study were common traits among those for whom the diet worked. They all seemed to crave carbohydrates, at times uncontrollably. But more than simply craving, the desire for carbohydrates would sometimes escalate to a feeling of greater and greater need until that need was finally satisfied.

She began to see that almost all of those who were successful on the diet had similar experiences or desires in relation to eating. In a high percentage of cases the answers to a few questions proved a strong predictor of how well someone was likely to do on the diet. A test emerged, one that we would soon be using to predict who would and would not be helped by the principles of the Carbohydrate Addict's Diet. But for all her success in predicting who would be helped, Rachael still didn't understand why the Carbohydrate Addict's Diet worked.

- Richard's contribution was fundamental to understanding the carbohydrate connection. He searched through the scientific findings of literally thousands of other researchers, seeking an understanding of the biological functions of the diet that worked so well for us and others. He found it; it was there to be seen in journal after journal. It had been observed and reported but never put to use.

The "discovery" wasn't new—"food addiction" had actually been observed as far back as 1947. Over the years many researchers had added other observations. Important aspects were and still are being discovered, some involving cutting-edge research on messenger chemicals in the brain called neurotransmitters.

Richard began to fit together the many pieces of the earlier research, which explained so many of our successes. We had known the diet worked, but with these additional clues, we could begin to understand why. And we could begin to explain it to others.

- As greater numbers of dieters succeeded on the diet, many other people heard about it and wanted our help. The Carbohydrate Addict's Center was the inevitable next step.

Founded in 1983 as the Center for Weight and Eating Control, its specific purpose was to gather information about the diet in a scientifically acceptable and controlled manner. But soon it became a way to help people who wanted to control their eating and weight. Within its first month, the Center had a waiting list of potential clients, all of them eager to find out if they were carbohydrate addicts.

More important, within a year, the successes were being documented. Most of our dieters had similar experiences. They had failed at other diets; they identified themselves as carbohydrate addicts. Our test results proved that more than 75 percent of those who came to us were carbohydrate addicts.

One important point emerged most clearly. Previous studies had found that other diets typically produced long-term weight-loss—defined as loss sustained over a year or more—in only about one in twenty cases. Compared to that level of performance—a mere 5-percent success rate—the people we worked with were succeeding at the rate of over *80 percent*.

We knew we had discovered an important treatment for a difficult and resistant problem, and the people with whom we worked had learned that they could find help for their problem. As the Center for Eating and Weight Control concentrated more and more on the problems related to carbohydrate addiction, we changed its name to the Carbohydrate Addict's Center to reflect our focus.

The Carbohydrate Addict's Center

Today, we are both professors on the faculty of New York's Mount Sinai School of Medicine; in addition, we are professors of Biomedical Science at the Graduate Center of the City University of New York. In addition, Richard is a professor of Biology and Medical Technology at Bronx Community College. Part of our research involves identifying the biological bases of eating disorders. Although we have been highly successful at reducing and, in many cases, eliminating the cravings, hunger, and excess weight that are often associated with carbohydrate addiction, we are now working to learn more about the causes of this disorder.

At the Carbohydrate Addict's Center our express purpose is to conduct research and educate people in the areas of eating and weight disorders, to gather information about the eating habits, symptoms, cravings, and weight-loss and weight-gain patterns of carbohydrate addicts. In the first six years of its existence, almost 600 clients were given dietary guidance at the Carbohydrate Addict's Center; many others have come to see us since, but it is the first 600 for whom we have the most complete data. We learned how changing their carbohydrate intake affected them.

These people actually used the diet. Their successes and failures have been studied and analyzed; they have helped us to modify and adjust—to individualize—the Carbohydrate Addict's Diet.

The 600 individuals are a diverse group. They range in age from nineteen to sixty-eight. Some are high-school dropouts, some are college grads, some are M.D.s and Ph.D.s. Virtually all occupations and social and economic levels have been represented.

Not surprisingly, the weight-loss goals of our clients are wide ranging. Some dieters told us that they simply wanted to maintain their current weight; some of those had been on liquid fasts and had lost weight. Now they were finding it impossible to keep the weight off.

Some people came to the Carbohydrate Addict's Center wanting to lose more than 100 pounds. Their excess weight was interfering with their health, their comfort, their self-esteem, their personal relationships; in some cases it made it difficult for them to live normal lives. Most of the people we worked with over the years wanted to lose fifteen to twenty-five pounds. Although women outnumbered men about six to one, we found that the problem of carbohydrate addiction was not limited to one sex.

Although weight levels, education, and occupation have all been diverse, there has been one constant: the results. By prescribing an eating plan designed to treat the carbohydrate addict's underlying disorder, we continue to show an unprecedented, long-term success rate higher than 80 percent.

Our research and work demands are great and, to date, our available time and facilities have limited us to working with only about 100 people annually at the clinic. With the publication of *The Carbohydrate Addict's Diet*, however, we aim to provide many more carbohydrate addicts the same program that is available at the Center.

If you are a carbohydrate addict, we welcome you to our ranks. The Carbohydrate Addict's Diet has been designed to enable you to cut your hunger and food cravings, to lose your excess weight and, most important, to keep it off.

Many people have described the diet contained in these pages as their "dream diet" because it seems so easy to live with. It's a happy surprise for many to find a diet that seems to have been developed especially for them.

And indeed it was.

The Carbohydrate Addict's Diet was designed for the carbohydrate addict who is tired of fighting the carbohydrate cravings, the deprivation, the self-blame, and the roller-coaster of "yo-yo" dieting. If you are tired of being hungry, of being afraid you are about to put back on the weight you struggled so hard to lose, then this book may provide the answer you have been seeking.

This program is intelligent and scientifically sound. No matter what your lifestyle, it is easy to follow. It involves no weighing or measuring. It is satisfying. And it works. It is a plan that will help you live the life you want.

We began by recounting key episodes from our dieting experience because we wanted to show that the Carbohydrate Addict's Diet works for a wide range of overweight people, for men and women, for the greatly overweight and for those who want simply to take off a few pounds.

By definition, the Carbohydrate Addict's Diet can work for all of us who have come to understand that we are carbohydrate addicts.

PART I

THE CARBOHYDRATE ADDICT

CHAPTER

1

What Is "Carbohydrate Addiction"?

A century ago, epileptics were thought to be taken over by "spirits." Today, epilepsy is a recognized neurological disorder.

Fifty years ago, everyone laughed at the town fool. Now the person who is mentally retarded is only rarely ridiculed and never blamed for his disorder.

Times have changed even for alcoholics. Alcoholism has been recognized as a disease, complete with hereditary and biological influences. A president's wife admitted her drug dependence, making it acceptable for sports and entertainment figures to talk openly about their problem. These public figures are applauded for admitting to their problem and seeking help.

But overweight? Like alcoholism, it is often genetic in origin; it runs in families. Yet overweight people are still the objects of ridicule and blame. It's considered in bad taste to tell jokes about the mentally retarded or someone struggling with alcoholism—but jokes poking fun at fat people are still commonplace.

People who are overweight suffer from a disorder that may not be any more their fault than epilepsy or mental retardation or alcoholism. In truth, we still have a lot to learn about the problem of overweight.

Myth Number 1: People Gain Weight Because They Eat Too Much

For decades, researchers have tried to discover a link between overweight and overeating. It seems logical, of course, in part because we've been taught since nursery school to believe that people who are fat must eat a lot (remember the Mother Goose rhyme? "Jack Sprat could eat no fat, his wife could eat no lean . . .").

The results of the studies are surprising. Some researchers have tried to make people of average or "normal" weight become overweight. They have failed—even when normal people were fed as many as 3,000 extra calories daily. Their weight tended to increase a little and then level off; tests showed that the rate at which their bodies processed (metabolized) the foods increased so that they burned off the extra calories. In other studies, some overweight people were shown to be able to maintain their excess weight even when their food intake was severely restricted. Experiment after experiment has shown that overeating does not always result in overweight; nor is overweight always the result of overeating.

Observations in rats and farm animals support these findings. A genetic propensity for weight gain has been discovered in many varieties of laboratory animals; one is the Zucker rat. When these rats are fed the same diets, in the same quantities, and are exercised to the same degree as other rats that don't have the same genetic tendency to obesity, the Zucker rats get fat whereas the other rats do not. Farmers, too, have found that certain strains of animals tend to be overweight—and they are willing to pay more for such animals as a result.

Why do we continue to think that humans are so different? Why do we insist that our weight is determined only by what we eat and not by the way our bodies use what we eat?

In the professional journals, scientists are likely to use terms like "energy intake" and "adiposity." But the fact is that time and again the tests lead to the same surprising conclusion: Many people who overeat do not get fat and many people who are overweight do not overeat.

Myth Number 2: Overweight People Have Emotional Problems

Overweight men and women have often been characterized as being angry, dependent, and stubborn. They are said to hate their mothers or to be afraid of sex.

Dr. Albert Stunkard, a noted researcher in obesity at the University of Pennsylvania, has said that despite the common categorization of overweight people as "sickies" or "neurotics," ". . . in almost every case, this was not found to be true."

In study after study, overweight individuals have failed to reveal any consistent differences in emotional or mental health from those who are of normal weight. Simple obesity appears to be a *physical disorder*. According to the American Psychiatric Association, it is not, in most cases, to be associated with any distinct behavioral or psychological syndrome.

Myth Number 3: People Who Are Overweight Have No Willpower

Many believe that overweight people got that way because they couldn't keep themselves from eating too much. Overweight and nonoverweight persons alike have adopted as true the idea that people with weight problems have no willpower.

On the contrary: Overweight people have not been shown to differ from their normal-weight counterparts in either behavioral or psychological ways. However, the blame placed on them—"It's her own fault; she just eats too much"—produces an added frustration for the overweight person.

Overweight People Are *Different*

A great deal of scientific research suggests that overweight people differ in physical ways from their thinner counterparts. Their bodies respond differently to many foods they eat, producing an increased or recurring hunger, a seeming drive to eat, and a tendency to store fat.

More and more scientific research suggests that many overweight people suffer from what is called a "food addiction," caused not by some sort of character flaw or psychological problem, but by an imbalance in body chemistry.

The notion of a food addiction isn't new—researchers have been attempting to understand food addiction and its relationship to overweight since 1947. And scientists are discovering more and more about food addiction and carbohydrate dependence. A review of *Index Medicus* reveals that roughly a thousand articles that appeared in

1989 alone revealed new information about the processes that may underlie carbohydrate addiction.

But before we explain the workings of carbohydrate addiction in scientific terms, let's see what carbohydrate addiction feels like. As we will continue to do throughout this book, we will tell you the actual case history of one of the people we have treated at the Carbohydrate Addict's Center.

Let's meet Carol.

Carol's Story

Carol T. walked into our offices the day before her thirty-second birthday. We saw a soft-spoken, attractive woman who clearly put energy into looking her best. Her strawberry-blond hair was carefully styled, her dress well cut and fashionable. We learned she was an administrative secretary with managerial aspirations.

Her manner and bearing were such that her twenty-plus pounds of extra weight didn't seem very important on her five-foot, four-inch frame. They were important to her, however. She told us that when one of her old boyfriends had teased her about her weight (he had called her "chubby"), she had become very, very angry.

"Hearing this guy make some comment about my weight made me mad," she said. "I really hated it."

We asked her about her dieting history. She admitted there was a part of her that felt she was making "too much of this weight thing," but there was another part of her that "just wanted to be skinny and feel great." She also told us that sometimes she had "the feeling that the weight thing and the diet thing" were out of control.

When we got down to details, we found Carol's history was one we have seen repeatedly in many of the carbohydrate addicts with whom we work. Carol would, for a time, manage to control her food intake, eating so-called diet meals that contained small portions of carbohydrates. The initial phase of "being perfect" would change almost without her knowing it, and Carol would find herself eating the same foods—but in larger portions than the diet recommended or she had planned. (It's not really cheating, she would tell herself.) But a little extra chicken, meat, or fresh vegetables shortly gave way to extra fruit. (Fruits are healthful, she would rationalize.) Then she would find herself craving starches: bread, rolls, pasta, and potatoes. Powerful desires for sweets and snack foods followed. Carol told us that she would find herself hand-delivering work to another part of the building in which she worked so that she could walk past the candy machine. Even if she successfully held out at first, eventually she found herself, as she put it, "eating anything in sight!"

When she came to see us, Carol summed it up this way: "I'm not happy with the way I look, and I don't want to keep going on and off diets for the rest of my life."

We gave her the Carbohydrate Addiction Test that we had developed. (You can take it, too, when you reach Chapter 3.) But Carol almost didn't need to take it. We've seen hundreds of carbohydrate addicts—and from our first conversation we were pretty sure that she was indeed a carbohydrate addict and probably a candidate for the diet.

SIGNS AND SYMPTOMS OF CARBOHYDRATE ADDICTION

Do you ever experience these symptoms?

- ***A frequent focus on eating.***
  Do you spend a great deal of time thinking about food, dieting, or your weight?

- ***Lack of satisfaction or the desire to eat again a couple of hours after eating.***
  Do you get the feeling you aren't really satisfied after eating, no matter what you eat? Are you hungrier two hours after eating than if you hadn't eaten at all?

- ***A sense of fatigue or tiredness.***
  Do you get a sensation of sluggishness, almost of feeling drugged after eating? Do you feel like lying down, perhaps

even drifting off for a nap? Do you put off work or planned activities because you just don't have the energy for them? Do you get hungry/tired in the middle of the afternoon?

- ***An unexplained feeling of anxiety or anger.***
  Do you have a certain unexplained nervousness or irritability? A desire to be alone? Do you find that you are angry at or blaming yourself?

- ***A heightened emotionality.***
  Do you find yourself feeling sad or weepy without reason? Do you ever experience a feeling of hopelessness; an intense feeling of loneliness; a generalized feeling of fear? Do you ever go to extremes, with a feeling of euphoria or heightened happiness, only to feel later inexplicably sad or hopeless?

If you are overweight or are constantly fighting the battle of the bulge and recognize some of the preceding symptoms, you may be a carbohydrate addict. Many of these symptoms have been cited in literally thousands of interviews with people looking for weight-loss programs. In most cases, the symptoms can be attributed to carbohydrate addiction.

What Causes Carbohydrate Addiction?

Scientists writing in *The New England Journal of Medicine*, *The Lancet*, *The Journal of Clinical Investigation*, and many other journals have reported a physiological dysfunction that leads to overweight in many people. This dysfunction results in the wrong amount of insulin in the blood. Although overweight may be caused by a number of different disorders, an insulin imbalance appears to be very important to understanding some of the underlying mechanisms involved in many people who are overweight.

In order to understand what goes wrong in the carbohydrate addict, it is important to know what happens in someone who is not a carbohydrate addict.

If carbohydrate consumption continues for a prolonged period of time, additional insulin is released. Again, the amount of insulin is appropriate to what is needed, in proportion to the amount of carbohydrates eaten at that particular time. When a normal person consumes carbohydrates, his or her body releases insulin within a few minutes of eating. The amount of insulin released is based upon what that person has eaten in previous meals. When the system is functioning normally, just enough insulin is released to help deliver the carbohydrate energy (in the form of the blood sugar glucose) to the liver and to muscle or fat cells throughout the body.

As the cells take in the glucose, the level of insulin in the blood drops. The drop in insulin also results in the release of a brain chemical called serotonin. The presence of serotonin produces a feeling of satisfaction.

Insulin is sometimes called the hunger hormone because it stimulates people to eat. When insulin is released in normal people minutes after they start eating, it may cause them to feel hungrier than they thought they were when they started eating. But upon completing their meal they feel satisfied—their insulin level drops and their brains get the signal to stop eating.

Hours later, after the body has used some of the glucose that remains in the blood, the insulin-to-glucose ratio in blood changes. It appears that this increase signals the body to eat again. We recognize this signal as the sensation of hunger. The normal person then eats, and the whole process begins again.

The balance of carbohydrates and insulin is a delicate one—and it can malfunction. Within a few minutes of eating carbohydrates, in fact, the carbohydrate addict's body releases far more insulin than is necessary. If the carbohydrate addict has recently consumed another serving of carbohydrates, the amount of insulin that is released will be greater still. The overabundance of insulin "insults" the cells that should be taking up the carbohydrate energy (glucose), interfering with the normal absorption of glucose.

An excess of insulin remains in the bloodstream. As insulin levels fail to drop, the brain levels of the chemical serotonin fail to rise, and the carbohydrate addict may not feel satisfied. Some carbohydrate addicts report that they do feel satisfied after eating, others that they find that they again feel like eating within two hours or so. And if the carbohydrate addict attempts to satisfy his or her hunger by again consuming carbohydrates, the insulin release that follows will be even greater and the sense of satisfaction even less.

The repetition of this cycle appears to form the physical basis of what we call carbohydrate addiction.

WITH ALL THIS TALK ABOUT INSULIN, WHAT ABOUT DIABETICS? WHAT ABOUT HYPOGLYCEMICS?

Although many diabetics and hypoglycemics may be overweight, the mechanisms of carbohydrate addiction, hypoglycemia, and diabetes should not be confused.

Diabetes is a disorder in which the body produces insufficient insulin or is unable to use it. If untreated, the malfunction results in too much glucose in the blood. Hypoglycemia is a condition characterized by low blood-sugar levels. Cold sweats, dizziness, faintness, headaches, and head-pounding may be experienced within about two hours after eating a carbohydrate-rich meal.

Our continuing research suggests that the Carbohydrate Addict's Diet is associated with weight loss and a general improvement in health. We believe that this diet presents no danger to the health of the healthy person.

Conversely, there are certain physical ailments that may argue against using this eating regime. For these reasons, it is important that you check with your physician before using this diet or varying in other significant ways from your regular regime. This is true particularly if you have diabetes, hypoglycemia, a history of heart disease, or kidney or liver disorders.

We also recommend under any circumstances that you seek to have your physician monitor your weight and progress as you continue on the program.

What Does Too Much Insulin Mean?

Assume you eat a carbohydrate-rich meal, perhaps a simple one of two slices of pizza and a bottle of cola. If you're a normal person, four or five hours will pass before you become hungry again. If you're a carbohydrate addict, however, you might feel hungry only two hours later—with a craving for more sweets or starchy foods (because of the excess insulin released into the bloodstream). Some carbohydrate addicts report that they feel hungry immediately after eating carbohydrates. They never feel satisfied.

Carbohydrate addicts recognize the desire to eat isn't logical, because they know they're not really hungry in the sense of requiring nourishment. But the drive to eat is hard to deny. You may find yourself eating out of habit, almost unconsciously satisfying a compulsion. You may snack, realizing to your surprise that you are eating out of boredom or to relieve stress. Simple fatigue may provoke hunger, too. Sometimes the desire to eat can be overwhelming, virtually compelling you to satisfy it. Sometimes you may be unable to identify any apparent cause.

Many carbohydrate addicts report that their cravings grow stronger each time they eat carbohydrates. In short order, they find themselves in a continuous cycle of eating, craving, and eating again.

For carbohydrate addicts, consuming carbohydrate-rich foods produces a compulsion to eat. At first the consumption of high-carbohydrate snacks or meals produces a feeling of pleasure or satisfaction. Shortly, however, pleasure is followed by an anxious sensation, perhaps a feeling of weakness. Hunger, tiredness, and a desire to snack often follow.

Unfortunately, the problem doesn't end there. In the presence of the excess insulin, the body also becomes very good at conserving energy. So while the carbohydrate addict gets hungrier with each carbohydrate-rich meal, the body gets better at storing energy—in the form of fat.

When we talk to our professional colleagues, we use terminology such as "mesolimbic dopamine system" and "decreased cellular insulin receptors." (In Chapter 2, there is a more detailed explanation of the physiological workings of carbohydrate addiction.) Yet the bottom line can be stated quite simply: In carbohydrate addiction, the carbohydrate-insulin/carbohydrate-serotonin connection has gone awry.

While other research scientists have reported this phenomenon, we were the first to recognize how the mechanism could be "corrected," and the experience of hunger cravings and fat storage could be minimized. We acted on these discoveries and created the Carbohydrate Addict's Diet.

In the past, diet experts have failed to treat the problem—whether they knew it by these names or others—by reducing the total daily intake of carbohydrates and distributing carbohydrates equally to all meals. We know that these strategies don't work for carbohydrate addicts.

Between 95 and 98 percent of the people on standard weight-loss diets regain all lost weight within one year. Until now, no one has found any alternative to these nearly sure-to-fail treatments. Through our research we discovered that it isn't only the amount of carbohydrates eaten that matters—it is also *how frequently* they are eaten. Frequency governs, in large measure, the hunger response for millions of people. Personally and professionally, we discovered that any weight-loss diet that prescribes three or more small meals each day containing anything more than minor amounts of carbohydrates will ultimately fail with the carbohydrate addict. Such a diet will trigger the insulin response and signal the carbohydrate addict to eat once again.

In general, we direct our dieters to eat two low-carbohydrate meals each day and to confine their carbohydrate-rich foods to one, daily sixty-minute sitting that makes up the third meal. In this way, the fundamental mechanism causing excessive hunger, recurring cravings, and weight gain is corrected. Insulin release is dramatically reduced. The carbohydrate addict feels satisfied—and stays satisfied for many hours. Weight drops off naturally, fat deposits decrease, and the addictive cycle is broken.

What Are Carbohydrates?

To the chemist, carbohydrates are chemical compounds consisting of the elements carbon, oxygen, and hydrogen. The categories of carbohydrates include the sugars and starches.

To the nutritionist, carbohydrates are the principal component of any diet. They may take the form of either simple sugars or complex carbohydrates.

The term "simple sugars" refers to carbohydrates, such as cane or beet sugar, known technically as sucrose, and corn syrup, which contains the sugar known as fructose. Fruits and fruit juices, table sugars, and honey contain simple sugars. The principal sources of complex carbohydrates, or starches, are breads and cereals, vegetables, rice and pasta, and peas and beans.

Carbohydrates are a basic source of energy in the diet. The digestive process breaks down carbohydrates into glucose for absorption from the small intestine. The glucose then is distributed by the bloodstream and to the muscle cells for fuel and to the liver and fat cells for storage.

Carol's Story, Part II

Now, let's return to Carol's story and her progress after we introduced her to the Carbohydrate Addict's Diet.

We told her about the scientific basis of her addiction, namely her overabundance of insulin, or hyperinsulinemia, and explained how that made her hungry. We told Carol that the diet was intended to reduce her craving for carbohydrates and, thus, her desire to cheat. We predicted she would find it easier to stay on this diet than she had with other diets.

She listened carefully but admitted to a certain skepticism.

For Carol, the diet unfolded this way:

Day One. Carol admitted that she was surprised at how little she ate at lunch the first day—she attributed it to beginner's enthusiasm rather than to her body's response to a low-carbohydrate breakfast. She enjoyed her first Reward dinner, but she couldn't quite bring herself to eat all the foods she wanted. She had a roast beef sandwich and French fries, but decided against eating the piece of lemon meringue pie she really wanted.

Days Two and Three. Carol said her second and third days were "as easy as the first." Most diets will deliver an initial weight loss of water weight in the first few days. Often this is seen as something of a payoff for the sacrifices of dieting. Yet Carol was pleasantly surprised. She found on the morning of the fourth day that, without having experienced the feelings of hunger or discomfort, she had lost two pounds.

Day Four. Carol's weight loss prompted her to put the diet to the test. That night she had veal parmigiana as well as pasta at a local Italian restaurant. She had bread, she confessed, "although, for some reason, I didn't smother it with butter as I usually do." She had a large salad with dressing and ate spumoni for dessert. When she got on the scale the next day, expecting to be punished, her weight was unchanged.

Week One Results. At the end of the first week, Carol had lost two and one-half pounds. She had mixed feelings, she confided: she was thrilled to be able to eat, enjoy herself, and still lose weight; but disappointed, too ("I sometimes think that I'd have to lose the whole twenty pounds in one week to be satisfied"). We reminded her, as we do all our dieters, that a one-half to two-pound weekly weight loss is the ideal rate for health reasons and weight-loss maintenance. For her twenty-pound weight loss, we recommended a rate of about a pound a week.

Week Two Results. By the close of week two, Carol admitted that she felt like she was doing "something wrong" every night as she ate her Reward Meal. But at the end of the second week she loved the fact that she had lost four and one-half pounds. We cautioned her that she was losing rather quickly.

A Few Weeks Later. . . . Weeks five, six, and seven proved to be a plateau. Carol told us that in the past such weight plateaus had usually meant cheating and, eventually, giving up on the diet. But this time, she told us with a wide smile, "I don't care. I've lost almost ten pounds, and I'm having a ball every night. I wouldn't even mind if I stayed at this weight." She didn't give up—and she didn't stay at that weight either.

A Few Months Later. . . . Week eight saw her losing weight once again. By week fourteen, she hit her target weight, twenty-three pounds lighter than the day she had entered our offices. We helped her individualize her eating program, encouraging her to increase slightly the quantities consumed at her Low-Carbohydrate Meals. Her weight was established *without* requiring a jarring or inappropriate maintenance program, a problem common to other diets.

Two Years Later. At her second annual checkup, Carol weighed two and one-half pounds less than her target weight. She told us that she loved "looking like this" and that she was happy to be "in control."

She added: "It's a wonderful way to live."

Carol's experience doesn't tell the whole story. We will recount other stories that show how flexible the diet is, how it can be adapted to any lifestyle. There are also important psychological aspects of the diet, like handling the individual triggers that can wreak havoc upon us. And there will be strategies to help in the individualizing of the diet for lifelong maintenance.

But Carol's experience *is* typical. We helped her to recognize that she was a carbohydrate addict. She learned what that meant in terms of her body chemistry and her behavior.

Then she, like more than 80 percent of the other dieters who have used this program, lost—and kept off—the pounds she wanted to be rid of.

SHOPPING FOR DIETS

The standard diet plans don't work for carbohydrate addicts—and carbohydrate addicts blame themselves. We have now come to understand that they have been trying to follow diets that are simply not suited to their physical needs.

When you're shopping for shoes, you don't buy just any pair. If the salesman brings you a pair of shoes that don't fit, you don't blame yourself, do you? Maybe they're too small, too large, or too narrow.

Say a friend or relative brings you a pair of shoes, and they don't fit either. You won't try to wear them anyway; you'll find a pair that suits you. Right?

The same is true with eyeglasses, medical prescriptions, top hats, and false teeth. They are right for you or not. Period. You accept that.

But diets are different.

With diets, most of us forget common sense. We pick a diet at random, giving little thought to our needs, our preferences, our strengths, our weaknesses, or specific metabolic levels. We take what may (or may not) be appropriate for someone else, and assume that it should be correct for us. We don't look at what *we* need.

Then we blame ourselves when, in the long run, it doesn't work. The diet that fails us is interpreted as our own failure.

Maybe, just maybe, that's because it wasn't an appropriate plan in the first place.

And the Carbohydrate Addict's Diet just might be.

CHAPTER

2

The Insulin Connection

The notion of food addiction is not new. As long ago as the 1940s, scientists were reporting early findings that suggested people could become addicted to certain kinds of foods. In the early 1960s, other observations led to the recognition that carbohydrates, in particular, could be addictive foods.

Carbohydrate addiction was first described in the literature in 1963 when researcher J. Kemp reported in the scientific journal *Practitioner* that ". . . many obese subjects show an addiction to high carbohydrate diets."

Although other scholarly articles gradually appeared reporting further exploration of the process that underlies carbohydrate addiction, it wasn't until the mid-1980s that a virtual explosion in research began. There seems to have been a remarkable interest in the area, most likely as a result of emerging research that began to explore brain chemicals, including the neurotransmitter serotonin. A review of *Index Medicus* reveals that in 1986, some 500 articles appeared on the subject; in 1987, there were more than 650. By 1988, some 900 appeared, and well over a thousand were published in 1989.

The interest is still growing. Some of the finest scholarly journals continue to include important articles on the subject, including *New England Journal of Medicine, The Lancet, American Journal of Clin-*

ical Nutrition, International Journal of Obesity, Annals of the New York Academy of Science, American Journal of Physiology, Journal of Clinical Endocrinological Metabolism, Metabolism, American Journal of Medical Genetics, British Journal of Clinical Psychology, Journal of Clinical Investigation. And innumerable others.

A small sampling of excerpts suggests something of the emerging knowledge. In a 1987 article in *Pediatric Clinics of North America*, L. Kathleen Mahan reported:

> Some of the physiological factors in the obese . . . that give rise to rapid weight gain and eventually obesity and that tend to maintain the obese state, are . . . abnormal levels of neuro-regulators like serotonin . . . and abnormal levels of hormones such as insulin.

In 1988, J. Rodin, R. Reed, and L. Jamner reported the following in the *American Journal of Clinical Nutrition*:

> The fact that the relationship between early insulin response and food intake was especially strong for obese subjects merits special attention because obesity is associated with changes in insulin sensitivity and responsiveness.

and

> A strong relationship obtained between food intake and insulin secretion within the first thirty minutes after sugar consumption was accounted for almost entirely by obese subjects.

and

> These data suggest that a more dynamic aspect of insulin secretion, such as rate of change over time, may be more important in determining subsequent food intake than absolute level of secretion per se.

Other authors offer up observations that buttress these findings regarding insulin release and obesity. Among them are these:

> Hyperinsulinemia can be genetically linked and precedes obesity.
> —F. Contaldo in *The Body Weight Regulatory System* (1981)

> High insulin levels in the blood are often found in obese individuals and these levels are excessively raised after glucose [intake].
>
> —I. McLean Baird and A. Howard in *Obesity: Medical and Scientifc Aspects* (1981)

> In some obese persons weight gain is caused by selective consumption of excess carbohydrate calories. It is likely that treatments based on an overall food restriction, or on diets that tend to inhibit further brain serotonin output, such as protein-sparing formulas, will have little chance of success in these individuals.
>
> —L. Altomonte, *et al.*, in *Pharmacology* (1988)

The citations could continue for pages and pages. But the inference to be drawn is quite clear: the evidence for a link between weight problems and a basic, underlying, biologically based mechanism is overwhelming. We may not as yet understand many of its nuances, but the fundamental connection is undeniable.

Thinking About Hunger

Traditionally, researchers have distinguished two hunger-related states in the person of normal weight. The first is essentially what the layperson would regard as hunger, the state in which we desire to eat. This desire to eat initiates the eating response, meaning we reach for food to relieve the hungry sensation.

The second state is characterized by the satisfied feeling that follows eating. Satiety signals that the time has come to stop eating, that the desire for food that initiated the eating episode has been appeased.

Those two hunger-related states have been identified as typical of people of normal weight. However, we are finding the sequence is more complicated, especially in the carbohydrate addict.

At the Carbohydrate Addict's Center and at the Mount Sinai Medical Center, our research has identified *four* hunger states.

They are as follows:

Generalized or Common Hunger

This is the strong urge to eat food of any kind. Though intense, this hunger passes in time and later reappears. "Normal" hunger belongs in this classification.

Most carbohydrate addicts report that they have the least difficulty controlling their eating responses to this hunger state.

Specific Hunger or Craving

Craving is the strong desire to eat a specific food (or food group). A craving is not likely to disappear for good and often increases in intensity. Although normals as well as carbohydrate-addicted people experience cravings, this hunger state recurs more often and more intensely in the carbohydrate addict. Craving may escalate in intensity and frequency to a point of addiction.

Discomfort or Dissatisfaction Hunger

This may be thought of as the "nibble-need." It is a less intense sensation than craving, but is nonetheless a persistent desire to snack. There is often a vague accompanying sense of discomfort; there may also be an accompanying belief that just the right food will "hit the spot," relieving the sense of dissatisfaction, but the "right food" is illusive.

Rarely is there any awareness of which food or food group will be satisfying. The eater in a state of dissatisfaction will often go from food to food in search of satiety. The classic image for this hunger state is the person standing in front of an open refrigerator, just looking for something to eat. In the carbohydrate addict, this hunger state may typically appear more often, though not necessarily more intensely, than in the normal person.

Subconscious Hunger

This hunger often does not enter one's awareness before the impulse to eat takes over. Subconscious hunger is characterized by a strong and often uncontrollable desire to eat; it results in the consumption of food without plan or anticipation.

Carbohydrate addicts often describe what we call an impulse-eating incident as occurring with only little awareness of loss of control or of psychological conflict on their parts. Normal eaters and lower-level carbohydrate addicts attribute the impulse-eating incidents to habit, though occasionally they admit that they are unable to stop even when they want to. During impulse eating, food is often consumed quickly with little chewing.

Just as some basic researchers are beginning to explain some of the biological and chemical underpinnings of carbohydrate addiction, the clinical research that we and others are conducting is helping us to understand more about the behavioral-biological links of this disorder.

Glucose-Transport Disorder

As discussed in Chapter 1, in many people it is an insulin imbalance that leads to the physiological dysfunction that characterizes carbohydrate addiction. There are a range of models and explanations for overweight conditions in general (almost a dozen have been identified and described in research animals). In humans, we have found hyperinsulinemia to be the one that best explains the recurring craving and hunger and the body's tendency to store fat that we have identified in our work with carbohydrate addicts.

Our research suggests that overweight may be better described as a symptom of an underlying disorder rather than the disorder itself. A variety of underlying biologically based imbalances can result from altered interactions between the factors involved. Precipitating factors may include the kinds of foods eaten, the frequency and quantities in which they are consumed, and less easily understood factors, like the body's use of the foods due to inherited metabolic tendencies and the interactions and nature of neurotransmitters, enzymes, hormones, and hormone receptors.

We believe that, at least in part, all of these factors in a significant portion of the population may contribute to what we call glucose-transport disorder. In examining the dysfunctions characteristic of glucose-transport disorder, however, it is necessary to understand the basic workings of part of the body's endocrine system—namely, the pancreas and its hormones.

The pancreas is an elongated, narrow organ approximately the length of the human hand. Located behind the stomach, the pancreas plays an essential role in controlling the fuel that is made available to the cells of the body. It manages this fuel through the release of three hormones—insulin, glucagon, and somatostatin.

After carbohydrates are consumed, the level of the basic fuel from which the cells of the body derive energy, the blood-sugar, glucose, begins to rise. The pancreas responds to the intake of carbohydrates by releasing insulin.

The insulin reaches the cells via the bloodstream. There it binds with receptor sites on the membranes of the cells, increasing their ability to "transport" the glucose from the blood to the interior of the cells themselves. This means the so-called insulin receptor sites located on the surface of the cells are activated. In that way, muscle and fat cells are stimulated to absorb the elevated levels of glucose through these "doors" in order to fuel their activities.

The insulin also facilitates conversion of glucose to glycogen and triglycerides for storage in the liver. A second pancreatic hormone is concerned with another stage of the glucose-glycogen cycle. That hormone, glucagon, is called upon to break down the stored glycogen when energy is required. It is also released into the bloodstream, and its action is effectively to raise the blood sugar level. The role of the third pancreatic hormone, somatostatin, is not yet fully understood, but it is thought to play a role in regulating the production and release of both the insulin and glucagon.

Insulin also acts directly on central nervous system regulators, serving as an intermediary to communicate the need to eat or stop eating. Insulin keys the action of substances that function as regulators—norepinephrine, serotonin, and mesolimbic dopamine—in a complex way that is still not fully understood. In normal functioning, that means insulin alerts the brain to release the neurotransmitter serotonin after each meal. This neurotransmitter then advises the cells of the body to no longer feel hungry.

In a normal person, glucose levels in the blood change in response to a wide variety of events but always remain within set limits. The pancreas of the normal eater releases just enough insulin to support the person's nutritional needs; the receptors allow the cells to receive the right amount of glucose; the insulin helps convert the proper amount of blood glucose to glycogen. Changes in brain chemistry are also cued, leading to the sensation of satiety. The ratio of insulin to glucose changes gradually.

It is important to understand that in normal persons and carbohydrate addicts alike, the body releases insulin in two phases. Researchers call the nature of this process biphasic.

The first phase is termed the *preload phase* and begins within minutes of consuming carbohydrates. In this phase, the pancreas releases a fixed amount of insulin, regardless of how much carbohydrate is being consumed at the time. The amount of insulin is determined by previous carbohydrate intake—that is, by the amount of carbohydrate eaten in the preceding meals. It doesn't seem to matter if the insulin release is cued at a given time by the consumption of one slice of cake or four—the initial phase of insulin release will be a set amount.

Conversely, the second phase of the insulin release, which takes place about seventy-five to ninety minutes after eating, is dependent upon how much carbohydrate is actually consumed at that meal. The body will recognize whether the first phase of insulin was sufficient to handle the carbohydrates consumed. This phase adjusts insulin production and release to the need of that particular meal. If the amount of carbohydrates consumed requires more than the initial quantity of insulin released, then a second measure of insulin will be issued.

In the carbohydrate addict, several of these biological processes fail to perform as they are supposed to, starting at the stage of the glucose transport. For reasons that are not yet clearly understood, sustained high levels of insulin in the blood (hyperinsulinemia) result. Studies have found that overweight people have much higher serum (in-the-blood) levels of insulin than do normal individuals.

High levels of insulin have been observed to coincide with a decrease in the number and sensitivity of insulin receptor sites in the muscle and adipose (fat) cells. This state, in which the cells are less able to absorb insulin and glucose, is called insulin resistance. Although the cause-and-effect relationship has not yet been clearly demonstrated, there is a clear suggestion of such a causal relationship between the decrease in insulin-binding sites and the occurrence of insulin resistance. This is reinforced by findings in many overweight people of changes in insulin responsiveness and sensitivity. In genetically obese mice, hyperinsulinemia has been observed to *precede* the occurrence of obesity.

That means that when too much insulin is in the blood for too long, the cells, paradoxically, change in such a way that *less* insulin is able to enter the cells and facilitate the entry of serum glucose to the tissues. Just as a floodgate may close as water levels rise, in an ever larger spiral, the longer the levels of insulin remain high, the greater is the *decrease* in the number of insulin receptor sites.

Taking an alternate route, the glucose, facilitated by the insulin, appears to be converted to glycogen and triglycerides via the liver. In animals, insulin injections have produced obesity, because insulin appears to stimulate fat synthesis, which means, in the simplest possible terms, overweight occurs in the presence of excess insulin.

Malfunctions extend to the brain chemistry as well. The sensation of being satisfied is never delivered, so the person continues to eat. The disordering effect of the excess insulin is such that a craving for carbohydrate foods results; an attempt is made to satisfy that craving, yet it seems impossible to do so. Thus, the pattern of sustained hyperinsulinemia contributes both to weight gain and continued carbohydrate hunger.

To make matters worse, this pattern can also mean a higher loading of insulin for the next episode of carbohydrate consumption. Researchers have demonstrated that overweight people have a significantly greater insulin release at the preload phase than do thin normals. That means that too much insulin will be released when carbohydrate foods are next consumed, continuing and exaggerating the biochemical cycle.

There are other ramifications of the excess insulin as well. Some of these are only now being studied and observed for the first time. Among these avenues of research are the effects of insulin on the metabolism of amino acids (the building blocks of proteins) and lipids (fats) in the blood, as well as on other intracellular processes.

In summary: the carbohydrate addict falls victim to this sequence of events:

1. Too much insulin is produced for the amount of carbohydrate that is consumed.
2. This excess of insulin results in a decrease in the number of receptors (with an accompanying decrease in removal of insulin and glucose from the blood).
3. Serotonin levels do not rise sufficiently to cause the sensation we identify as satisfaction; the carbohydrate addict does not get the signal to stop eating and continues to eat carbohydrate-rich foods.
4. Production of insulin rises with each subsequent carbohydrate intake.
5. Greater and more frequent quantities of carbohydrates may be consumed with no increase in satisfaction.

Normal Metabolism

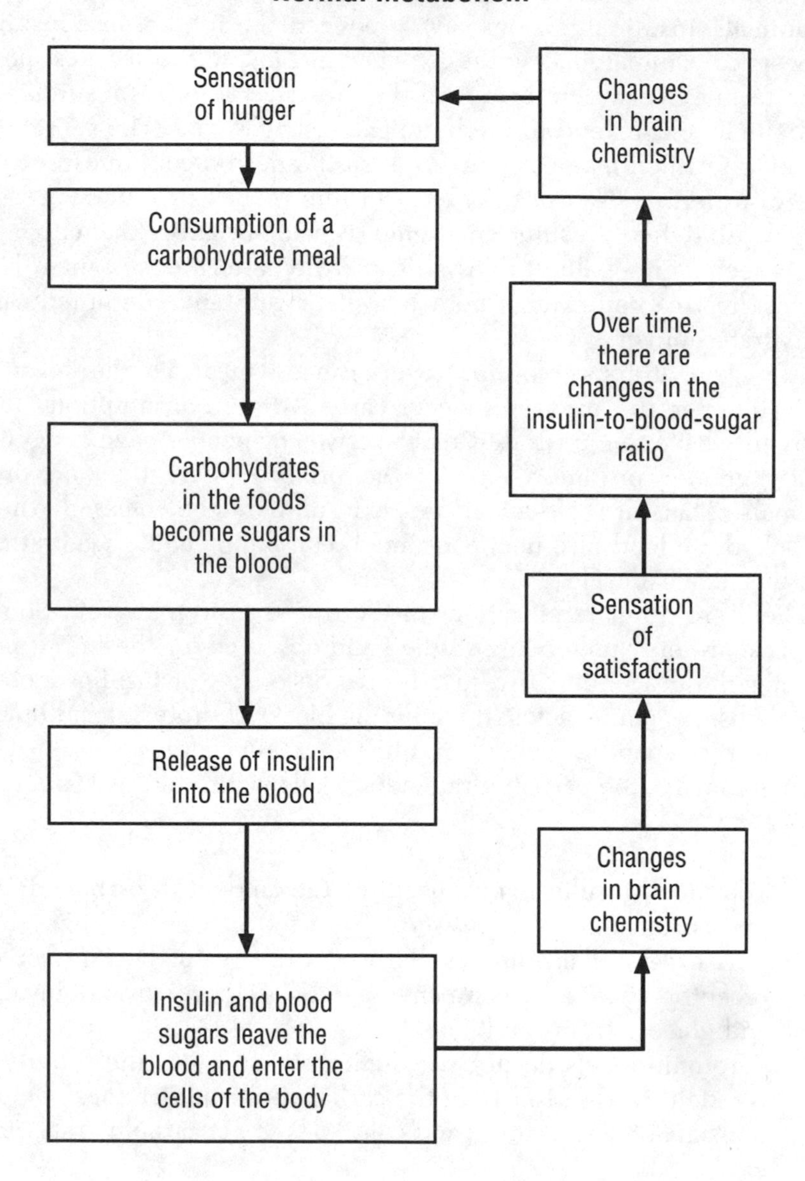

Carbohydrate Addict Metabolism

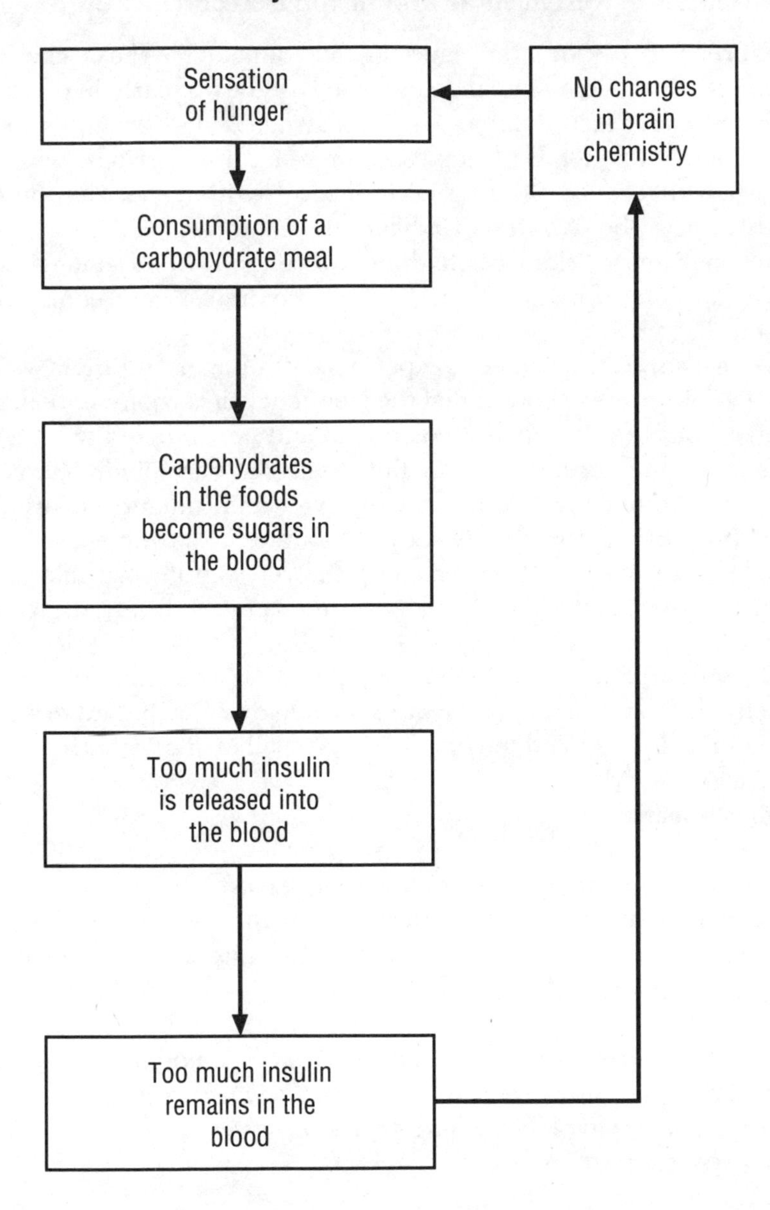

Current Research at Mount Sinai Medical Center

In order to explore the effect of food intake on these chemical workings, we have conducted controlled studies of carbohydrate addicts and nonaddicted subjects. We instructed both groups to consume comparable foods during two four-week time periods, with one important difference—during each of the two time periods the distribution of carbohydrates was different.

For one period, the carbohydrates were distributed among three meals each day; for the other, the carbohydrates were confined to one meal.

We measured the subjects' experience of hunger and their weight change. The results showed that the frequency of carbohydrate intake affected both the carbohydrate-addicted and nonaddicted group's experience of hunger and weight. But it affected carbohydrate addicts at a much higher level. Both weight levels and hunger increased in direct proportion to increases in carbohydrate meal frequency. In the carbohydrate addict, these changes showed significant differences when the total daily food intake was the same and only the carbohydrate frequency was changed.

In summary, we have found, then, that by consuming only one carbohydrate-rich meal per day, the carbohydrate addict experienced less intense hunger and fewer cravings as well as significantly greater weight loss.

This appears to be caused by:

1. Lowered insulin production and/or release
2. An increase in receptor sites (due to the decrease in insulin), with an accompanying increase in the rate at which insulin is removed from the blood

For carbohydrate addicts, this means that by changing the number of times they consume carbohydrates each day, they can reduce the intensity and recurrence of hunger and cravings and increase their body's tendency to lose weight.

We are pursuing other avenues of research involving triglyceride levels and cholesterol levels in relation to frequency of carbohydrate intake.

Our research and that of others indicate that carbohydrate addicts differ greatly in the biological processes that govern their food cravings. Carbohydrate addicts are also different in the ways in which their bodies use and store food energy.

Scientists have discovered that these differences in biological processes can make some people predisposed to overweight. These people find themselves craving carbohydrates, and often have difficulty controlling their eating; their bodies may actually, in some sense, be destined to store fat. These processes have been observed in animals that are genetically predisposed toward obesity.

The research suggests that, because of their genetic makeup, many overweight people are carbohydrate addicts and have strong, biologically based tendencies to become fat. If their underlying disorders are left untreated, they are equally predestined to remain overweight.

At the same time, the evolving body of research reveals a new understanding of the cause of the underlying biological problems, and offers new hope to the carbohydrate addict.

CHAPTER

3

The Carbohydrate Addict's Test

The Carbohydrate Addict's Diet was designed, as its name suggests, for carbohydrate addicts. It isn't the right diet for everyone—because, quite simply, there is no diet that works for all of us. Although the Carbohydrate Addict's Diet may help the nonaddict in the short term, it is unlikely to deliver the pleasure and freedom the carbohydrate addict gets from the plan.

That leaves us with an obligation: at the Carbohydrate Addict's Center and for the readers of this book, we must help carbohydrate addicts distinguish themselves from people with other eating disorders. For that purpose, we have devised the Carbohydrate Addiction Test.

You will find the complete test, including instructions, in the pages that follow. The test itself requires only that you be honest and nonjudgmental with yourself as you answer the questions.

INSTRUCTIONS

1. Please take the Carbohydrate Addiction Test alone, and complete it at one sitting.
2. For each of the questions, answer yes if it *usually* applies to you and no if it *usually* does not. But answer every question.

3. Answer as if you were *not* on a diet or worrying about calorie consumption or about your weight.
4. If you are unsure of an answer, take time to think it through. Don't worry about defending or explaining yourself. Answer candidly about your tendencies or impulses to eat.
5. This test is based on statistical research in the area of eating patterns. It is designed to compensate for guesses. So don't be overly concerned about the "right" answer. In the long run, guessing will not influence the accuracy of the test.
6. Answer each question as if it stands by itself—don't try to link it to any other question. Try not to be concerned about how many yes or no answers you mark. Just answer as honestly as you can without concern for your score.

A CLASSIC CASE: CARMEN'S STORY

Carmen R. wasted no time. "I'm a carbohydrate addict," she assured us, on the phone, even before her first visit to the Center. "I've been one all my life."

Carmen had been referred to us by a cousin who had been following the Carbohydrate Addict's Diet. She called us because she had just seen her cousin for the first time in several months.

"She looked wonderful," Carmen told us. But it wasn't the success of the diet so much as its identity that excited Carmen. "When she used the term 'carbohydrate addiction,' I almost jumped out of my seat. I mean, I *know* that I'm one."

We made an appointment to see Carmen. She was so eager that she arrived a half hour early for our meeting. She was about fifty-five. Her hair was dark, but streaked with gray. She was burdened with about forty extra pounds.

"Something goes haywire in my body when I eat bread or pasta or desserts," she said. "Instead of feeling satisfied, I feel, I don't know, kind of dissatisfied. Not complete. I can feel full, I can even feel stuffed, but I don't feel satisfied. And two hours later, I'm starving."

Carmen poured forth in detail virtually all the classic signs of carbohydrate addiction. The consumption of carbohydrates seemed to let loose an uncontrollable hunger in her. "It's not even that I'm enjoying it that much, it's just that I can't stop."

She recognized the addictive character of her problem as well. "I remember seeing a TV special where they said something about a drug addict taking drugs at first for the good feelings. Later, they said, the drug addict wants a fix to avoid the feelings of withdrawal. I feel like that's me."

She had the symptoms, so we gave her the Carbohydrate Addiction Test. We weren't surprised to find that she fell into the severe addiction range.

We put her on the diet, and it worked. Her weight dropped, steadily and pleasurably, about a pound and a half a week. She told us she planned and shopped specifically for her Reward Meals. "I have an eating plan that I can live with for the rest of my life. It doesn't feel like a diet at all."

As of this writing, she has kept her weight off for four years. She moved to Florida and reports that she now wears shorts "for the first time in years."

The Carbohydrate Addict's Test

Answer yes or no to every question.

1. ______ I get tired and/or hungry in the midafternoon.
2. ______ About an hour or two after eating a full meal that includes dessert, I want more of the dessert.
3. ______ It is harder for me to control my eating for the rest of the day if I have a breakfast, containing carbohydrates, than it would be if I had only coffee or nothing at all.
4. ______ When I want to lose weight, I find it easier not to eat for most of the day than to try to eat several small diet meals.
5. ______ Once I start eating sweets, starches, or snack foods, I often have a difficult time stopping.

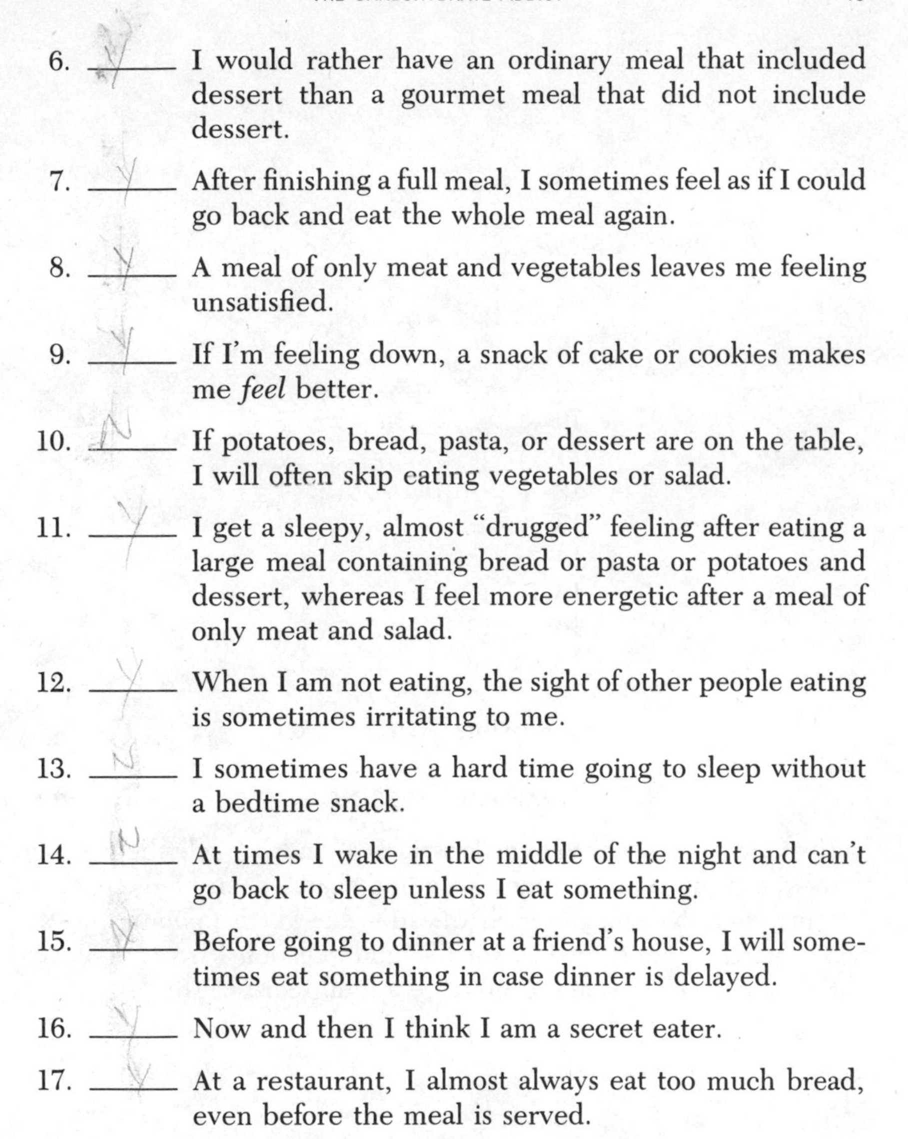

6. ______ I would rather have an ordinary meal that included dessert than a gourmet meal that did not include dessert.

7. ______ After finishing a full meal, I sometimes feel as if I could go back and eat the whole meal again.

8. ______ A meal of only meat and vegetables leaves me feeling unsatisfied.

9. ______ If I'm feeling down, a snack of cake or cookies makes me *feel* better.

10. ______ If potatoes, bread, pasta, or dessert are on the table, I will often skip eating vegetables or salad.

11. ______ I get a sleepy, almost "drugged" feeling after eating a large meal containing bread or pasta or potatoes and dessert, whereas I feel more energetic after a meal of only meat and salad.

12. ______ When I am not eating, the sight of other people eating is sometimes irritating to me.

13. ______ I sometimes have a hard time going to sleep without a bedtime snack.

14. ______ At times I wake in the middle of the night and can't go back to sleep unless I eat something.

15. ______ Before going to dinner at a friend's house, I will sometimes eat something in case dinner is delayed.

16. ______ Now and then I think I am a secret eater.

17. ______ At a restaurant, I almost always eat too much bread, even before the meal is served.

Scoring the Carbohydrate Addict's Test

To determine your score, add the values for each question to which you answered yes.

Question	*Value*
1	4
2	5
3	3
4	4
5	3
6	3
7	5
8	3
9	3
10	3
11	4
12	4
13	3
14	3
15	5
16	3
17	2
Total Possible Score:	60

SAMPLE SCORING

If you answered yes to questions 1, 3, 4, and 7, circle the numbers for those questions on the preceding chart. Then read across the line to find the value for each (question 1 is worth 4 points; question 3 is worth 3; question 4 is worth 4; and question 7 is worth 5). Add the values (4, 3, 4, and 5 produce a total score of 16).

HOW THE TEST WAS DEVELOPED

We asked the people we work with at the Carbohydrate Addict's Center to provide us with daily eating inventories in order to identify significant trends in their eating habits. This test is the result of a close analysis of hundreds of daily eating inventories, detailed logs of all foods consumed.

We also pored over the personal histories of more than 600

carbohydrate-addicted subjects and those of a control group of several hundred normal subjects (nonaddicts) in order to distinguish behavioral patterns characteristic of the carbohydrate addict.

Our goal was twofold. First, we needed to be able to identify which of the dieters who came to us were carbohydrate addicts so that we could predict success in their use of the Carbohydrate Addict's Diet. In scientific terms, then, this goal was to establish the *validity* of the test.

It was also essential to screen out those dieters who were not carbohydrate addicts, for whom the diet was not likely to prove helpful. To our research colleagues, that goal is understood as establishing the *specificity* of the test.

In the seven years since we first devised the test, we have reconstructed and retested it five times. The first version of the test predicted accurately 78 percent of those who were carbohydrate addicts. However, it also identified 26 percent of the normal people who took it as carbohydrate addicts; such cases are called false positives in testing terminology. Clearly, the test needed to be more specific.

In the versions of the test that followed, we improved both validity and specificity. The current version identifies an impressive 87 percent of carbohydrate addicts who take it. The specificity of this version is also outstanding. It identifies only 4 percent of normal individuals as carbohydrate addicts. (The remaining 9 percent of those tested have been found to have a carbohydrate addiction that is compounded by other eating disorders.)

What Your Score Indicates

In brief, the higher the score, the stronger the carbohydrate addiction. A high score also suggests you have probably experienced difficulty in trying to stay on weight-loss programs *not* designed with the carbohydrate addict in mind.

Your total score will identify you as having a *doubtful addiction*, a *mild carbohydrate addiction*, a *moderate carbohydrate addiction*, or a *severe carbohydrate addiction*. More detailed descriptions follow.

DOUBTFUL ADDICTION	(21 or less)
MILD CARBOHYDRATE ADDICTION	(22–30)

MODERATE CARBOHYDRATE ADDICTION (31–44)
SEVERE CARBOHYDRATE ADDICTION (45–60)

Doubtful Addiction

A score of 21 or less suggests that you probably are not having difficulty controlling your eating or your weight. If you are experiencing such difficulties, however, the odds are that your problem is not related to carbohydrate intake. We would, therefore, recommend that you see your physician.

Although some people who test as having a doubtful addiction have been successful when following the Carbohydrate Addict's Diet, this diet was not designed to address the eating patterns or problems of those with doubtful addiction.

Mild Addiction

A score in the 22 to 30 range suggests that you may have some tendency to carbohydrate addiction, but that you are often able to control the impulses.

Sometimes you may experience episodes of eating greater amounts of carbohydrate-rich foods than you intended to eat. You may sometimes eat out of habit or when you are bored, tired, or under stress. You may reward yourself (or the people around you) with food for having accomplished tasks that you didn't really want to do. You may eat simply because "it's there." There's pleasure, even joy, in eating in social situations.

It is doubtful that your weight is a *major* area of concern, though you may want to lose some weight for health or appearance reasons. In the past you may have found that other diets were too restrictive, regimented, or frivolous and you may have concluded they were not worth the effort.

The Carbohydrate Addict's Diet can prevent you from progressing to higher levels of addiction. It can help you to lose weight and feel better about eating—without the artificial calorie counting, food exchanges, and the weighing and measuring of other weight-loss programs. You will find that you can eat the foods you love, in the quantities you want, and still lose weight.

Moderate Addiction

A score in the 31 to 44 range suggests that you experience recurring hunger and food cravings that may vary in intensity but make dieting difficult. You may sense an underlying urge to eat or snack, but at times are able to summon your resources to control it. At other times, when demands or stress levels are high, or when you are tired or ill, your ability to control your eating may slip away.

Most people who have a moderate addiction have recurring concerns about their weight and/or their eating. They often pressure themselves to take off some weight. Moderately addicted carbohydrate addicts are often angry at themselves—until they realize they may have a physical disorder.

If you're moderately addicted, the Carbohydrate Addict's Diet can help you to reduce your desire for snack foods, starches, and/or sweets. As a result, it can help you to lose weight and keep the weight off—without the sense of being deprived you may have felt in the past while dieting. The Carbohydrate Addict's Diet will provide you with a livable, satisfying plan that will allow you a daily reward of the foods you enjoy the most. Most of the people we work with find that they feel a great deal more energetic as well.

Severe Addiction

A score of 45 to 60 indicates that your eating or your weight is probably of great concern to you. Most of the people that we work with who fall within the severe-addiction range experience recurring hunger or food cravings, which at times can be very strong, even overwhelming.

People with a severe carbohydrate addiction are able to stay on diets for a limited time. Typically, they soon find that they just can't keep it up. Sooner or later they find themselves eating the very foods they had been trying to avoid.

The severe carbohydrate addict is likely to have recurrent mood swings and may even experience physical symptoms, such as alternating tiredness or listlessness, and nervousness or irritability. You may have felt trapped, hopeless, and very likely out of control. Severe carbohydrate addicts become "yo-yo" dieters, going on and off diet after diet, trying to find one that can take and keep the weight off.

For you, the severely addicted carbohydrate addict, the Carbohydrate Addict's Diet should be easier to follow than any of the diet plans you have tried in the past. It has been designed to reduce your hunger and food cravings, which reduces the temptation to cheat. The Carbohydrate Addict's Diet is not a temporary program that will abandon you (with only a few words of wisdom for assistance) when it comes to weight-loss maintenance. Rather, it will guide you to a permanent and struggle-free weight-loss maintenance for the rest of your life.

Is She or Isn't She?
Ann's Story

We've had a lot of practice, so perhaps it's not surprising that we both have a sixth sense about carbohydrate addiction. When a new client arrives at our office, we usually know whether she is or isn't even before the talk turns to food and eating habits. Sometimes, though, it isn't obvious, even to us. Ann is a case in point.

She was a trim five-feet-four, 118 pounds, when she came to see us. She'd never been overweight and only recently had developed a problem with carbohydrate cravings. We tried to get a sense of her to begin with, and it didn't take long for some key facts to emerge.

A recent boyfriend had told her she was fat. Ann thought she loved him and wanted very much to please him. Despite the fact she was old enough to know better (she was twenty-eight), she starved herself to near anorexia. But though Ann was below her ideal weight, her boyfriend was still not satisfied.

Ann then began to see herself as fat, too. She had tried a commercially available liquid diet that claimed to be high-protein (but which was, we knew from experience, also high in carbohydrates, with high levels of sucrose, the familiar white table sugar). She did lose some weight, but she also found herself developing recurring food cravings. She began sneaking food and gradually began to gain the weight back. Then her boyfriend left without any real explanation.

By the time we knew all these facts, we had a pretty good idea as to what Ann's problem might be. We gave her the Carbohydrate Addict's Test, and our suspicions were confirmed. Ann tested as a moderate carbohydrate addict, but from what she told us it was apparent that there were other factors that had made her problem worse—namely, her severe, unnecessary, and repeated dieting and her destructive relationship.

The first challenge we put to Ann was to admit that she was a carbohydrate addict. She found it difficult to accept at first, but as we drew her out about her eating habits, the conclusion was inescapable. Finally, she admitted that she had a problem that she just couldn't solve by herself.

The next step was to get her eating regular food in a controlled fashion. We introduced her to the Carbohydrate Addict's Diet. Ann admitted she was a bit frightened. "My eating has been so mixed up," she said. "I change my plan from day to day. I don't know if I can be that disciplined." We explained that the diet would help curb her desire to cheat, and we urged her to try it.

Ann succeeded with the plan, though success wasn't a matter of weight loss in her case. Her success concerned her release from her addiction. "I never knew what normal people felt like," she told us. "I can't believe I've been living with this most of my life.

"I feel different now. I feel like I can think. There's a calmness in me now. I don't feel driven. Do you know what I mean?"

We did.

Remember . . . Not Everybody's a Carbohydrate Addict

Not everyone who is addicted to carbohydrates is overweight, and not everyone who is overweight is a carbohydrate addict. If the Carbohydrate Addict's Test reveals that you are a carbohydrate addict and you are overweight, however, then the chances are better than eight in ten that the Carbohydrate Addict's Diet can help you to lose weight and keep it off.

Please note, as well, that there is no direct relationship between overweight and test scores. The Carbohydrate Addiction Test measures only an exaggerated hunger response created by what appears to be an imbalance in the carbohydrate-insulin-serotonin connection.

We developed the Carbohydrate Addict's Test because we needed to identify candidates for whom the Carbohydrate Addict's Diet was appropriate. We soon found that the test also helped the carbohydrate addict to recognize more of the signs and symptoms of addiction.

Now, it's time to learn how the disorder called carbohydrate addiction influences your feelings and your behavior and how the Carbohydrate Addict's Diet helps correct the physical causes of the addiction itself.

CHAPTER

4

The Carbohydrate Addict's Profile

Our documented research has shown that 75 percent of overweight adults identify themselves as "carbohydrate addicts." Clinical and laboratory findings suggest an even higher percentage is more likely. Evidence indicates that there is an 85 *percent* incidence of carbohydrate addiction in overweight Americans. The bread, pasta, potatoes, sweets, and other carbohydrate-rich foods that they consume testify to their carbohydrate addiction. Some report that they don't enjoy the food, that it doesn't make them feel good, or that they don't find it satisfying. Yet, they often feel a powerful drive to eat.

Addiction is a strong word, yet most carbohydrate addicts seem to understand the concept well. It fits, they say; it describes what they have known and felt. By definition, "addiction" is a dependence on a substance (food or chemical) that produces a habitual or an excessive need for its continued use or consumption. Accompanying notions of withdrawal from and an addictive response to carbohydrates are also familiar to carbohydrate addicts. If you are a carbohydrate addict, you probably recognized the symptoms even before you took the Carbohydrate Addict's Test in the previous chapter.

Not all carbohydrate addicts are the same. There are, however, certain patterns of behavior that are common to many of us. For example, most carbohydrate addicts feel the compulsion to eat when they aren't genuinely hungry. They crave rich, carbohydrate-dense foods like bread or sweets only an hour or two after finishing a meal. It is common for carbohydrate addicts to report that at times they are less satisfied after eating than before; it is also common for carbohydrate addicts to find they have difficulty stopping once they begin to eat bread or pasta, snack foods, or (sometimes) sweets.

Once they begin to eat carbohydrates, the impulse to continue is often difficult to control. Even though they want to stay true to the rules and regulations of their diets, carbohydrate addicts frequently eat foods that are not on their eating programs. This drive to cheat usually builds until the need is satisfied. As this pattern repeats, the carbohydrate addict loses his or her motivation and, over time, the will to diet loses out to the need to eat.

The carbohydrate addict's determination to lose weight is sabotaged by a biologically based disorder.

It usually isn't personality, it's biology.

When a carbohydrate addict eats carbohydrates, his or her body releases too much of the "hunger hormone," insulin, into the bloodstream. Rather than telling the brain the hunger has been satisfied, this excess of insulin (hyperinsulinemia) causes the carbohydrate addict to desire more food after eating. Carbohydrate addicts often feel driven to eat. Yet the more often sweets, starches, and snack foods are eaten, the more insulin is produced and the more frequent and stronger are the cravings for carbohydrate-rich foods.

This seeming compulsion to eat produces weight gain. Even more often, the effects of the insulin on the metabolism will make losing weight much more difficult for the carbohydrate addict than for the normal person.

Most carbohydrate addicts are entirely unaware of their biologically based disorder. Thus, they continue to try to eat and diet as if they were normal people. But following diets designed for normal people usually results in a cycle of disappointment and frustration. The inevitable failure of other diets, the increasing tendency to cheat, and impulses that prove uncontrollable, all lead to self-blame. Rarely do carbohydrate addicts question the appropriateness of their diets. "If my friends manage to lose weight, why can't I?" is a familiar question.

Although carbohydrate addicts often find themselves eating when they had no intention of doing so, the pattern isn't always constant. Strangely, the carbohydrate addict sometimes finds it relatively easy to keep from eating almost anything for a long period; at other times the addict cannot refrain from eating for even short spans of time. The drive to eat often follows the intake of carbohydrates.

One carbohydrate addict we've treated described some of her feelings in this way. Her words are typical of many of the people with whom we have worked.

> It seems like an uncontrollable craving at times. I think I should be able to control myself but I don't. I know I'm not weak-willed. I keep most other aspects of my life together—but not my eating.

Another carbohydrate addict told us:

> Each time I say, "This time I'll do it," but I fail on diet after diet. I often think I'll just give up trying, but I can't. I want to be able to control my eating, lose weight, and look good—and feel good about myself, too.

These are not weak-willed people. Most carbohydrate addicts know, deep inside, that they do not lack willpower. In fact, over the years, we have learned that our dieters are likely to be strong-willed people who are able to control many parts of their lives. But the key point is that, because of the way their bodies react to certain of the foods they eat (i.e., because of their metabolism), most carbohydrate addicts experience hunger or recurring cravings much more intensely and more often than do normal people. They may feel a sense of irritation, anxiety, or anger. They often tell us of feeling tired or sleepy after eating carbohydrate-rich foods. And these responses seem to get stronger over time.

Many carbohydrate addicts tell us their eating baffles them, that they feel betrayed. All too often, they feel like they are betraying themselves.

Maybe you'll recognize some of Rita's frustrations.

With her red hair and expensive attire, Rita made a striking appearance when she came to see us. She had given up her acting career a few years earlier, but was married to a successful businessman who enjoyed seeing her dress well. And so she did.

But Rita found she was outgrowing her clothes as fast as she bought them. "Last week was the last straw," she told us. "I put on a dress that had seemed a bit tight, but certainly fit, a month ago. I had sent it out to be cleaned and when I went to put it on last week, I couldn't get the zipper together. I was furious.

"I called the cleaners and complained that they had shrunk my dress. They were very courteous and said they would check it out. They asked for the number on the receipt. It was still attached to the plastic bag so I gave it to them and they traced the cleaning process.

"They called me back and explained that the item had been cleaned two months before. I was mortified as I realized that the dress didn't fit because I had gained so much weight in that time that I had gone up a complete size or more. If there had been a hole in the floor, I would have dropped in it. Can you imagine?"

We could imagine. Many carbohydrate addicts can understand her feeling of being out of control. That is what this diet is all about.

A Dietary Demon Disguised

When Cindy K. came to the Carbohydrate Addict's Center, she told us she was ready to give up on dieting. She had tried to follow to the letter the various dietary instructions she had been given in the past, yet despite her attempts to do "everything right" (as she put it), she had been unable to lose weight and keep it off.

"It's like something is working against me," she told us. "I'll go along determined that this is the time that I'll do it and *bingo!* before I know it, I'm eating again. I just don't know what happens.

"I really want to stick to it, but I just find myself eating. At this point, I just don't care."

She was angry and frustrated—and unsuccessful in her dieting attempts.

Cindy took the Carbohydrate Addict's Test and talked a good deal about herself and her dieting. It was obvious that her problem wasn't that she just gave up on her diets. It wasn't a lack of willpower. Her problem was that the foods she had been taught were "diet" foods were making her addiction worse.

Cindy, along with hundreds of other people we have treated, had been taught to believe that fruit was a free or safe food. It was, she had been told, a good diet food, and she ate it several times a day. For some dieters, fruit is a perfectly appropriate, low-calorie snack. For the carbohydrate addict, however, fruit is frequently T-R-O-U-B-L-E.

This is why.

Carbohydrate addiction is characterized by a reaction to an entire class of food. This food group is, of course, the carbohydrates, which include breads, starches, sweets, most snack foods—and all fruits, which contain the natural sugar fructose.

When you throw a rubber ball against a hard surface, it bounces back, right? When the carbohydrate addict consumes food rich in carbohydrates, simple or complex, his or her appetite will also "bounce back." And each bounce goes ever higher and higher. The comparison is a bit simplistic, but one cookie will produce the desire for another. Or two or three or a good many more.

The food doesn't have to be a personal favorite of the carbohydrate addict, and may even be one that the dieter was eating while trying to avoid more "fattening" foods. Many carbohydrate addicts reach for fruit instead of candy, thinking that fruit is okay. Although apples and oranges and the rest are traditionally regarded as essentially harmless to the dieter, in the carbohydrate addict a small serving of fruit—even a few grapes—can set off a biochemical chain reaction that produces a strong and recurring desire to eat.

So there was Cindy, dutifully following one dietary regimen after another, all of them promising to help her lose her a few pounds. Unknown to her, her very body chemistry was busily undermining her hopes and her plans. She could force herself to skip her morning Danish, replacing it with an innocent piece of fruit, say an orange. But that orange would cause too much insulin to be produced, and an increase in hunger would result. A piece of fruit would often produce the desire for another; eventually, her desire broadened, and Cindy's fruit fantasies gave way to carbohydrate snacks, foods high in starches and sweets.

We put Cindy on the Carbohydrate Addict's Diet. She reported to us within days that she felt as if she had been freed. "I never knew dieting could be like this. I can't believe it. It's so easy. And all of these years I thought I was 'being good.' I was eating the wrong foods! No wonder I was hungry.

"It's wonderful. It doesn't even feel like dieting. I just didn't realize I was different. I treated myself like every other dieter. And I'm not."

Cindy's carbohydrate addiction is not unique. In fact, she was so happy with the diet that she brought her brother to see us. Alan is a very large man, a weight lifter who stands over six and one-half feet tall. He weighed better than 300 pounds. But he admitted to cowering before an uncontrollable compulsion to eat huge quantities of carbohydrates.

His case was trickier than his sister's. He had noticed on his own that bread and other starches seemed to make him hungry, so he skipped carbohydrates at breakfast and lunch. He even skipped dessert at most dinners. Yet he often felt almost uncontrollable urges to eat. "Suddenly, I'm starving. I eat anything in sight. I don't know what gets into me. I go along fine for a while and then I can't stop," he reported.

We questioned Alan more thoroughly, but the source of his addiction wasn't apparent at first. He didn't share his sister's love for fruit; naturally, we asked him that. We were as puzzled as he—until he dropped the answer before us in living color. It was in lemon yellow and orange orange . . . it was fruit *juices*. He drank them by the gallon, all day long. He consumed a literal stream of carbohydrates that pumped up his insulin level and produced an appetite rebound that Superman couldn't have controlled.

We unmasked Alan and Cindy's dietary demon—that natural fruit sugar, fructose—and limited those foods to a once-a-day satisfying intake. We introduced them to the Carbohydrate Addict's Diet. It worked for both of them and continues to work for them to this day.

The Addictive Process

Many of the carbohydrate addicts with whom we have worked have told us that their inability to stay on their diets grows worse over time. Their desire to cheat seems to grow. At first, they can manage to ignore their urge for forbidden foods. Gradually it becomes a deeper craving. Eventually, their desire becomes uncontrollable.

At the Carbohydrate Addict's Center, we have developed detailed descriptions of what appear to be definable Levels of Addiction. Many dieters regard their failure to stay on a diet as a kind of haphazard eating free-for-all; they think that they are eating anything in sight. But we have found that the carbohydrate addict does not elect to cheat at random. While the carbohydrate addict may believe that he or she is eating more or less by chance ("Who could have known the boss would bring donuts in this morning?"), chance has very little to do with it.

In fact, there is usually a clear pattern to their selection of foods. We have discerned that pattern, and we can pretty much predict the sequence of food cravings. The sequences of predictable eating make up the Levels of Addiction. We have found that we can usually predict with a high degree of accuracy what kinds of foods carbohydrate addicts are likely to eat at any given stage in the addictive process.

The carbohydrate addict's eating is almost always progressive. While the desire to cheat at times seems to disappear, it is never truly gone. Even if the addictive process seems to vanish for extended periods of time, it will always return. The carbohydrate addict's movement through the Levels of Addiction is marked by strong and increasing urges to eat.

Let's take a look at the three Levels of Addiction.

Addiction Level 1

At this level, the addict's desire for carbohydrates is partly hidden by his or her desire for food of all kinds. The carbohydrate addict seems to feel satisfied by eating what he or she has been taught is a good, balanced diet.

The carbohydrate addict rationalizes that vegetables, whole-grain breads, potatoes, and meat, fish, or chicken are healthful foods. When dieting, the Level 1 carbohydrate addict gives in to the desire to eat by consuming great quantities of foods of all kinds without feeling that anything has been lost. "These foods aren't really that fattening" is a common rationale. In the later stages of this level, there may be a desire for fruit as a regular snack. Fruit juices may also be the beverage of choice.

Carbohydrate addicts at Level 1 tend to think that they simply love to eat. For a time they may think that they are in control of their eating.

For the carbohydrate addict, this sense of control is only an illusion. Level 1 is only rarely recognized for what it is—the *first stage* of a progressive disorder. "There's no harm in eating a lot of good food," they tell themselves. But soon the drive to eat progresses and the carbohydrate addicts' weights will often rise as well.

Addiction Level 2

The kinds of foods that the carbohydrate addict eats begin to change at Level 2. Although a wide range of foods is still eaten at this level, the desire for vegetables, protein, and fruit soon begins to fade. In its place, starches such as bread, bagels, pasta, rice, and potatoes begin to seem very important and highly satisfying. Snack foods, such as potato chips, popcorn, and pretzels, become more attractive.

Part of the appeal of starchy and snack foods at Level 2 is that, when they are eaten, they deliver an initial sense of physical satisfaction, a sense of relaxation. Unfortunately, this sense of satisfaction is temporary, and within a few days the same starches and snack foods begin to produce a new and greater urge to eat more of them. At the same time, satisfaction seems to decrease.

Some people have reported a desire for beer or wine at this level, though many do not. Level 2 is often marked by the experience of recurring tiredness, especially after meals or in the middle of the afternoon.

When carbohydrate addicts first reach Level 2, they often deny their own fear ("I'm not out of control"). Gradually the dieter becomes increasingly concerned with issues of eating, weight, and weight loss. The false confidence of Level 1 begins to fade, and more concern is focused on progress (or rather, the lack of progress) in the weight-loss program.

Gradually, the carbohydrate addict realizes he or she is only rationalizing and is in fact no longer in control.

Addiction Level 3

While cravings for starches and snack foods (e.g., bread products, pasta, rice, potatoes and potato chips, pretzels, and popcorn) continue at Level 3, the drive for sweets can become very strong. At this level, snack foods and desserts are preferred.

With the consumption of cakes or cookies or chocolate, the earlier desire for vegetables and even fish, meat, or fowl as well as fruits decreases or even disappears. Most meat or other protein is consumed with bread as a sandwich.

Meals seem incomplete without a sweet dessert. Although sweets provide an initial surge of relief, they soon lose their ability to satisfy the carbohydrate addict.

At this level, many of the people we work with report eating when they are not hungry, when they don't have an urge to eat, and when they don't even *want* to eat. Food doesn't seem to taste especially good. The experience of eating becomes more of a compulsion or duty. The carbohydrate addict at Level 3 is eating because of a driving *need* to eat—a physical, inner demand to eat—rather than out of enjoyment.

Normal mealtimes, periods of eating that are distinct from periods of noneating, gradually disappear. The carbohydrate addict may eat at any time, usually small or large snacks that include sandwiches, snack foods, and/or sweets. Rather than separate meals, the carbohydrate addict finds him- or herself eating continuous snacks. Sandwiches take the place of meals. Some people report that they have a diminished consciousness of their eating habits. As one dieter who came to the Center expressed it, "It's almost like being half-aware of what you're doing, like being half-hypnotized."

Others have commented that they felt as if they were not really aware of what they were doing until after they had put food into their mouths. Tiredness, self-blame, and feelings of hopelessness often mark this level.

RECOGNIZING THE THREE "LEVELS OF ADDICTION"

LEVEL 1

Food Cravings: Good, wholesome meals are desired and enjoyed at Level 1. There is a desire for a wide variety of foods. Typical favorites are salads, vegetables, fruit and fruit juices, red meats, fish, fowl, and cheeses in combination with breads, pasta, potatoes, and desserts.

Psychological Characteristics: At Level 1, the carbohydrate addict is usually confident of his or her ability to control food intake. The carbohydrate addict usually thinks about the weight-loss potential of the foods he or she consumes, rationalizing that "good food never hurt anyone." In general, there is no consciousness of the presence of a progressive, biological disorder.

LEVEL 2

Food Cravings: An increasing desire for carbohydrates emerges at Level 2, especially for breads and baked goods, potatoes, rice, pasta, snack foods (e.g., potato chips, popcorn, pretzels, cheese puffs).

Sometimes there can be a desire for beer or wine. The desire for vegetables and salads lessens.

Psychological Characteristics: The feeling of control found at Level 1 gradually gives way to worry about eating and weight. A feeling of fatigue at midafternoon or following the evening meal is common. The desire for snack foods is most likely to get very strong in the evening.

LEVEL 3

Food Cravings: Snacks and sandwiches become the principal foods at Level 3. Cakes, candy, potato chips, popcorn, cookies, chocolate, pies, puddings, and other carbohydrate-rich foods are the staples at this stage to the exclusion of other foods. Meals are replaced by less defined periods of intermittent snacking.

Psychological Characteristics: The pleasure of eating may fade for the Level 3 carbohydrate addict; there is less a desire to eat than a compulsion or drive to eat. Many people report feeling ashamed and trapped and overwhelmed. An accompanying tiredness and self-blame are also typical. Often there is a sense of failure and the carbohydrate addict may even isolate himself or herself, feeling a desire to be left alone. The dieter may even find himself or herself hiding snacks in a desk or briefcase or pocket as snacking becomes a way of life.

Addiction Triggers

Our bodies are not machines. We do not move from one Level of Addiction to the next in the same way we change gears in a car. The Levels of Addiction themselves are not clear-cut. But in our years of research, we have found that, for most carbohydrate addicts, movement through the Levels of Addiction often proceeds in much the same manner.

When we find differences in our carbohydrate addicts, they can often be attributed to what we call "addiction triggers." These are situations or stresses that cause the carbohydrate addict to progress to higher addiction levels. Even when there are no obvious triggers, the apparent underlying biological disorder that causes carbohydrate addiction itself can press the carbohydrate addict to move to higher

Levels of Addiction. In most carbohydrate addicts, however, we have seen, time after time, certain triggers that move the carbohydrate addict to higher levels of addiction more quickly.

Consider Linda's case history.

Linda's Story

Linda P. came to the Carbohydrate Addict's Center as a last resort. "I've done everything," she said, "but I just can't take this weight off."

She explained. "I gained it when I was pregnant with my daughter and I just can't get rid of it. It's been four years now. My husband and I both want another baby but I'm afraid I'm going to gain another twenty-five pounds with the next one. Maybe even more."

She attempted to explain to us how her body had changed.

"I don't know, it feels like my metabolism has changed or something. I didn't think I ate that much when I was pregnant but I had nothing to compare it with. Anyway, I know I don't eat that much now but everything I eat seems to stay. If I manage to take off a few pounds I put it on the first time I go off the diet or even if I just relax a little. I don't want to keep putting off getting pregnant but I'll die if I gain even more.

"I don't know what to do," she concluded.

Linda's story had a very familiar ring to us. We confirmed that she was in fact a carbohydrate addict with the Carbohydrate Addict's Test. Then we were able to tell her that we thought we could help her. We recognized that for Linda her addiction trigger had been her pregnancy.

She had been of average weight during her childhood, teenage, and early adult years. It was only with the advent of pregnancy that her carbohydrate addiction had been activated. We had learned from other women in Linda's situation that there is a sort of genetic time bomb that explodes into action with the hormonal changes that take place during pregnancy. Linda told us the same changes had taken place when her mother became pregnant. We had seen this family pattern many times.

Not all women have the problem, of course; even those whose pregnancies trigger their carbohydrate addiction don't experience it in the same way. In some, the carbohydrate addiction disappears shortly after they give birth, whereas in others it continues for quite a while. In still other women, their carbohydrate addiction simply doesn't go away until it is corrected.

In most of the cases of pregnancy-triggered carbohydrate addiction we have seen, the women have been able to regain control of their eating and their weights with use of the Carbohydrate Addict's Diet. Many of these women have gone on to have additional children, confident of their ability to avoid the same pregnancy-overweight syndrome the next time they had a child.

Linda, however, surprised us. With the help of the Carbohydrate Addict's Diet, she succeeded in freeing herself of the carbohydrate addiction spiral. That was evident immediately when she returned for a follow-up interview five months after first coming to us. By then she was thirty pounds thinner.

Almost before we could say "hello-how-are-you," she blurted, "I have some exciting news." We expected to hear that she felt ready to become pregnant once again or perhaps that she was already expecting. That wasn't it.

Linda informed us that because she "felt so wonderful with her new figure and newfound freedom" (from worries about her weight and her desire to eat) that she and her husband decided to postpone having a second baby.

She had been promoted ("I'd been doing good work all along but no one ever recognized it or gave me any more money for it"). Rightly or wrongly, she attributed her promotion to her weight loss, her new clothes, and her positive attitude. She was enjoying her life, and she wanted to relax and take advantage of the feeling.

"This isn't a diet that I'm afraid I'm going to go off within a few weeks. I know I will be able to keep this weight off all of my life and, for now, I'm not in such a hurry to change a thing."

Don't Pull the Trigger

In the carbohydrate addict, individual triggers—sometimes situations or stressful events—can affect the body's biochemistry. There may be an effect upon the neurotransmitter balance in the brain, which controls the experience of hunger and satisfaction and therefore the complex mechanisms involved in fat storage. This translates to a difficulty in losing weight or an increased or recurring hunger.

In general, weight-loss programs that do not treat the cause of carbohydrate addiction do not address such triggers. Most programs are unable to help the dieter to counteract them. The result is that carbohydrate addicts find themselves trying to cope with strong impulses to eat or snack with no alternative strategy available to help.

Some particularly strong-willed people are able to resist for a short time the urge to snack, eat, or binge. If the trigger situation or stress continues for a prolonged period, however, few carbohydrate addicts are able to withstand the resulting drive to eat. When several different trigger situations or stresses occur one after another or even simultaneously, they seem to have a multiplying effect, making it even more difficult to resist that powerful urge to eat. The Carbohydrate Addict's Diet was designed to help the carbohydrate addict reduce the recurring desire to eat that is brought on by these triggers. The eating plan that makes up the diet was especially designed to reduce the hormonal backlash that the triggers can bring on.

Almost all of the carbohydrate addicts with whom we have worked over the years have found that they are better able to handle everyday stresses and strains with less anger, internal conflict, and aggravation when using the diet. When they put it to use, our dieters experience the benefit of a more balanced system. The system itself acts to enable carbohydrate addicts to deal with trigger situations or stresses and help them to stay firmly in control.

There are different triggers for different people, as the stories of Adrian, Mary, and the others that follow suggest.

Adrian's Story

Adrian looked frazzled the first time she came to see us. Attractive and well groomed, Adrian was in her late forties, but her pent-up tension and anger made her look older.

"If I were an alcoholic, we would say that my boss was driving me to drink. Instead, he's driving me to eat. I don't mean this as an excuse, but I really feel that he's making me eat.

"I am so angry at him, I tear into food. I literally bite into a roll like I'm biting into him. I don't leave my anger at the office, either. I bring it home with me and overeat at home, too."

Adrian looked sad and hopeless as she told us, "I'm stuck. I can't leave the job." With a child in college and another in law school, she and her husband needed the money. Yet her physician had found her blood pressure had grown dangerously high, and she had put on twenty pounds since taking her high-pressure job. "I have more food in my drawers than the guy on the coffee cart. I'm getting to the point that I stuff my face without even knowing what I'm eating," she said.

Adrian lost her weight and regained control of her eating—though it took a confrontation with her boss, as well as the Carbohydrate Addict's Diet, to do it.

Mary's Story

One of the most frequent addiction triggers for the women we work with are changes that occur immediately before the monthly onset of menstruation. Mary O.'s case is typical.

Mary made her appointment several weeks in advance. "I want to come and see you when I'm in the middle," she told us on the phone. "I want you to see how bad it is."

When she arrived, we were struck almost immediately by her anger. She was frustrated at her plight—and she had a deep sadness about her. It became apparent that she was very tired of fighting and feeling frustrated at her periodic loss of control.

"Four, five, maybe six days a month, I'm a mess. I'm miserable. And I can't stop eating. I eat everything in sight. I'm like a crazy person. I've given up even trying to control myself. And I end up starving myself the rest of the month to try and limit the damage I've done during these few days.

"Nobody seems to be able to do anything to help me. They all agree that it's probably hormonally related, but nothing they have done has helped. If you could just help me to stop eating, maybe I could get the other things under control."

She unburdened herself of her fears. "I feel like my life is falling apart. It's not getting better. If anything, it feels like it's getting worse."

The result of Mary's Carbohydrate Addict's Test placed her in the severe range during her premenstrual days, so we recommended she start on the Carbohydrate Addict's Diet immediately.

She was reluctant at first because we advised her to remain on the diet all month long, not just on the days when she usually experienced her eating problems. She said when she decided to come to us that she had "hoped this diet was only going to be necessary during those four or five days."

We finally convinced her to try the diet full-time by explaining that a balanced eating program was necessary all month long. Only by its sustained use could the diet help her reduce or even eliminate the swings of mood and eating that she had experienced.

Mary called us within days; her own words speak most clearly for the results. "Why didn't you tell me it would be like this?" she exclaimed. "I feel better than I have in years. Better than I ever felt. I can't believe it. I wouldn't go off this diet on a bet.

"The cravings are gone. I'm losing weight, and I *never* lose weight at this time of the month. I feel human again. It's like I'm not expecting it at all."

Chris's Story

Chris L. presented us with a different kind of problem. She was a carbohydrate addict all right, her test scores revealed that. What wasn't so apparent was the reason why.

"You have to understand that a couple of years ago my test results would have been entirely different," she told us. "Something's changed and, so help me, it's making me a carbohydrate addict."

Like detectives, we tried to trace the changes that had taken place in Chris's life that might have set off an addictive response. At first, the only life event that seemed to correlate with her change in eating habits was that she had moved to a new apartment on her own, after having lived with roommates.

We asked her to keep a food diary to help us pinpoint the culprit. She was to note everything she ate, the times and places she ate, and the level of her hunger. Sure enough, a pattern emerged. When she ate with other people, whether it was at a restaurant, at her home or theirs, or at work, she didn't experience the drive to eat. But when she ate alone, she often felt the compulsion to eat. But that still wasn't the whole story, because it didn't *always* happen when she ate alone.

Another week of keeping her food diary offered the answer. Her addictive response to food invariably occurred after eating at a restaurant in her neighborhood. She always ate alone there; it was kind of a second home for her. The people knew her, she liked the food, and she felt comfortable there.

We asked Chris to experiment. The test worked: when she stayed away from the restaurant for a week, her cravings stopped, confirming her and our suspicions. But we all wanted to know exactly what was the cause. A talk with the head cook provided the answer.

We had briefed her on food sensitivities, on the several foods and additives that we had found had brought about an addictive response in other people with whom we had worked. Chris called the next afternoon.

"Bingo." She laughed with relief. "We got it. It's MSG. Monosodium glutamate. They put it in the casseroles, they put it in corned beef hash, they put it in the vegetables." Her trigger was the additive MSG, which is often used in preparing Chinese cuisine but may also be present in a variety of other foods, among them salad dressings.

Chris L. eliminated monosodium glutamate from her diet; with that gone, her cravings disppeared as if by magic.

We've had people who, because of changes in their daily habits, found themselves snacking and gaining weight. One recently widowed woman had begun spending time with a group of women in her building. They played cards, went to the movies, lunched, and dined together. This also meant a significant change from her previous eating history. She had kept her husband company at meals, she told us, but "food was never very important to him, and not to me either." When she suddenly found herself around food all the time, she started eating a lot more than she ever had.

Another woman who came to us drank quantities of a certain diet soda that triggered her carbohydrate addiction. Caffeine seemed to be the culprit in her case. Other people, too, have found that changing seasons seem to provoke an addictive response—the cravings and the pounds accumulate in the fall and winter and they struggle (but fail) to take them off in the spring.

These varied problems suggest how everyday foods, activities, and other factors can trigger a carbohydrate addiction. Be alert for such life-events. If your carbohydrate addiction occurred suddenly, or if your addiction intensifies rapidly, there may be a simple explanation. Finding it may help you resolve or more easily gain control over your addiction.

But now it's time to learn about the diet itself in detail.

ADDICTION TRIGGERS

The events of any given day may bring on a desire to eat. The familiar and obvious smell of fresh baked goods when you walk past a bakery can trigger an addictive attack, as can a more subtle (and seemingly irrelevant) event like a disagreement with a colleague at your place of work.

We call these day-to-day experiences "addiction triggers." Here is a list of some of the most common triggers we have observed in the carbohydrate addicts we have treated at the Carbohydrate Addict's Center.

EMOTIONAL STATES

The following feelings may provoke a desire to eat:

- Anger you can't express
- Anxiety
- A sense of being out-of-control or of being powerless
- Depression
- Excitement
- Frustration
- Self-blame

DAY-TO-DAY ACTIVITIES

Many quite unexceptional day-to-day activities can cause the carbohydrate addict to progress to higher addiction levels. These include:

- Changes in home life
- Changes in working conditions
- Exercise
- Illness

- Pregnancy
- Premenstrual changes
- Quitting smoking
- Stressful situations of almost any kind

EATING HABITS

Not surprisingly, a range of dietary and nutritional factors can also trigger addictive responses. Among them are:

- Extreme dieting
- Fasting
- The sight or smell of food
- Rapid weight gain
- Rapid weight loss

HIGH-CARBOHYDRATE FOODS

Consuming high-carbohydrate foods is another surefire way to trigger the desire for more carbohydrates. Among the foods that most of our dieters have found trigger their addictions are:

- Bread and other grain products, including bagels, cookies, cereals, cakes, crackers, pastries, doughnuts, and rolls.
- Fruit of all kinds, including grapes (and raisins), bananas, cherries, dates, apples, and oranges. Juices too.
- Sweet dessert foods, including ice cream, chocolate, candy, puddings, sherbets.
- Snack foods like popcorn, potato chips, pretzels, cheese puffs, and nuts.
- And other foods, too, including some beans (Boston baked beans, rich with molasses, is a classic trigger); all kinds of pasta, from simple spaghetti and egg noodles to ziti and ravioli; rice (alone and in other dishes); French fries; and—don't forget—plain sugar, too, even just a spoonful of it in your coffee or tea.

PART II

THE DIET

CHAPTER

5

The Carbohydrate Addict's Diet

This diet requires a willingness to learn a new way to eat and to forget lots of the old rules and myths about dieting that have failed to help you in the past. Remember: this diet is designed to treat the *cause* of your excess weight or recurring cravings.

The Carbohydrate Addict's Diet is an eating plan designed by carbohydrate addicts for carbohydrate addicts. It includes some new approaches to treating carbohydrate addiction and helping you to lose weight.

No weighing, no measuring. The Carbohydrate Addict's Diet is not a living-by-the-numbers approach to dieting. It does away with the weighing and measuring, calorie counting, and exchange plans common to many other diets. Instead, your body's own biological mechanisms are used to reduce your carbohydrate cravings, your intake of calories, and the desire to cheat.

You needn't give up your favorite foods. In his first inaugural address, Franklin Delano Roosevelt said, in reference to the Great Depression, "The only thing we have to fear is fear itself." In a similar vein, the Carbohydrate Addict's Diet requires only that you give up the notion that dieting means you must be deprived. The Carbohydrate Addict's Diet doesn't require you to put your appetite on hold for weeks or months on end. It doesn't require you to give up "forbidden" or fattening foods.

The Carbohydrate Addict's Diet is not one of those starvation diets that produce short-term weight loss usually followed by an appetite rebound—and by rapid weight gain. The Carbohydrate Addict's Diet has proven that for one of your meals each day, every day, you can eat what you want, in the quantities that satisfy you—and still lose weight (in the short term) and keep it off (in the long term).

You aren't limited to small portions. Most diets advise eating small meals several times a day. In contrast, the Carbohydrate Addict's Diet does not restrict you to small portions.

The other diets base their advice on the assumption that all dieters will find small, frequent meals containing carbohydrates satisfying. Although this may be true for other dieters, such a regimen plays havoc with the metabolic chemistry of the carbohydrate addict. As a result, standard diets do not produce a comfortable and permanent weight loss for the carbohydrate addict. Instead, these diets, with their frequent small carbohydrate meals, actually feed the addiction and eventually lead to a loss of control of eating.

That's why such diets don't work for the carbohydrate addict. Just as you can't expect an alcoholic to drink small quantities of liquor several times a day, we have found that no one can expect the carbohydrate addict to eat small or "sensible" portions of carbohydrates several times daily.

As you will see, our approach is different.

Portrait of an Addict: Ellen's Story

We sensed immediately that Ellen was a very giving person. Forty-two years old, she was a homemaker, happily married and the mother of two teenage daughters.

"I think most girls are dissatisfied with their weight," she told us, "and I was no different. But when I look back at my pictures I was absolutely normal. I was twenty-five when I got married and I wore a size eight. But I'm twice that size now." She looked older than her years, too, with her soft brown hair going gray.

"Right after I got married, I got pregnant with my first girl. I ended up twenty pounds heavier. With my second daughter, I gained another twenty, and somewhere along the way I picked up a few more.

"I need to lose at least forty pounds, maybe even fifty," she concluded.

She knew about Carbohydrate Addict's Center because a friend had consulted us. She'd even looked over her friend's Carbohydrate Addict's Test and determined that she would test even higher than her friend had.

"Last week, I really saw how bad things had gotten. I baked a square chocolate cake for Susan, my fourteen-year-old, because she was having friends over for a slumber party. I was finished baking by around one o'clock in the afternoon and the cake was cooling before I put on my famous butter-cream frosting." Ellen's manner was reserved, her voice soft.

"Each time I walked past the cake, I would smooth an end of it, picking up some crumbs to even it out. Then I would stick a knife into the frosting and smooth it out and lick it off. By the time I actually got around to putting on the frosting, the cake was about a quarter gone.

"Then I cut the cake in half in order to put one square layer on top of the other, but the shape looked strange. You know, too small to be a normal cake and too large for a small cake. I continued to pick and snack at the cake in order to make it look right, then I put it into the refrigerator.

"Then I went into the bedroom and fell into a heavy sleep. I got up just as the girls were getting home from school." Ellen was very sheepish by the time she reached this part of her story.

"They went to the refrigerator and found this ridiculous little cake that looked really strange. They wanted to know what had happened to the rest of the cake. Then—and here's what really got to me—I lied. I said that my sister had come over—they know how she can eat—and that she ate up quite a bit of the cake. But the girls looked at me like they knew something was wrong."

Ellen finally went to the store to buy a cake for her daughter's party. "I felt like a drug addict or alcoholic, covering up my addiction from my family. And I felt so frightened of them seeing through my story. Here I was frightened of my own kids. It's a really lousy way to feel.

"That's when I called you. I thought that you might be able to do something for me."

You can adjust the diet to special situations. The Carbohydrate Addict's Diet is a dynamic, flexible plan that can accommodate day-to-day changes in your life and your lifestyle.

Important food-related events—whether it's the once-a-year anniversary celebration at the fanciest restaurant in town or the everyday family dinner—can be enjoyed while you still follow your diet and lose weight. Business lunches, entertaining, holidays, parties, and special affairs will no longer present you with temptations to cheat: with a little planning, you can eat normally with your family or friends, and still remain true to the diet and to yourself.

You don't need to feel guilty anymore. The Carbohydrate Addict's Diet offers the incredible experience of being blameless—something many of us have rarely felt. The hundreds of subjects who followed the diet in its first few years used it without guilt-ridden cheating sessions. The diet does not require that you deprive yourself; you don't need to starve yourself for days or weeks; you don't have to eat tiny "diet meals."

You won't be left high and dry. The diet doesn't just abandon you when you reach your target weight as many other diets do.

We haven't taken the Band-Aid approach that many other diets have. These diets fail to help dieters to keep their weight off and then blame dieters for regaining the weight. Losing weight isn't like a small cut that can just be protected for a week or two and then will disappear forever. Weight problems in most people require ongoing attention and concern. The Carbohydrate Addict's Diet will help you to change your lifestyle to treat your addiction for the rest of your life.

The Carbohydrate Addict's Diet isn't a hit-and-run program that will leave you alone and defenseless after a while. Instead, the diet helps to curb your own biological urge for the rest of your life. Best of all, you need no longer fear bingeing, cheating, or regaining those pounds.

The goal is permanent weight loss. The goal of the Carbohydrate

Addict's Diet isn't *quick* weight loss; our purpose is *permanent* weight loss. Physicians and scientists agree that the faster you lose weight, the faster you are likely to regain it. It's like the old story of the woman who lost 1,000 pounds—50 pounds, twenty times over. That's just what our program is about.

We have found the best way to lose weight (so it will remain lost) is to take it off at a measured and sensible pace. *At the Carbohydrate Addict's Center we have found that the best weekly rate of loss should be no more than about 1 percent of the dieter's current weight*. Thus, a 200-pound person should lose no more than two pounds a week, a 150-pounder no more than one and one-half pounds, and so on. This view is shared by the medical community and is endorsed by the National Council Against Health Fraud, Inc., which warns dieters to "beware of weight-loss programs that promise or imply dramatic, rapid weight loss."

Weight-loss programs that promise quicker rates of weight loss do so because their diets are difficult to follow for more than a limited time. On such deprivation diets, even the truly motivated dieter can continue for no more than a few weeks or months. Thus, on these diets, quick weight loss is important because it is the principal reward the diet offers.

The result—and bitter experience is speaking here, both firsthand and on behalf of countless others—is money spent, a quick loss of weight, and then abandonment. It's a lonely feeling, being left to the wiles of a metabolism that has slowed from the fast weight loss. And to the inevitable fear that you're about to gain back the weight. And the self-blame that follows when you do.

This diet isn't for everyone. Most people do not have the same metabolic response to carbohydrates that the carbohydrate addict does. Nonaddicted people can eat "normally." But if you're a carbohydrate addict, you cannot eat "normally" without eventually losing control. Trying to eat and diet like a normal person can only lead to frustration and failure. If you have taken the Carbohydrate Addict's Test in Chapter 3, you know whether or not you are a carbohydrate addict. If you are, then you can be confident that this diet program was designed for you.

Try it out. The authors of this book both suffer from carbohydrate addiction, and as scientists we were committed to finding a way out of our addiction by using our knowledge, skills, and training. "After all," we reasoned, "if we are working on treatments for other kinds of disorders, why shouldn't we be working on something that will help us as well?"

As scientists, we knew that our personal success would not, in itself, provide sufficient clinical information for acceptance of the scientific community, so we tested the Carbohydrate Addict's Diet on others. Over a seven-year period, hundreds of people who have used the diet under our guidance have, in more than eight out of every ten instances, found it a successful means to permanent weight loss. As they lost weight, our carbohydrate addicts also reported decreases in cravings and hunger, as well as great increases in energy levels.

Dieters who use it have reported a number of other dividends as well. Some say they sleep better, waking more refreshed than they ever have. Others say they have discovered a renewed sense of energy, even a "sense of peace" upon adopting the diet.

Such improvements aren't surprising really, because a physical battle with an addictive substance is being brought to a successful end. This doesn't mean that the Carbohydrate Addict's Diet will solve all of your emotional or physical problems. It isn't a substitute for diagnosis and treatment of physical or psychological ailments. But if carbohydrate addiction is your problem, the Carbohydrate Addict's Diet may well contribute to an enjoyable and improved quality of life.

Staying on the Carbohydrate Addict's Diet is easy and fun. It does away with the triggers that have, in the past, brought about your failure. Instead of blaming you, the Carbohydrate Addict's Diet works with your strengths—the strengths that every carbohydrate addict naturally has. The strengths are there, in the biochemistry of your metabolism, and we have found that you can make them work for you.

Putting the Guidelines into Practice

The Carbohydrate Addict's Diet works on entirely different principles than other diets.

Once we came to understand the mechanism behind carbohydrate addiction (the overproduction of insulin, or hyperinsulinemia), we needed to help the carbohydrate addict to avoid it.

We could have cut out carbohydrates as a way to reduce insulin.

But it wasn't reasonable to ask anyone to eliminate all carbohydrates from his or her diet indefinitely—nor would it be healthy to do so. So that was out.

Fortunately, we have found eliminating carbohydrates isn't necessary.

Carbohydrate addicts have the greatest difficulty controlling their eating when they consume carbohydrate foods several times a day. Conversely, when the number of meals or snacks at which carbohydrate foods are eaten is decreased, eating becomes controllable and cravings decrease dramatically.

When carbohydrates are eaten less frequently, less insulin is produced. The body has a lowered tendency to store the excess calories in its fat cells and is more capable of breaking down stored fat. In that way, the carbohydrate-insulin-serotonin connection functions more effectively for weight loss. We have found that the less often the carbohydrate addict consumes carbohydrate-containing foods, the more satisfying the foods are—and the greater the control of eating that is possible. In short, we found the overweight-carbohydrate-addiction cycle can be broken.

Our research has also revealed that when the carbohydrates are consumed during a limited period of time, it appears that the usual overproduction of insulin is decreased. Thus, a long evening—say, several hours or more—of eating and drinking presents a special difficulty to the carbohydrate addict. Perhaps the evening involves a leisurely dinner of, say, hors d'oeuvres, soup, salad, entrée, and dessert. Drinks may be served before and after the meal. This kind of extended consumption of food and drink (in particular, of carbohydrates) is practically guaranteed to produce an exaggerated insulin response in the carbohydrate addict. Because an excess of insulin is produced, the long dinner actually leaves the carbohydrate addict unsatisfied or craving carbohydrates that evening or during the day that follows.

If, on the other hand, that same food is consumed within a single hour, the carbohydrate addict experiences far less hunger. The reason for this difference in satisfaction is that the body is able to produce only a limited amount of insulin at any time. Thus, if the time during which food is consumed is limited, the time during which your body is called upon to produce insulin is limited also. The result is that the amount of insulin produced can be controlled to the degree that hyperinsulinemia (production of excess insulin) can be prevented.

We have discovered that there are two primary factors that negatively affect the eating behaviors of the carbohydrate addict: the *frequency* at which carbohydrates are eaten (i.e., at more than one sitting daily) and the *duration* of the consumption (i.e., when that one sitting exceeds sixty minutes).

An ideal diet for the carbohydrate addict, then, is a diet that, first, limits the number of times each day that carbohydrates are eaten (though it does *not* appear to require reducing the *amount* of carbohydrates eaten at that meal); and second, that limits the time allotted for eating that meal.

The Carbohydrate Addict's Diet Plan

The Carbohydrate Addict's Diet is a dynamic eating plan that will allow you to eat Low-Carbohydrate Meals and daily Reward Meals (see page 106) in combinations that will help you to greatly reduce your hunger for carbohydrates while you lose weight and permanently maintain the weight that you desire.

Each week, you will follow an eating plan that is based on (1) the amount of weight you lost that week and (2) the amount of weight you want to lose in the coming week.

Most diets are one-size-fits-all plans that do not take you, as an individual, into account. Just as no two people can be expected to respond in exactly the same way to a single medical treatment, no two people can be expected to respond in the same way to a single eating plan. One person may lose weight, another may not. You've seen it yourself. You starve yourself all week to find that you've put on half a pound, while your spouse or a friend eats twice as much and gets away with it.

Different people respond differently to different diets. Even the same person may lose at different rates at different times. The Carbohydrate Addict's Diet takes into account many factors that may influence your body's response to dieting, factors like your age, gender, metabolic rate, and activity level.

Just as a medication or treatment needs to be adjusted to fit *your* particular system, each week the Carbohydrate Addict's Diet will help you to choose the correct diet plan that will help you to reduce your hunger and successfully meet your weight-loss goals.

All five plans (Entry Plan and Plans A, B, C, and D) consist of combinations of Low-Carbohydrate and Reward Meals. Each plan will have a different effect on you and on your weight loss.

Directions

As you begin the Carbohydrate Addict's Diet, follow the Entry Plan for two weeks. Weigh yourself every day and record your weight (see Chapter 7). At the end of two weeks you will be able to see your weight loss for that period.

Then decide if you want to continue to lose weight in the coming week or if you would prefer to maintain your weight. Based on that information, the Carbohydrate Addict's Diet Guide (page 86) will tell you which diet plan (Plan A, B, C, or D) to follow in the coming week in order to meet your weight-loss or weight-maintenance goal.

Each week, the Carbohydrate Addict's Diet Guide will help you to select the most appropriate diet plan for *you* based on how much weight you lost in the previous week and how much weight you would like to lose in the coming week.

Some people find that they can stay on one particular plan for many weeks, losing weight steadily, feeling satisfied and content. Others find that their bodies are more changeable. They need the variety of plans offered by the Carbohydrate Addict's Diet to avoid the exasperating and defeating plateaus of past single-plan diet programs.

Remember:

When you begin the Carbohydrate Addict's Diet, follow the Entry Plan for two weeks and record your weight daily (see Weighing Yourself, page 118). At the end of your second week on the Entry Plan, The Carbohydrate Addict's Diet Guide (on the following pages) will help you to select the best diet plan (Plan A, B, C, or D) for you to follow for the next week. Continue to weigh yourself daily.

At the end of each week, go back to the Carbohydrate Addict's Diet Guide that follows in order to select your following week's plan.

The Guidelines

The Carbohydrate Addict's Diet allows you to change your eating habits without depriving you of the foods you love in the quantities that satisfy you.

THE DIET PLANS

Note that detailed Reward Meal and Low-Carbohydrate Meal guidelines are included in Chapter 6.

ENTRY PLAN

Each day eat:

- a Low-Carbohydrate Breakfast,
- a Low-Carbohydrate Lunch,
- and a Reward Dinner*

PLAN A

Each day eat:

- a Low-Carbohydrate Breakfast,
- a Low-Carbohydrate Lunch,
- a Reward Dinner*,
- and a Low-Carbohydrate Snack

PLAN B

Each day eat:

- a Low-Carbohydrate Breakfast,
- a Low-Carbohydrate Lunch,
- and a Reward Dinner*

* Your Reward Meal may be eaten at breakfast or lunch if desired. See p. 106.

It's simply a matter of biology. People who are not carbohydrate addicts feel satisfied after eating. That's because their metabolism responds in two ways to the food they take in: first, insulin is released so that the body can use the food energy that has been consumed; and, second, it releases the brain messenger serotonin in quantities great enough to issue the "stop-eating" order.

We now know that in the carbohydrate addict these mechanisms malfunction. We devised the Carbohydrate Addict's Diet in order to correct these malfunctions. If these malfunctions are not corrected, the carbohydrate addict can expect to continue to feel hunger or

THE DIET PLANS (*continued*)

PLAN C

Each day eat:

- a Low-Carbohydrate Breakfast,
- a Low-Carbohydrate Lunch,
- and a Reward Dinner* plus Salad

On Plan C, it is important to *begin* your Reward Dinner with at least two cups of salad. Since this is your Reward Meal, any vegetables may be included in this salad. Top salad off with your favorite salad dressing. After you have finished your salad, go on to enjoy your Reward Meal.

PLAN D

Each day eat:

- *Either* a Low-Carbohydrate Breakfast
- *or* Low-Carbohydrate Lunch
- and a Reward Dinner* plus Salad

On Plan D it is important to *begin* your Reward Dinner with at least two cups of salad. This is your Reward Meal so you can include any vegetables you want in this salad. Add your favorite salad dressings. After salad, go on with your delicious Reward Meal. This diet plan may result in a too-rapid weight loss. If weight loss is more than two pounds per week, return to Plan B or Plan C.

* Your Reward Meal may be eaten at breakfast or lunch if desired. See p. 106.

recurring cravings, to feel unsatisfied, and to regain weight that has been lost.

Because there are so few rules, it is very important that you follow them exactly. Most dieters have very little trouble in doing so because the diet suits them and addresses their needs. The diet itself makes it easy to follow. You will not feel deprived.

In fact, you may not even feel like you are on a diet—*but don't be fooled*. The diet won't work if you don't follow the basic guidelines.

Guideline #1: Eat Low-Carbohydrate Meals Daily

When you keep the carbohydrate intake low during your Low-Carbohydrate Meals, your body responds by producing and releasing *less* insulin. Less insulin means less hunger, fewer cravings, and a feeling of satisfaction. Best of all, a lowered level of insulin prods your body to take fat out of storage and to use it.

It is important to create a daily routine, in which the same two meals are designated as your Low-Carbohydrate Meals. The foods that you eat at these meals must be low in carbohydrates. We have found that many of our most successful dieters eat their Low-Carbohydrate Meals at breakfast or at lunch. In the next chapter, we will give you detailed advice in planning for your Low-Carbohydrate Meals.

In general, your Low-Carbohydrate Meals should consist of average servings (about four to six ounces) of meat, fish, or fowl, or two to three ounces of cheese, and roughly one and one-half to two cups of vegetables or salad. These meals will satisfy you and help you to lose weight while keeping your insulin levels low. Low-Carbohydrate Snacks (Plan A) are equal to about half the quantity of Low-Carbohydrate Meals.

Yet we all desire—and need—carbohydrates as part of our daily food intake. These needs are met by the Reward Meal.

Guideline #2: Eat a Reward Meal Every Day

Once a day at your Reward Meal, you can eat any food you desire (allowing for any dietary limitations imposed by your physician). *All* foods are allowed at the Reward Meal, and quantities are *not* limited, though your Reward Meal should be nourishing and well balanced.

Some of the people we have worked with are concerned when they first hear that Reward Meal quantities are not limited. They do not realize that when people are deprived of insulin-releasing carbohydrates for two consecutive meals, their bodies appear to adjust. The body comes to expect the food in the Low-Carbohydrate Meal; it will not be expecting a heavy carbohydrate load.

Having been fooled by two consecutive Low-Carbohydrate Meals, the body will release far less insulin than if you had been eating carbohydrates at every meal. An entire chain of metabolic events is changed, too: less insulin is released; less fat is stored; and more fat is used up. The lowered level of insulin also allows the brain chemical, serotonin, to act as it should—as an appetite regulator. You will probably eat far less than you would if you had been eating three consecutive carbohydrate-rich meals.

We have to be careful, however, because the body has a way to compensate for an unexpectedly high intake of carbohydrates, a sort of double-check mechanism. As we continue eating carbohydrates, a second phase of insulin is released.

But there is a way to control this second insulin release and to keep the insulin level low. It is the Reward Meal's one-hour time limit.

Guideline #3: Complete Your Reward Meal Within One Hour

It all has to do with timing. The second phase of insulin release occurs about one and one-quarter to one and one-half hours after you begin eating. This insulin release comes from a reading made by your system as to how much carbohydrate you have eaten at that meal.

If you are still eating at that point, seventy-five to ninety minutes later, the amount of insulin in the second release will compensate for its original low release. Conversely, if you have finished eating, this second phase of insulin release appears to be kept low.

So a very important guideline to enjoying the Reward Meal is a time limit: you may eat whatever you desire, in whatever quantity you wish, but you have to complete that meal *within one hour*.

Guideline #4: Consume All Alcoholic Beverages During Your Reward Meal

Alcoholic beverages such as beer, wine, and cocktails can be enjoyed during your Reward Meal. If you have a favorite wine, save it to enjoy immediately before or along with your Reward Dinner. Be sure to finish your drink, and your meal, within the 60-minute time limit.

Some of the people we have worked with have found ingenious ways of dealing with prolonged cocktail parties by choosing club soda or diet soda until they were about to begin their dinner. They were then able to indulge themselves with their favorite wine, beer, or mixed drink without fear of recurring carbohydrate cravings or of gaining weight.

So buy the wine that you enjoy, or mixings for your favorite drink, and save them for your Reward Meal hour.

THE CARBOHYDRATE ADDICT'S DIET GUIDE

If you have been following the Entry Plan . . .

. . . and you have lost more than 2 pounds in the past week:

and you want to continue to lose weight,
then **FOLLOW PLAN A** for the next week.

and you want to maintain your weight,
then **FOLLOW PLAN A** for the next week.

. . . and you have lost ½ pound to 2 pounds in the past week:

and you want to continue to lose weight,
then **FOLLOW PLAN B** for the next week.

and you want to maintain your weight,
then **FOLLOW PLAN A** for the next week.

. . . and your weight stayed the same during the past week:

and you want to lose weight,
then **FOLLOW PLAN C** for the next week.

and you want to maintain your weight,
then **FOLLOW PLAN B** for the next week.

. . . and you gained weight during the past week:

and you want to lose weight,
then **FOLLOW PLAN D** for the next week.

and you want to maintain your weight,
then **FOLLOW PLAN C** for the next week.

If you have been following Plan A . . .

. . . *and you lost more than 2 pounds in the past week:*

and you want to continue to lose weight,
then **increase your Low-Carbohydrate Meal portions** and **FOLLOW PLAN A** for the next week.

and you want to maintain your weight,
then **substitute one or two Reward Breakfasts for your Low-Carbohydrate Breakfasts** during the week and **FOLLOW PLAN A** for the next week.

. . . *and you have lost ½ pound to 2 pounds in the past week:*

and you want to continue to lose weight,
then **FOLLOW PLAN A** for the next week.

and you want to maintain your weight,
then **substitute one or two Reward Breakfasts for your Low-Carbohydrate Breakfasts** during the week and **FOLLOW PLAN A** for the next week.

. . . *and your weight stayed the same during the past week:*

and you want to lose weight,
then **FOLLOW PLAN B** for the next week.

and you want to maintain your weight,
then **FOLLOW PLAN A** for the next week.

. . . *and you gained weight during the past week:*

and you want to lose weight,
then **FOLLOW PLAN C** for the next week.

and you want to maintain your weight,
then **FOLLOW PLAN B** for the next week.

If you have been following Plan B . . .

. . . and you have lost more than 2 pounds in the past week:

and you want to continue to lose weight,
then **FOLLOW PLAN A** for the next week.

and you want to maintain your weight,
then **FOLLOW PLAN A** for the next week.

. . . and you have lost ½ pound to 2 pounds in the past week:

and you want to continue to lose weight,
then **FOLLOW PLAN B** for the next week.

and you want to maintain your weight,
then **FOLLOW PLAN A** for the next week.

. . . and your weight stayed the same during the past week:

and you want to lose weight,
then **FOLLOW PLAN C** for the next week.

and you want to maintain your weight,
then **FOLLOW PLAN B** for the next week.

. . . and you gained weight during the past week:

and you want to lose weight,
then **FOLLOW PLAN D** for the next week.

and you want to maintain your weight,
then **FOLLOW PLAN C** for the next week.

If you have been following Plan C . . .

. . . and you have lost more than 2 pounds in the past week:

and you want to continue to lose weight,
then **FOLLOW PLAN B** for the next week.

and you want to maintain your weight,
then **FOLLOW PLAN B** for the next week.

. . . and you have lost ½ pound to 2 pounds in the past week:

and you want to continue to lose weight,
then **FOLLOW PLAN C** for the next week.

and you want to maintain your weight,
then **FOLLOW PLAN B** for the next week.

. . . and your weight stayed the same during the past week:

and you want to lose weight,
then **FOLLOW PLAN D** for the next week.

and you want to maintain your weight,
then **FOLLOW PLAN C** for the next week.

. . . and you gained weight during the past week:

and you want to lose weight,
then **FOLLOW PLAN D** for the next week.

and you want to maintain your weight,
then **FOLLOW PLAN D** for the next week.

If you have been following Plan D . . .

. . . *and you have lost more than 2 pounds in the past week:*

and you want to continue to lose weight,
then **FOLLOW PLAN C** for the next week.

and you want to maintain your weight,
then **FOLLOW PLAN C** for the next week.

. . . *and you have lost ½ pound to 2 pounds in the past week:*

and you want to continue to lose weight,
then **FOLLOW PLAN D** for the next week.

and you want to maintain your weight,
then **FOLLOW PLAN C** for the next week.

. . . *and your weight stayed the same during the past week:*

and you want to lose weight,
then **check your low-carbohydrate foods for hidden carbohydrates** and **FOLLOW PLAN D** for the next week. Make sure that your Reward Meal lasts no longer than one hour.

and you want to maintain your weight,
then **FOLLOW PLAN D** for the next week.

. . . *and you gained weight during the past week:*

and you want to lose weight,
then **check your low-carbohydrate foods for hidden carbohydrates** and **FOLLOW PLAN D** for the next week. Make sure that your Reward Meal lasts no longer than one hour.

and you want to maintain your weight,
then **check your low-carbohydrate foods for hidden carbohydrates** and **FOLLOW PLAN D** for the next week. Make sure that your Reward Meal lasts no longer than one hour.

Guideline #5: Absolutely No Between-Meal Snacking Is Allowed

Even small quantities of carbohydrates can stimulate insulin release—and a few nibbles of potato chips or a single piece of chocolate can produce powerful cravings for more carbohydrates.

One piece of fruit, eaten other than during your Reward Meal, can reverse the whole metabolic process that is emptying your fat cells. That apple or banana or whatever can be the difference between weight loss and weight gain. Even low-carbohydrate foods should not be eaten between meals.

If you're thinking this might be a problem, remember: the Carbohydrate Addict's Diet will cut your desire to cheat or to snack between meals.

Double the Pleasure

The Carbohydrate Addict's Diet offers a dual reward, too—the joy of permanent weight loss and the ability to eat *anything you want* once a day.

Most diets ask you to put your appetite on hold, giving up the food you love for the weight loss you desire. But by changing your patterns of carbohydrate eating, you can have both the food and the weight loss.

OVERCOMING THE CRAVING: BEVERLY'S STORY

She was tall, with long blond hair, in her late twenties. She wasn't very much overweight when she came to us ("I only want to take off five or ten pounds," she said), but she did have a problem.

"I came to you because of the fight I have with food," Beverly told us. "A friend of mine heard you talk at the hospital where you work. I don't know if you'll think I'm a carbohydrate addict but as soon as I heard the term, I knew I was."

Beverly had an air of determination about her as she talked. The skin around her dark blue eyes revealed a certain tension. The more we listened, the more we saw how strong she was—and how desperate.

"If I eat some cake or cookies or chips at a party, especially corn chips, I can't stop. All I can think about is the food.

"The other night I went to a party. I can't tell you the name of any of the guys there but I can give you a detailed description of all the food that they served. This is crazy. I'm addicted to food. No, I'm addicted to carbohydrates.

"And I can pack it away. I'm five-foot, ten-inches tall, and I can eat like a man, even more. I can eat a whole chocolate cake myself and finish a pint of ice cream for a snack."

She described her symptoms in more detail.

"The problem is," she confided, "I'm never satisfied. I eat and eat and I don't feel finished. I don't even know what it means to feel satisfied. I don't know if I've ever felt it in my life. I'm always hungry."

Beverly's case was an unusual one. Most people might say that she had no need to diet. She was trim. She was physically active, working as a swimming instructor ("I burn lots of energy at work," she said). She was healthy and, in most respects, happy.

But she was worried. "I wonder if it's just a matter of time until I get tired of the fight to keep my weight under control and I just give up. That scares the hell out of me. I'm really tired of fighting, of never feeling satisfied."

You can probably guess at Beverly's test results. She tested at the very top of the scale, a 100-percent, severe carbohydrate addict. We recommended she try the diet on for size.

She agreed willingly.

Although she wasn't scheduled to come back for two weeks, we got a call from Beverly only four days into the diet.

"It's gone," she said. "The hunger is gone." We could hear the excitement in her voice.

"I was perfect. I did everything you said and now I know what a normal person must feel like. The first two days I was afraid to eat carbohydrates with my dinner. I figured that I would be willing to do without them completely if that would eliminate the hunger. But then I remembered what you said about this being for life and that I couldn't cut them out for the rest of my life. Besides, I really wanted a goody. So two nights ago I tried and it didn't come back. The hunger. I feel incredible."

At her two-week appointment, Beverly had lost only one pound, but she didn't care. "I only have five to lose. It can take forever as long as I don't feel hungry." She shrugged, a much less tense person than the one we had met only fourteen days before.

"I'm not sure, but I think I've been feeling satisfied. Not only after the Low-Carbohydrate Meals so much, but especially after my Reward Dinner. I eat, and I don't need to keep an eye on how much I should eat. I just seem to taper off naturally. I don't even know if that's what people mean when they say that they're satisfied, but I feel good and finished and ready to stop eating.

"That's the first time in my whole life that's ever happened to me."

Beverly's path wasn't all so easy, it turned out. After she had been at her weight-loss goal for a few weeks, she admitted to us that she would often go off her diet by extending her dinner hour beyond sixty minutes. She sometimes added carbohydrates to other meals, too.

Perhaps it was just a kind of testing-the-limits that a part of her felt she had to do. We explained to her that she was sabotaging the diet and probably releasing higher levels of insulin. We talked her through the process. She admitted she was acting like a spoiled child ("I guess I want it all," she said). She regained a firm commitment to the diet and found it worked for her.

It was only months later that we were invited to Beverly's wedding. On the invitation she wrote us a personal postscript: the serving of dinner at the reception was to be completed within one hour.

What About Alcoholic Drinks?

The Carbohydrate Addict's Diet does not prohibit alcoholic beverages. However, since the alcohol in beer, wine, and liquor may act in ways similar to carbohydrate-rich foods, you should drink any alcohol that you desire with your Reward Meal.

Remember, though, that all alcohol-containing drinks *must* be consumed within the sixty-minute period designated for the Reward Meal.

Some Dos and Don'ts that Lead to Success

Do not mix and match diets. Don't try to apply rules from other weight-loss diets and use them with the Carbohydrate Addict's Diet.

Do use the Carbohydrate Addict's Diet food lists: see Low-Carbohydrate Meal Foods (see page 98), menus (page 182), and recipes (page 194) in planning your Low-Carbohydrate and Reward Meals. They are essential to your success.

Do not assume that what previous diet programs have called "fattening" or "dietetic" foods can be eaten during your Low-Carbohydrate Meals. You may eat *any* food during your Reward Meal—but don't consume any food containing carbohydrates at any time other than your Reward Meal. That means no fruit and fruit juices, no potatoes, rice, pasta, sweets, or snack foods at any time other than during your Reward Meals. Only designated vegetables should be included in Low-Carbohydrate Meals. (See page 102).

Do not snack between meals—not even low-carbohydrate foods.

Do not consume alcoholic beverages except during the sixty minutes of the Reward Meal.

CHAPTER

6

More About the Diet

You have your guidelines; now it's time to get behind the wheel and go where you want to go. To help you reach your goals, we'd like to ride along awhile. Think of us as helpful navigators, trying to make sure you don't make any wrong turns, and helping you to get back on track if you do.

In the previous chapter, we explained the Carbohydrate Addict's Diet. In this chapter, we will get specific, and talk about individual foods and where they fit into your daily eating plan.

First, it's important to distinguish between low-carbohydrate foods and carbohydrate-rich foods. Although there are no forbidden foods on the Carbohydrate Addict's Diet (subject only to any dietary restrictions your physician recommends), carbohydrate-rich foods should be eaten only during your one-hour Reward Meal. We're defining carbohydrate-rich foods as those containing more than four grams of carbohydrates per average serving. So let's look at what you should eat at your other two meals of the day, your Low-Carbohydrate Meals.

Low-Carbohydrate Meals

Depending on your plan (Entry, A, B, C, or D) the Carbohydrate Addict's Diet includes two to four meals a day, one to three low in carbohydrates, in addition to a Reward Meal.

Which meals should be Low-Carbohydrate Meals? Many of our most successful dieters choose breakfast and lunch as their Low-Carbohydrate Meals, but the choice is yours. If you are following Plan A, you may have your Low-Carbohydrate Snack at midday or in the evening. In deciding which meal is to be your Reward Meal, keep in mind that you should try to maintain the same schedule each day, eating the Low-Carbohydrate and Reward Meals in the same sequence. On special occasions, you may want to make a switch; we'll talk more about that later. In general, however, you should try to keep the same meals as the Low-Carbohydrate Meals as often as possible.

How much should I eat? Though quantities are not limited at your Reward Meal, at Low-Carbohydrate Meals your portions should be of average size. "Average portions" are what you might get at a restaurant—about four to six ounces of meat, fish, or poultry; or two to three ounces of cheese; and one and one-half to two cups of salad or vegetables with two to three tablespoons of salad dressing or a pat or two of butter or margarine. Low-Carbohydrate Snacks are equal to about half the quantity of Low-Carbohydrate Meals. You need not weigh nor measure. Portion sizes are given to help you gauge what an "average portion" is.

How should my food be cooked? Low-carbohydrate foods may be broiled, boiled, sautéed, baked, poached, roasted, or even fried. However, no breading or batter should be used. In keeping with the recommendations of researchers concerned with preventing heart disease, we recommend you use polyunsaturated oils or olive oil if you sauté your food.

Which foods are low in carbohydrates? Your Low-Carbohydrate Meals or Snacks should be chosen from the list of foods that follows. These foods enable you to balance your insulin levels, reduce your hunger, and lose weight.

If a food is not listed here, don't eat it during your Low-Carbohydrate Meals or Snacks. Eating carbohydrate-rich foods during your Low-Carbohydrate Meals or Snacks can set off an addictive reaction—which can undo the entire eating and weight-loss program.

When in doubt, save the food for the Reward Meal. Eat it then, without worry.

Planning Ahead: Matthew's Story

When Matthew P. came to us, we knew already he was a busy man. He'd called from his car phone to make an appointment, and despite a certain urgency in his voice, he had told us that he couldn't fit in a meeting with us for two weeks. His schedule was too jammed.

Matthew's easy manner upon meeting him came as a surprise. He was a finance attorney whose rugged good looks and solid build would have fit a man in a more physical line of work. But the extra pounds (perhaps twenty-five) he was carrying were unmistakable.

He told us a good deal about himself (he'd struggled with his weight much of his life), his job (his work kept him on the road a great deal), and his family (his father was very much overweight: "His doctor says it's killing him"). And he confided in us his fear that his own eating and weight would get truly out of control.

We tested Matthew, and he proved to be a moderate carbohydrate addict. We recommended that he follow the diet, and he agreed. When we explained to him how the diet works, he did express one concern.

His worry was how to fit low-carbohydrate lunches into his hectic business schedule. He had several meetings a week that took the form of business lunches, and the times and places were often chosen by other people. As he described the problem, we felt that he wanted us to allow him to be an exception to the rules—but of course we could not.

We reminded him that his primary concerns had to be with his weight, his eating control, and his addiction. Matthew rose to the challenge.

"Certainly," he decided then and there, "I know I can work this out if I really want to."

At our next appointment, a relaxed Matthew appeared. He began telling of his triumphs while we were still walking through the halls into our office.

"I did it," he said, beaming. "It was really terrific. It wasn't as hard as I thought. Except for one time, I didn't have any trouble."

He had devised a series of sensible strategies. He would call ahead to the people with whom he was to meet and suggest restaurants in which he knew he would be able to get a tasty Low-

Carbohydrate Meal. For a meeting in another city in which he knew of no restaurant, Matthew called ahead and asked his host if they might meet at a Japanese restaurant. He knew that there he could get a meal of simple protein (chicken, beef, or fish) and plain vegetables (no rice). Sometimes he would suggest that they have a seafood lunch so that he could enjoy shrimp or lobster or the catch of the day—and a large salad.

Matthew proved even more resourceful and was really enjoying being in control. At one conference lunch, he told us, everyone was served the same casserole dish, one in which the foods—including some that were rich in carbohydrates—were mixed together. Matthew ate his salad, drank a diet soda, and then excused himself. He went down the street, found a fast-food restaurant, and ordered another diet soda and two hamburgers with cheese. He removed the buns and completed his Low-Carbohydrate Meal. He said that he felt great. Then he returned to the conference and enjoyed a cup of coffee knowing that his Reward Meal was coming later that evening.

Matthew used his wits to stay on his eating plan. He didn't allow himself to be bullied by circumstance.

LOW-CARBOHYDRATE MEAL FOODS

Your Low-Carbohydrate Meals may include any of the foods in the following list. Remember that your portions should be of average size. In preparing the Low-Carbohydrate Meals, you may broil, boil, sauté, bake, poach, or roast. Eggs may be fried in a pat or two of butter or margarine. Low-Carbohydrate Snacks contain the same low-carbohydrate foods but are about half the quantity.

Meat and Poultry

★ Up to four to six ounces of any of the following meats, poultry, or meat substitutes at each of your two Low-Carbohydrate Meals:

- Bacon (or breakfast meat substitutes that contain fewer than four grams of carbohydrate per serving)
- Beef
- Cheeseburgers (with regular or with low-fat cheese)

- Chicken
- Chicken roll (without filler or added sugar)
- Chicken wings
- Corned beef
- Dried beef
- Duck
- Frankfurters (beef, chicken, or other all-meat varieties only; none with sugar or fillers are allowed)
- Ham or smoked turkey
- Hamburgers
- Lamb
- Liver (chicken only)
- Luncheon meats, including salami and bologna (all-meat varieties only; none with sugar or fillers are allowed). You may want to choose low-fat, low-salt varieties of luncheon meats.
- Pastrami
- Pork
- Sausages (all-meat varieties only; none with sugar or fillers are allowed)
- Turkey or turkey loaf (no sugar or fillers)
- Turkey wings
- Veal

Fish and Shellfish

★ Approximately four to six ounces of any of the following fish or seafood at each of your two Low-Carbohydrate Meals. In tuna, salmon, and other seafood salads, be sure to **avoid any filler, bread crumbs, or relish.**

- Bass
- Bluefish
- Clams
- Cod or scrod
- Crabmeat
- Flounder
- Haddock
- Halibut
- Lobster

- Mackerel
- Oysters
- Perch
- Salmon (cooked, canned, or fresh)
- Sardines (in oil or tomato sauce)
- Scallops
- Shrimp
- Smelt
- Sole
- Sturgeon
- Swordfish
- Trout
- Tuna

Fats, Oils, and Dressings

★ Two to three tablespoons of any of the following fats, oils, and dressings at each of your Low-Carbohydrate Meals, less if you are following low-fat dietary guidelines.

- Butter or margarine
- Corn oil
- Mayonnaise (regular, substitute, or light)
- Olive oil
- Peanut oil
- Safflower oil
- Sesame oil
- Sunflower oil
- Soybean oil
- Vegetable oil
- Commercially available prepared salad dressings (note that low-cal varieties are *higher* in carbohydrates)

Eggs and Dairy Products

★ Up to two ounces daily of milk, cream, or half-and-half in one cup of coffee

★ Two eggs (or equivalent egg substitutes); two to three ounces of any cheese; or one-half cup of cottage or farmer cheese.

★ You may also combine two eggs with one ounce of cheese in preparing an omelet.

★ Low-carbohydrate dairy foods include:
- Sour cream or low-cholesterol substitute
- Eggs or low-cholesterol equivalents

Regular or low-fat varieties of these cheeses: (Watch out for added sugar or wine.)
- American
- Blue (Stilton, Gorgonzola, Roquefort, or varieties)
- Brick
- Brie
- Camembert
- Cheddar
- Colby
- Cottage, regular or low-fat*
- Cream cheese or cream-cheese substitute
- Edam
- Feta
- Gouda
- Gruyère
- Havarti
- Hot pepper cheese
- Jarlsberg
- Monterey Jack
- Mozzarella
- Muenster
- Parmesan
- Pasteurized processed: American, Swiss, cheese food or spread
- Provolone
- Ricotta (regular, *not* skim-milk variety)
- Romano
- String

Vegetables and Salads

★ One and one-half to two cups of any of the following vegetables or salad fixings at each of your Low-Carbohydrate Meals. Vegetables may be eaten raw or boiled or sautéed.

* If you are particularly sensitive to carbohydrates, you may find that cottage cheese will lead to rebound hunger or reduced weight loss. If so, eliminate it or save for Reward Meals only.

- Alfalfa sprouts
- Arugula
- Asparagus
- Bamboo shoots
- Beans (snap, green, or wax)
- Bean sprouts
- Cabbage, all kinds
- Capers
- Cauliflower
- Celery
- Chicory
- Collard greens
- Cucumbers
- Cabbage
- Dill pickles
- Eggplant
- Endive
- Fennel
- Kale
- Kohlrabi
- Lettuce
- Mushrooms
- Mustard greens
- Okra
- Onions (up to two tablespoons)
- Parsley
- Peppers
- Radishes
- Scallions
- Spinach
- Squash (summer varieties only)
- Tomatoes (raw; one-half only per meal)*
- Turnip greens
- Turnips
- Watercress
- Zucchini

* Tomatoes and tomato products such as catsup border between acceptable and unacceptable low-carbohydrate foods for Low-Carbohydrate Meals. They do not seem to bring about an addictive reaction when eaten in small quantities. Keep quantities limited to one-half tomato or about one to two tablespoons of catsup.

Desserts

- ★ You may have a low-carbohydrate gelatin dessert with homemade whipped cream or a low-fat, low-carbohydrate (no sugar added) whipped cream substitute at any of your Low-Carbohydrate Meals.
- ★ At Low-Carbohydrate Meals, you should *not* have the usual sweets or desserts sold in stores, markets, or restaurants. Even though many of these desserts are labeled "low-calorie," they may be high enough in carbohydrates to produce an insulin rebound.
- ★ Do *not* consume fruit as a dessert at a Low-Carbohydrate Meal. This is a common mistake—don't make it yours.
- ★ Save your regular desserts for the Reward Meal. Or, try the low-carbohydrate dessert recipes on page 243.

Other Foods: Where Do They Fit In?

Fiber: Adequate fiber is an essential part of any healthful diet. Choosing vegetables and salads from the low-carbohydrate foods list will provide you with a fine fiber-rich program for those two meals. For your Reward Meal, you may select any fiber-rich food, including vegetables or any of the grains. Among our favorites is popcorn.

Condiments: At Low-Carbohydrate Meals (as well as the Reward Meal) you may use bouillon, consommé, all herbs, vinegar, mustard, olives, pepper, salt, soy sauce, garlic, garlic or onion powder, hot sauce, and white horseradish. Avoid or limit catsup and relish. (See footnote on the opposite page.)

Breads and cereals: Do not eat any of your usual breads, pancakes, cereals, or other breads and grains at your Low-Carbohydrate Meals. Even small amounts of most breads and cereals eaten at times other than during the hour of your Reward Meal will increase your insulin level, along with your appetite and your weight. However, we have provided recipes for special, low-carbohydrate alternatives (see page 200).

Beverages: You may drink unlimited quantities of carbonated water, seltzer, club soda, or black coffee or tea.

Diet soda that has no fruit juice added is also acceptable. Read the label: if it contains more than four grams of carbohydrates per serving, avoid the drink except during your Reward Meal. You may add about two tablespoons of lime or lemon juice to tea or club soda.

If you prefer your coffee with milk or cream, you may have one cup of coffee each day with up to about two ounces of milk, cream or half-and-half. Cream substitute is also acceptable—if it contains two grams of carbohydrates or less per serving. Read the label. Be sure to complete your coffee within fifteen minutes.

Add sugar only at Reward Meals. Any sugar substitute that you use must have no more than two carbohydrate grams per serving.

All alcoholic beverages should be consumed during your Reward Meal only.

Fruits: Do *not* eat any fruits or drink any fruit juices except at your Reward Meal. Although fruit and fruit juices are healthful foods, consuming them even in small amounts can result in high insulin levels. High insulin levels, in turn, will almost certainly produce a hunger, a desire for more carbohydrates, and a slowing or stopping of your weight loss.

You may use one or two tablespoons of lime or lemon juice in tea, soda, or in cooking, at your Low-Carbohydrate Meals.

Drink Plenty of Water

Be sure to drink six to eight glasses of water or other noncaloric liquid each day. This is particularly important because many carbohydrate addicts do not drink enough liquids and may think they are craving foods when their bodies are actually thirsty.

Water is essential to your continued good health—drink at least six glasses daily.

READ THAT LABEL!

Most commercially prepared foods are required by law to bear a label listing their ingredients. As a carbohydrate addict, you owe it to yourself to become a label reader. Even if you *think* a certain food is safe for one of your Low-Carbohydrate Meals, make sure; you need to *know* whether the food you are about to eat has carbohydrates in it or not.

Be on the alert for any ingredient ending in -ose, such as sucrose, fructose, and dextrose. These are common kinds of sugar and are forbidden at Low-Carbohydrate Meals.

Other high-carbohydrate ingredients include corn syrup, corn solids, malt-dextrin, and starch; hydrolyzed starch, fruit solids, sugar, and juice; and beet sugar.

Read those labels carefully—and save any food that you discover to be carbohydrate-rich for your Reward Meal.

NOT ALL VEGETABLES ARE CREATED EQUAL

Yes, vegetables are good for you. And *most* vegetables are acceptable as part of a Low-Carbohydrate Meal. However, some vegetables can bring about an addictive response in the carbohydrate addict.

The following vegetables have more than four grams of carbohydrate per average serving. Enjoy them at your Reward Meal—but *don't* eat them at any other time.

At your Low-Carbohydrate Meals do *not* eat:

- Artichokes
- Avocados
- Beets
- Broccoli
- Carrots
- Chickpeas (garbanzo beans)
- Corn
- Kidney beans
- Legumes
- Lima beans
- Onions (if more than about two tablespoons)
- Peas
- Potatoes
- Snow peas
- Tomatoes (if more than one-half medium-sized tomato)
- Water chestnuts

Although both onions and tomatoes are carbohydrate-rich, you can include limited quantities of them at any of your Low-Carbohydrate Meals. Be sure to limit quantities as indicated. For a list of vegetables that can be included in your Low-Carbohydrate Meals, see page 101.

As always, during your Reward Meal you may include any quantity of these and any other foods.

The Reward Meal

The Reward Meal is fundamental in helping to control the excess insulin production that seems to cause carbohydrate addiction. The Reward Meal will also provide you a key incentive to remain on the diet—the opportunity to eat the foods you love even as you are dieting and losing weight.

To use the Reward Meal to your advantage, follow these guidelines in incorporating it into your daily eating plan:

Eat a balanced diet. The Reward Meal is to be a daily feast, not a binge. Make it a delicious, well-rounded meal. Select foods from each of the four basic groups. Include milk and dairy products; meat, fish, and poultry; fruits and vegetables (include a salad); and breads and grains.

Reward yourself once a day at a time of your choosing. The only inflexible rule regarding the Reward Meal is that it must be eaten within a sixty-minute time period. You can set aside any hour of the day for your Reward Meal, but you must remember that it cannot be thirty minutes at one time and thirty an hour later. The Reward Meal must be continuous and not exceed one hour per day. Period.

Most of the people with whom we have worked report they find it most satisfying to save their Reward Meal for dinner, although a number of dieters have chosen lunch as the designated Reward Meal hour. In some cases they have chosen a Reward Meal lunch because it suits their working schedules and expense accounts. A few dieters have tried breakfast, but that is the least popular choice.

What *is* important is that the Reward Meal, whatever its designated time of day, suits your schedule and lifestyle. And remember, the Reward Meal doesn't have to be at the same time every single day. The Carbohydrate Addict's Diet does not require that you choose between sharing in the fun of eating and partying versus staying on your diet. You can do both. But don't change your schedule on a whim. Except for special occasions, keep your Reward Meal in its regular spot. Make it part of your daily routine. Remember that you are changing your lifestyle, and keeping to a routine will help you do it.

Don't change your Reward Meal to breakfast just because you wake up in the mood for pancakes. And *don't* change your Reward Meal to lunch because you saw a new restaurant that looked like fun. We recommend that you save any changes in scheduling your Reward Meal for special occasions, like that buffet lunch at Christmas with your co-workers or the holiday family brunch.

Reward yourself with whatever you want. That's right, *anything*. Include meats, poultry, or fish. Enjoy breads and pasta, rice, beans, potatoes, and fruits. Eat anything you like, whether it is low or high in carbohydrates—unless otherwise advised by your physician. Have the foods prepared the way that you like them. Make sure that your meal is well-balanced and sensible.

Feel free to include any beverage you like—drinks (diet or other), fruit drinks, milk, or your favorite beer, wine, or mixed drink. Top off your meal with a dessert that you really enjoy. Or more. Just remember to complete your meal within one hour.

Reward yourself with as much as you want. Reward Meal quantities are not limited. Have two desserts if you wish. Have more of whatever you wish. At your Reward Meal, there are no limitations on how much you eat as long as the meal is well-balanced and sensible.

During your Reward Meal, you may find that allowing yourself to eat as much as you want, of what you want, is not as easy as you thought it would be. When you eat your Reward Meal alone, you may feel guilty. You may feel as if you are doing something wrong. The people we have worked with often report that, in the beginning, they feel as if they will be punished for eating all of the foods that have been forbidden to them for so long.

You need to remind yourself that past diets failed to lead you to your ultimate goal—that is, permanent weight loss. If these diets had not failed you, you would not be reading this book now. To attempt to follow the rules of diets that have not succeeded in the past makes no sense.

Our most successful dieters remember that for the first time in their lives, they are treating their addiction. These dieters are willing to try a new approach to dieting, one that has been proved successful, rather than continuing to follow the tried-and-untrue rules of past failures. In some cases, the Reward Meal, the most exciting and enjoyable part of the Carbohydrate Addict's Diet, presents the most difficult guideline of the diet. Dieters are not used to eating what they want, at *any* time, without fear of being punished. They feel guilty and perhaps frightened or concerned about indulging in the pleasure of the Reward Meal. Remember that the Carbohydrate Addict's Diet treats the biologically based cause of your drive for carbohydrates and your excess weight. The Reward Meal is an essential part of the Carbohydrate Addict's Diet.

Eating what you want at your Reward Meal will take some getting used to, but the Reward Meal is yours to enjoy. Tell that voice in your head to stop nagging and scaring you. Past diets did not work. Neither did the rules that they offered. Try this diet with an open mind and sit back and watch it work.

Eating your Reward Meal in the company of others presents another challenge. When you finally have calmed the doubting voices in yourself, along come friends and family to start the whole process all over again. Their questions, doubts, and concerns are predictable and are based on old diets that failed them as well as you. But people hold fast to established ideas, even if they are ineffective. We have listed some of the most frequent of these challenges on page 148. We think you will find that they are familiar.

In the beginning, if friends or family remark that your Reward Meal cannot be part of a weight-loss program, you might want to tell them that you are trying a new approach that deals with the biologically based cause of carbohydrate hunger and weight gain. You will probably find that, in a little while, as the pounds begin to drop, they will no longer challenge your ability to enjoy previously forbidden foods; rather, they will want to know how they too can take part in this remarkable program. Until then, you need not defend yourself. Follow the program that was made for you. Let others do or say what they want. Soon enough they will be coming to you to find out the secret of your success.

Reward yourself with a wide selection. The selection is unlimited. Choose a well-balanced meal, which might include such foods as:

- Apples, applesauce, apricots, apple juice, or cider
- Bagels, bananas, beef, or bread

- Cake, candy, hot or cold cereal, any kind of cheese, cherries, chicken, chocolate, cookies, crackers, cranberry sauce or juice
- Danish or other pastries
- English muffins or eggs
- Figs, any kind of fish, fruit pops, or French toast
- Grapes or granola
- Hamburgers or hot dogs (with buns)
- Ice cream
- Jams or jellies
- Kale or any other vegetable; kumquat or other fruit
- Lettuce, linguini, or lasagna
- Macaroni or any other sort of pasta, matzo, meatloaf (with or without carbohydrate-rich filler materials), milk or other dairy products)
- Nuts of any kind
- Oranges or any other variety of citrus fruit
- Pancakes (and syrup), peaches or pears or pizza, pie, popcorn, potato chips, potato, pretzels, pudding of any sort
- Quail
- Raisins, ravioli, rice, rice cakes, or rice pudding
- Sandwiches—of any and all sorts; salads, sherbet, squash, and stuffing, just plain sugar
- Turkey, tahini, or tonic of any sort
- Ugli fruit
- Veal, vanilla, venison, any vegetable you like
- Waffles, water chestnuts, Wiener schnitzel, wild rice, or watermelon
- Yams, yogurt (fruited or plain), or Yorkshire pudding
- Zucchini or, say, a serving of zuppa inglese or zabaglione.

Just remember. . . . You *must* eat your Reward Meal within sixty minutes—consecutive minutes, that is—per day. If you finish your Reward Meal before your sixty minutes are up, that's fine. Just don't let the meal go on longer than the one-hour time limit.

You *must* eat your Reward Meal at one sitting and you must *not* eat between meals. You may *not* consume anything at your other two meals except low-carbohydrate foods.

If you have finished your Reward Meal hour and you suddenly think of something you would like to have eaten, don't despair (and, most important, don't go back for more). Put the food away, and then eat the food guiltlessly at your *next* Reward Meal—no more than twenty-four hours away.

Don't forget: Your next Reward Meal is *always* less than a day away. You get to eat anything you want every day. What a great way to diet. What a great way to live.

WHAT ABOUT HEALTH-RELATED DIETARY RECOMMENDATIONS?

The National Academy of Sciences. The American Heart Association. The National Cancer Institute. The U.S. Surgeon General. The National Research Council. The U.S. Department of Agriculture.

These and numerous other powerful and prestigious organizations have, in recent years, offered dietary recommendations to aid in the prevention of common diseases.

These recommendations are completely compatible with the Carbohydrate Addict's Diet.

PUTTING THE RECOMMENDATIONS TO USE . . .

Your first concern is to follow any dietary advice your doctor offers. If you have trouble understanding how to integrate his or her recommendations with the diet, consult your physician with this book in hand. Listen to your doctor, that's rule number one.

The rest of the recommendations are a little more complicated. There is something of a consensus among these groups about selecting the foods you eat. In general, each of these institutions recommends reducing your intake of cholesterol and fat (in particular, saturated fats), salt, and simple sugars. Another common recommendation is to limit your consumption of alcoholic beverages.

On the other hand, strong recommendations have been made by several of these organizations about increasing the intake of fiber and complex carbohydrates (in particular whole grain foods, fruits, and vegetables). It has also been advised that adolescent girls and adult women should emphasize foods high in calcium. Iron-rich foods are also important, especially for women.

. . . WHILE USING THE CARBOHYDRATE ADDICT'S DIET

All of these recommendations are compatible with the Carbohydrate Addict's Diet.

We wholeheartedly recommend that you work to reduce the amount of fats of all kinds in your diet. This is true at both the Reward Meal and at the Low-Carbohydrate Meals. For any or all of your meals, you may want to choose low-fat cheeses, lean meats, fowl, or fish. Low-cholesterol substitutes for mayonnaise, cream cheese, sour cream, breakfast meats, and other foods are available at many stores. Cooking with olive oil and polyunsaturated oils is recommended. You may choose to use specially coated pans and sprays to further reduce your fat consumption.

As for increasing your intake of fiber and complex carbohydrates, that, too, is important. The Carbohydrate Addict's Diet requires, however, that you avoid carbohydrate foods except at the Reward Meal. That means you must make a special effort to eat a balanced Reward Meal, and to incorporate allowable vegetables and salads at Low-Carbohydrate Meals.

Always minimize your use of salt (we have done so in the recipes). Women should eat calcium- and iron-rich foods. (Calcium-rich foods include cheese, ice cream, yogurt, spinach, and milk; meats are especially high in iron.) The nature of the diet is such that your consumption of alcohol and simple sugars is limited to the Reward Meal, helping you to follow those recommendations as well.

As you plan your menus, follow the guidelines of the diet. But you should also keep in mind that you can—and must—eat a balanced diet along these recommended lines.

It's good for your health.

Adjusting to a New Lifestyle: Jimmy O's Story

Jimmy did construction work. At fifty-six he was an interesting mix of youth and age. His hair was light brown dappled with gray; his face was boyish, but pale and tense.

"My doctor says I've got to take off some weight. He's been telling me for years, but now it's serious." He went on to talk about his high blood pressure, his backaches, and his father, who died at age fifty-eight. "I have to take off at least thirty pounds," he said.

Jimmy had tried diets in the past but, he told us, "I couldn't work on cucumber sandwiches or child-sized portions. I get too hungry. It just doesn't feel like real food. It's not enough for me.

"And I can't carry a measuring cup and food scale with me to the twentieth floor of a construction job. Or those exchanges—they wanted me to eat one exchange of this and two exchanges of that. I can't live like that. I don't eat exchanges, I eat real food that gets all the exchanges mixed together. It got really ridiculous, trying to figure out exchanges while the guys are ordering sandwiches from the deli."

Jimmy's Carbohydrate Addict's Test revealed he had only a Mild Addiction. We told him about the three-meal-a-day plan, two of them low in carbohydrates, the third the Reward Meal. We explained the insulin connection, too, and he nodded in agreement. He'd try it.

Jimmy was between jobs, so for the first two weeks of the diet he had little difficulty following it. In fact, he was losing weight almost too quickly, at a rate of about three pounds a week. But then he was called back to work.

"Now let's see how the diet holds up on the job," he said with a laugh.

It proved to be a difficult challenge. A basic part of Jimmy's work, we learned, was an almost ritual approach to eating. Breakfast with the guys was first. Then after a couple of hours of work came coffee break. Then some more work and lunch. In the middle of the afternoon came another break. Then everybody went home for dinner.

The sum total of this eating-working schedule was five mealtimes daily. Not surprisingly, Jimmy didn't do as well the first week back on the job.

"Breakfast is no problem," he assured us. "Bacon and eggs I love and I don't really mind giving up the bread.

"The morning coffee break, though, that's tough. I don't know exactly what to do. For the first couple of days I just had coffee, but then I started adding rolls toward the end of the week. Lunch is okay, I bring that from home.

"The real tough one is the coffee break in the afternoon. By then I'm tired and cold and hungry and the thought of just coffee when everyone else is eating is impossible."

Even with his rule breaking, however, Jimmy lost three pounds. Still, from experience we knew we couldn't let him eat carbohydrates as often as he wanted to: it would inevitably lead to an appetite rebound and the end of his weight loss.

Given his rapid weight loss, we recommended that Jimmy follow plan A. This would help avoid hyperinsulinemia but still suit his needs. We recommended the following: his breakfast would remain the same Low-Carbohydrate Meal, and we reminded him that he'd have to forgo the rolls that he had added to his morning coffee break. He agreed, he could manage that. Lunch was to be as usual, low-carbohydrate foods. But Plan A added a Low-Carbohydrate Snack.

Jimmy was now able to follow a plan that included a snack at afternoon break, like a chicken leg and dill pickle. Jimmy suggested celery stuffed with cream cheese, a favorite snack of his. We told him that was perfectly acceptable, too.

It worked. Breakfast and lunch remained his Low-Carbohydrate Meals, dinner his Reward Meal. At the midafternoon break, Jimmy had some meat or his cheese and celery snack.

On his next visit, Jimmy told us a story about his daily throwing away of the bread that came with the deli sandwich he had started ordering for that snack. "So help me," he said, chuckling, "I swear the pigeons know I'm coming now and they head for the trash can nearest me." His weight dropped steadily—but not too fast. He reached his desired weight loss of thirty-two pounds in less than four months. And, two years later, his yearly check-in revealed his weight was still level.

The Carbohydrate Addict's Diet had worked well for him. "I'm thinner than I was in high school, and my blood pressure is like that of a kid. That's it for me—for life."

TWO STEPS TO SUCCESS

Over the years, our dieters have told us of a variety of approaches to the Carbohydrate Addict's Diet that they feel helped them be successful in adapting to its guidelines. Perhaps the most important of these involve planning, shopping, and preparing foods in advance for the Low-Carbohydrate Meals.

SHOPPING FOR SUCCESS

• Shop on a regular basis to buy the foods you need, both for the Reward Meal and your Low-Carbohydrate Meals. Marketing once a week—with a full menu plan in hand—is a wonderful way to help control what you eat.

• Plan ahead: keeping a chicken or a turkey, cans of tuna, fresh or frozen fish, and lots of low-carbohydrate vegetables on hand represents lots of Low-Carbohydrate Meals in the planning stages.

PREPARING FOR SUCCESS

• Many of our successful dieters have built once- or twice-a-week cooking times into their schedules. With only an hour or two of careful planning and cooking, you can prepare most of the Low-Carbohydrate Meals you need for an entire week.

• During a one-hour "cook-in," you might bake a chicken or turkey, and chop up a quantity of low-carbohydrate vegetables (except lettuce). Then you can freeze some cooked chicken or turkey for another day, and dice and freeze some for chicken salads or stir-frying. Store the vegetables and salad goods in airtight containers for later use; add the lettuce immediately before serving.

By buying the foods you need and preparing the food in advance, you will be able to have the food you need at hand to treat your addiction. Remember: successfully treating carbohydrate addiction means changing your lifestyle—and planning meals and preparing food in advance will help you do this.

Enjoying your food is an essential part of the Carbohydrate Addict's Diet. Satisfaction and enjoyment are an important part of what makes the Carbohydrate Addict's Diet a lifetime program. While the diet can easily be followed with little or no cooking, many of the people we work with, who never liked to cook prior to the program, now find that they greatly enjoy buying their food, experimenting with new recipes, and indulging in new feasts at their Reward Meals.

"It's wonderful," one of our current dieters exclaimed. "I used to spend all my time thinking about which foods I *couldn't* have. Now I spend my time planning what I'm going to have at all the Reward Meals to come."

"I've become really creative with my Low-Carbohydrate Meals," a second voice chimed in. "Last week, I stir-fried some shrimp, mushrooms, and green beans and added some teriyaki sauce and I brought it in for lunch for two days. It was fantastic."

"My husband loves this diet," another participant added. "He's not on the diet, but because of my Reward Meals he never ate so well."

Whether you choose to eat out or enjoy planning and preparing many of your meals yourself, there is one general rule: Within the guidelines of the diet, treat yourself well, eat foods that are nutritious and delicious and, best of all, the foods that you truly desire. This is an important aspect of the diet. If you truly enjoy your diet, if it offers all the rewards and pleasures you need, you will have no trouble staying on it and keeping your weight down, for life.

CHAPTER

7

Putting the Diet to Work

You now know what to eat and when you can eat it. You understand how making changes in your eating habits can affect your metabolism and help your body to adjust its basic mechanisms so that you feel more satisfied and less hungry.

The goal of all this is, of course, to help you to lose weight and to maintain your weight loss. In order to do this, you must establish a system whereby you can monitor your weight as you use the Carbohydrate Addict's Diet.

Defining Your Goal Weight

We must start with the obvious question: How much weight would you like to lose?

Patients often have far greater expectations for weight loss than do their doctors. Physicians and other scientists agree that it is best for your health to lose a reasonable number of pounds and to maintain this new weight; it may be hazardous to your health to "yo-yo," constantly losing and regaining great amounts of weight.

The choice is yours: *you* must decide how much you would like to weigh. Don't assume that the number that appears on some standardized chart next to specifications that match your height and bone structure is the only answer. *You* decide, with your doctor's guidance, what should be *your* weight.

Some of the dieters who have come to us have known from the start exactly what their final goal was; they were ready to go for it the moment that they heard the starter's gun. Others have had to think hard before they could establish an initial weight goal. In some cases it was a weight at which they felt comfortable, although it wasn't their ideal or their final goal. In other cases, they would reach their goal weight and decide to go further; in still others, they felt that their initial weight was quite acceptable. But no matter what their goals, almost all of these dieters moved steadily toward their goals, enjoying their Reward Meals with a sense of purpose and energy.

Whether you decide to go all the way right away or to lose your weight in stages is up to you. Some of the people we work with say that the staged weight loss offers some psychological benefits. They find it comfortable to pause between steps; stopping allows their bodies and their minds to adjust to weight loss, giving them new confidence. Some are convinced it helps them ensure the permanent success of weight-loss maintenance.

Some dieters who have opted for the staged approach found that upon reaching their initial goal, they were comfortable there. Some reported improvements in their health and energy levels, others experienced increased satisfaction with their personal appearance. Many of these people have happily maintained their weight at their initial goals for years with no particular desire to continue to another stage.

Many of our dieters do not want to lose in stages—they know what they want and just want to get there. In considering the weight that is to be your goal, make sure it is a reasonable one. For instance, trying to go back to the weight you were as a teenager probably isn't realistic.

Check with your physician and then follow the plans to your new weight-loss goal. Plans C and D will result in more rapid weight loss; Plans A and B will help you slow down your loss as you approach your goal weight and move naturally into your lifetime maintenance program.

Weighing Yourself

Weighing yourself is an important part of any eating and weight-control program. In the Carbohydrate Addict's Diet your weekly weight loss will help you to individualize the diet by choosing the plan that will help you meet your weight-loss goals. Whether you are trying to lose or maintain your weight, accurate weighing is essential to monitoring the process. Some people have superstitions about weighing themselves, or even peculiar little rituals. Others think they *know* how much they weigh: "I don't need a machine to tell me—I'll know if I'm losing weight."

We disagree. We do need to weigh ourselves, because it provides us with the information from which to judge our progress; it encourages us, it helps us determine whether any changes need to be made in our diets. It's a basic part of the process.

How often do I weigh myself? Even when you're not dieting, your weight may vary as much as five pounds a week. Premenstrual changes, heavily salted meals, hot weather, and other factors can produce significant day-to-day weight changes. As a result, a once-a-week weighing is not enough.

Why Average Your Weight?

Compare these three graphs. The first represents five weekly weights over a period of one month. The pattern, in general—and the fifth weekly weighing (Day 29) in particular—look a bit discouraging, don't they?

Weekly weighings, however, fail to show the daily fluctuations that most people experience. If you only weigh yourself once a week, a high-weight day may make it appear as if you are gaining weight for the entire week when, in general, you are not. Likewise, a low-weight day's weighing may make it appear as if you are losing weight at a greater rate than you are.

Now let's look at these same once-a-week weighings shown in context with the daily weights that have not been recorded in the first graph.

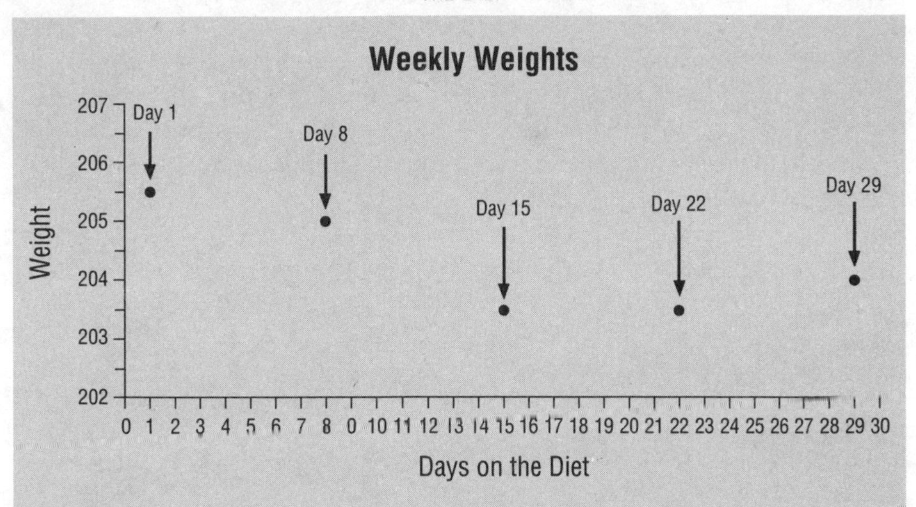

The addition of daily weights gives quite a different picture. The last week of dieting shows that there has, in fact, been quite a weight loss during the last week of the diet (Day 22–Day 29). By itself, Day 29 shows a single high-weight day, which often may be caused by water retention, premenstrual changes, etc. If they weigh themselves only once a week, dieters may see only the high-weight Day 29 and never see the entire week's weight-loss picture. The last week of lower weights are not seen in the once-a-week weighings of the first graph.

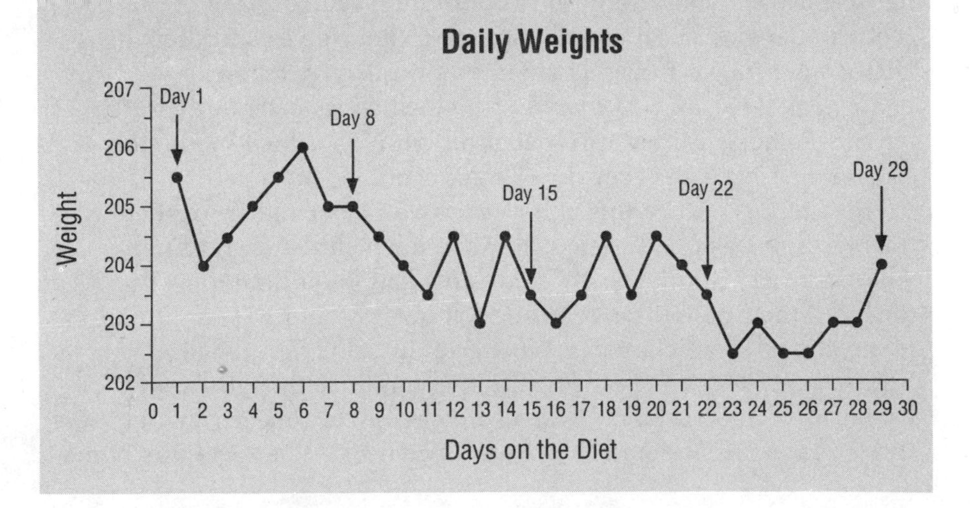

Now consider the same figures, only this time reported as a weekly average of weights. This graph most accurately represents the individual's weight loss over the twenty-nine days. This one is a little easier to take, isn't it? Yet, it most accurately reflects the true weight-loss progress.

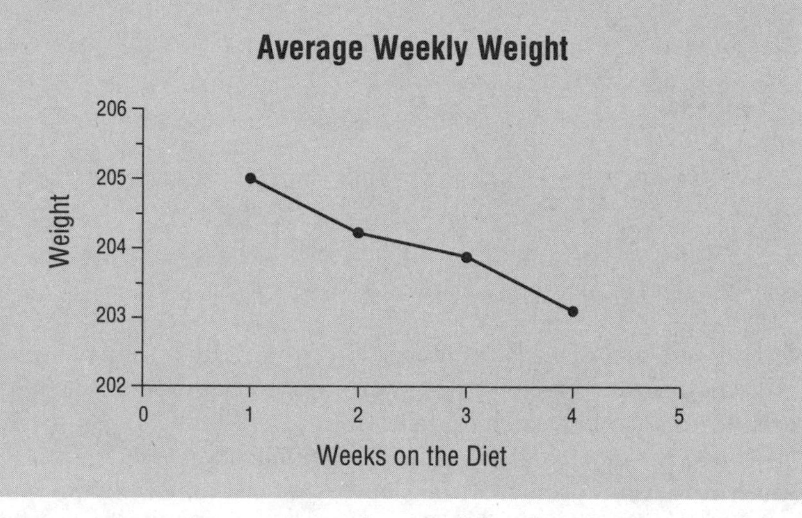

Bobbi's Story

Not everyone who comes to the Carbohydrate Addict's Center has a constructive attitude, but Bobbi did. Unlike many of the people who have come to us unhappy with themselves and their lives, Bobbi would have to be classified as a positive person.

She was forty-six when we first met. She was married ("pretty happily," she said), had two daughters in high school, and a job as an administrative assistant in a large insurance office.

Her dieting history was about what we have come to expect. Several times she had dieted, lost some weight, then regained what she lost. But her losses and gains had been limited to the ten- to fifteen-pound range. She took our test and was identified as being almost dead center in the moderate addiction range.

She wanted to lose "at least fifteen pounds, although twenty would make me ecstatic." She also expressed a concern that at times her eating seemed to get out of control. When she was home alone, she said, she would sometimes find herself eating without being able to stop. She had noticed that when marketing she would buy things in anticipation of being alone, although she often told herself the food was for others. On more than one occasion she had waited for everyone else to leave the house, taken out her store of goodies, then sat in front of the television and "pigged out." What bothered her most was that she found this to be probably the most pleasurable experience that she had had for a very long time and that she was finding that she wanted to do it more and more often.

We told her about the Carbohydrate Addict's Diet, explaining the normal mechanism of insulin release and how its dysfunction probably caused some of her behavior. Then we explained the diet's guidelines. Bobbi left our session bound and determined to lose weight.

When she returned two weeks later for her scheduled appointment, she was bitterly disappointed. She hadn't lost any weight, she said.

We asked to see her weight chart. To our surprise, she admitted she didn't have one. She explained that she had weighed herself on the first day, a week later, and then again that day. Wasn't that enough? she asked. Other diet programs she had used required that she weigh herself once a week or that she not weigh herself at all.

Daily weighing is critical, we explained. We gave her a scenario. Say she weighed 156 on the day she started the diet. Most people's weights vary a pound or two from day to day, so let's assume that although Bobbi's typical weight was actually 158, she happened to be at a low-weight point on that first day. Assume she stayed dutifully on the diet for a week, then, at week's end, weighed herself. Even if she had really lost two pounds she might well appear to have made no progress—having weighed herself at a day or time when the scale read 156.

People can use their weights as an excuse to eat. When they *lose* weight they tell themselves, Great, I can eat now. If they *gain* weight they say, What's the use? I tried so hard and I gained weight, so I might as well eat. If their weight *stays the same*, they say, "No matter what I do, I'm not going to lose, so I might as well eat."

That's why we recommend daily weighings, which are then averaged for the week. This routine helps avoid such counterproductive reactions. It gives the dieter a chance to see how he or she did over the entire week; it's the way scientists measure changes, taking as many readings as possible to average and compare them over time. It also helps you to understand the changes in your weight that take place naturally.

Several weeks later Bobbi was very much an advocate of daily weighing. "I can't tell you how important it is. Before, I would get on the scale after a week of torture and find that I had gained a half a pound. Or I would eat like a pig for a week and my weight would stay the same.

"Now I see that it was those stupid weekly weighings. Now I can see the ups and downs during the week but I can also see the *trend* of the weight loss beyond the false highs and lows.

"That's really important in keeping my motivation going."

Bobbi lost twenty-two pounds in four months. After two years, she has maintained her goal weight. And continues to weigh herself every day and to average her weight each week. "It's become second nature to me. It keeps me sane and it keeps me slim."

Averaging your weight. In order to measure the rate of your weight loss, your daily weights should be averaged. This averaging helps smooth out the highs and lows, and gives you a more realistic picture of what is really happening with your weight loss.

As Bobbi found, high-weight or low-weight days can make it appear as if you are gaining when you are losing (or vice versa). This accounts for people who have been cheating on a diet but find that when they report for a weekly weigh-in at another diet program, they are told that they have lost weight or stayed the same. But the cheating will usually catch up with them in a week or two.

By averaging your weights, you compensate for high- and low-weight days and get a more accurate reading of what is really happening with your weight level. Taking regular and frequent measurements compensates for the highs and lows of any natural phenomenon. The human body is the same—it isn't a machine, but it changes and adjusts constantly to countless factors.

HOW TO AVERAGE YOUR WEIGHT

Averaging your weight allows you to see how much weight you have lost, without being influenced by a particularly high- or low-weight day.

In order to find your average weight for the week, follow these steps:

1. Add up (total) all of the weighings in that week.
2. Divide that *total* by the number of weighings in that week.

Example #1: Your weights for the week were:
150, 149, 149, 150, 148, 148, 147
Adding up all of the weighings for the week gives a total of 1041.
Divide the total by the number of weighings (7).
You may use a calculator: 1041 ÷ 7 = 148.7 (rounded off to 149)

Example #2: You forget to weigh yourself one day, so you have only six weights that week.
Your weights for the week are:
140, 141, 139, 139, 138, 138
You may use a calculator: 835 ÷ 6 = 139.1 (rounded off to 139)

THE WEIGH-IN

What kind of scale should I use? The kind of scale you have is less important than having one that is dependable. Test its consistency by weighing yourself several times in succession. If it varies by more than a pound, get rid of that scale and invest in a new one.

If you are going to buy a scale, we recommend that you buy one with a digital quartz readout to the half pound. In this way you'll know whether your weight is 160 or 159.5. These scales typically cost about $40, but they're worth it for truly accurate readings.

Is there a correct way to weigh myself? Weigh yourself every morning at about the same time in your schedule (i.e., do it consistently before or after breakfast, clothed or unclothed, and so on). Weigh yourself only once today, and don't do it again until tomorrow.

Place the scale on a flat, hard surface and leave it there. Position yourself on the scale the same way every day. Don't pretend you're a ballet dancer and try to fool the scale by positioning one foot on the edge or whatever.

So that's it: every day, at about the same time, get on the scale. Wear the same amount of clothing (preferably none), take the reading, get off, *record it* on the chart on the opposite page—and get on with your day.

Assessing Your Progress

The combination of the enjoyable diet and your slow but steady weight loss will make daily weighings an enjoyable habit. If you are like most people who have used the Carbohydrate Addict's Diet, you will begin to look forward to the end of the week and the averaging—it promises you an accurate look at your progress rather than potentially misleading readings that can occur with the once-a-week approach.

When you weigh yourself, you must also give up the idea that one weight at that particular moment is your weight; it really isn't. That may sound strange, but look at it this way: that daily number cannot reflect minor and unpredictable fluctuations, for the same reason that a once-a-week weighing does not. Rather, your daily weight is to be thought of as but one part of seven parts of a week's worth of weights.

If your weight is higher or lower than it has been, try to treat it simply as a piece of information. Don't compare your weights from day to day—forget about it until week's end.

Record your weight each day on your weight chart.

For the weeks that follow, continue to weigh yourself every day and record your daily weighing, averaging your weight (instructions above) every seven days. After fourteen days, you can compare the second week's average with the first; that should be the first time you compare weights.

Again, you cannot compare single days and simple weighings, given typical day-to-day weight variations. Paying attention to such misleading indicators can lead you to a loss of confidence or a sense of

Week Beginning (date)	MON. (weight)	TUES. (weight)	WED. (weight)	THURS. (weight)	FRI. (weight)	SAT. (weight)	SUN. (weight)	Average Weight for Week

failure ("I'm not getting *anywhere*!"). Or to a false sense of success ("I can afford to cheat today—I lost *two pounds* yesterday!").

Don't overreact to your weight: don't abandon your eating plan just because your weight rises or falls. This program has been designed and refined by years of research, trial, error—and success. Stay with the program, and don't decide to cheat or be harder on yourself just because of a daily fluctuation in your weight. Trust the Carbohydrate Addict's Diet to work for you. This is a lifetime program, not a day-to-day diet.

Reaching Your Goal Weight

As you approach your goal weight, one of two things will happen: either your weight loss will slow or your weight loss will continue.

If your weight loss slows, that means you will probably level off at or near your goal weight. That means it's a good weight for you, and your maintenance program will consist of continuing the eating program you have been following. Continue to eat as you have, but if you feel you need additional techniques for individualizing your eating, see Chapter 5.

One of the most appreciated aspects of the Carbohydrate Addict's Diet seems to be that dieters enjoy a maintenance program that is essentially the same as the diet itself. In many cases, most of the people we work with find that they have to increase portions at their Low-Carbohydrate Meals after they have remained at their goal weights for a time. It appears the body adjusts to its new weight and is better able to handle a greater intake of food.

We must caution you, however: add only *low-carbohydrate foods* to your scheduled Low-Carbohydrate Meals and Snacks.

Your Weight Chart

Record your weight every day.

Compare only your weekly averages to determine if you are losing weight. (To get your average for the week, add up all the weights in that week, and divide by the number of weighings.) For more averaging instructions, see page 123.

What About Exercise?

Many researchers have reported over the years that there is a relationship between activity levels and weight loss. In general, our findings support their reports, yet we have also observed that a rigorous exercise regime is *not* essential to the success of the diet, and other scientists have supported our findings.

Do these findings seem odd? They aren't, really.

The explanation lies in the distinction between exercise and physical activity. Today, the word exercise is usually used to mean a programmatic pattern of activity, a planned regimen of regular running or swimming or other vigorous workouts. On the other hand, physical activity is less well defined: a job that requires considerable walking, for example, involves what we would term physical activity.

Thus, while exercise may make you feel good, look good, and stay healthy, it is not an integral part of the weight-loss component of this diet. At the same time, we do emphasize that you need to maintain a moderate level of physical activity (not necessarily a rigorous exercise plan) to help make the diet work for you.

So run or swim if you wish; there are many health benefits, and it may make you look good and feel better. But don't do it solely to advance your weight-loss goals. Recall that it is a return to normal insulin balance that eventually produces weight loss in the carbohydrate addict.

In short, you don't have to be in training for the marathon to lose weight; but you also can't expect reasonable weight loss when you never get out of your easy chair.

As always, follow your physician's recommendations, too.

THE EX-SMOKER'S EXTRA POUNDS: MAC'S STORY

We all know ex-smokers who tossed out the butts and immediately thereafter started taking on pounds. Arnold McD. (known to all as "Mac") came to us with exactly that story to tell.

He'd quit smoking three months earlier at his doctor's insistence. In the intervening weeks, he had gained about a dozen pounds. Added to the "six or seven pounds I didn't need in the first place," that meant Mac was carrying around twenty pounds he wanted to be rid of.

At forty-four, Mac had reached the age when many of us start to examine our habits to determine how they impact on our health and longevity. Mac's doctor had, too, and as well as telling him to abandon the cigarettes, he had told him it would be necessary for him to drop some weight.

Mac had tried by himself. "I had heard that some people gained weight after they stopped smoking, but I didn't think it was anything that I couldn't handle. Now I'm finding it isn't so easy."

Oddly, he reported, "I don't think that I'm eating that much more. I know that doesn't make sense, but it's true."

That's why he came to see us.

He tested in the moderate addiction range, so he appeared a good candidate for the Carbohydrate Addict's Diet. We explained the diet to him and also talked about research on post-smoking physical changes, which often result in increases in the body's tendency to hold on to or gain weight.

Mac said that he didn't quite grasp the biological underpinnings, but he was willing to give the diet a try.

He may not have been a scientist, but Mac trusted that we knew what we were doing. The first week he lost four pounds. We needed to slow down his weight loss, to bring it closer to the ideal of 1 percent of body weight per week. We advised him to increase his intake of low-carbohydrate foods at breakfast and at lunch. It worked, and several visits later his weight-loss rate was down to two pounds per week.

Mac lost his twenty pounds, then decided to "lose a few more while I'm at it." At twenty-five pounds lighter, his weight leveled off. "I could probably lose more if I cut down on my Low-Carbohydrate Meals, but I don't need to. I'm five pounds thinner than I planned, I haven't smoked in almost a year, and I look better than I did at eighteen."

About three years after his first visit, Mac was in the neighborhood and stopped by to see us. His weight was holding constant, and he felt good about himself. He was even running stop-smoking groups for the organization that had helped him to stop in the first place.

CHAPTER

A Day in the Life of One Carbohydrate Addict

Elaine T. had been shown into our office and was waiting for us when we returned from dinner. She was the first of our evening appointments. Elaine was finishing her third week on the Carbohydrate Addict's Diet, and it was obvious that she was not happy.

At forty-one, Elaine was a very successful literary agent. Several of her clients had been on the bestseller list during the past few years. Starting as a would-be author herself, Elaine had found that she was more talented at recognizing good writing and negotiating the sales of books than at writing the books herself. She said that she loved the business but that it took its toll, too. Most of all, she had left writing because of the stress.

"The stress," she had said half-laughing, "can you imagine? I thought that was stress. Now, a single negotiation can go down the tubes if I say the wrong thing to the wrong person at the wrong time. I never know whether I'm pushing when I should pull back or pulling back when I should be pushing."

During her first session, Elaine had told us about the pressures of her work—conference after conference, one meeting after another with authors, editors, other agents. Business luncheons were part of her daily routine. "It sounds exciting but it's insane. My livelihood can hang in the balance over the dirty luncheon dishes. I have no one to support me; my parents are dead and I have no one I can count on but myself. If I don't make the sale, there's no paycheck coming in. The pressure is incredible.

"During a meeting, if I say too much, I could let the cat out of the bag and ruin the whole deal. If I don't speak up, I may have missed my chance. I have to always be super-careful about what I say. I have to watch every word. And all of this takes place over lunch. Most of the time I eat with a knot in my stomach and a lump in my throat. Half the time, I don't even taste what I'm eating. I just look down and it's gone."

At the end of this, her third week on the diet, Elaine had the same tight, stressed expression that she had had when she described her work during that first session. We started the session, as we always did, getting an overview of the preceding week.

"It's been rough. I know the diet should be easy. And it *was* easy the first week or two, but now I'm having a hard time. My sister and my sister-in-law are really enjoying the diet and saying that they can't believe how easy it is. I don't know if it's me or what, but I always feel as though I'm doing something wrong. I don't know. I just don't feel as if I have a grip on it. I don't understand." At that point Elaine shook her head, shrugged a little, and seemed to withdraw into her own feelings of frustration.

For a moment it looked as if she might cry, then her face hardened. We explained that we needed to understand what was happening to her so that we could help. We gently asked Elaine to tell us what happened during her day, from start to finish, so that we could know the problems she was encountering and so that we could help her through the obstacles that she had been facing alone.

Elaine recounted a day that was to start with meeting an old friend, who was also a client, at the airport. He had an outline for an exciting new book and was interested in having Elaine serve as his agent. It looked quite promising; Elaine also knew of an editor who was looking for just that kind of story. But before Elaine could get to the airport, she had to deal with one mishap after another.

Her day began with a toilet that simply would not stop running. She had no time to wait for the superintendent, and when she searched for a tool to help turn off the cold-water valve the contents of the top shelf of her closet landed on her head. She finally succeeded at getting the waterfall down to a moderate rate but in the process she tore her nail and cut her hand.

"By this time I was forty minutes behind schedule. I knew that this was not going to be my day."

She still attempted to prepare a low-carbohydrate breakfast of bacon and eggs at home, trying to "use up" the defrosted bacon that she had been keeping in her refrigerator for several days. But she felt rushed and knew that she didn't really have time to prepare her Low-Carbohydrate Meal. "All I could think about is how much easier it would be to just pick up a bran muffin and a cup of coffee from the deli on the corner."

Elaine remembered that she had done this in the past and was determined to avoid the same old easy habits that had been her downfall. She reported that she was "feeling incredibly good at times and the carbohydrate cravings were essentially gone," so she decided that she would cook the bacon in the broiler while she showered. But she did not realize that the cold water valve that she had shut off for the toilet also shut off the cold water in the shower. She almost burned herself in the shower and ended up half-washed, half-shampooed, and totally miserable. She completely forgot about the bacon, went to her bedroom, and turned on the air conditioner.

"By the time I finished dressing and opened the bedroom door the place was filled with the smell of burned bacon grease. I had to leave the window open when I left (not a great idea when you live in a second-floor apartment) in order to keep the smoke alarm from going off. In my imagination, the bran muffin was looking better and better. But I held out—partly because I knew that I really didn't want to start craving carbohydrates again and partly because I was so late."

She got to the airport ten minutes before her friend's scheduled arrival, but with the time that it took to get from the parking area to the terminal, she arrived fifteen minutes late. "After all that his plane was delayed for at least an hour. I was so mad and frustrated. He didn't get in for almost two hours and I just sat there feeling more and more powerless and angry. By that time I just gave up. I didn't care about eating or the diet or anything."

When her friend arrived and they picked up his baggage and her car, they went for lunch. By then it was almost one o'clock. "By this time I was feeling a little better and I was ready to enjoy my lunch. I purposely chose a restaurant that had this wonderful grilled chicken and salads and side orders of green beans sautéed in olive oil and garlic. I was feeling really good about having a delicious low-carbo lunch and then Steve said that he insisted on paying. Now the prices in this place are really high and I felt embarrassed to order what I really wanted. I would have needed two salads—they're really small. What made it worse was that I had picked the place. I didn't mind paying for him but I didn't want him to pay for me. But he insisted."

Elaine ordered only the chicken and one salad. She did not want to impose on her friend, so, because they were too expensive, she chose not to order the other salad and side order of green beans that she wanted. "I felt cheated and hungry. First, I didn't have the breakfast I had coming, and then, part of my lunch. I don't usually feel hungry anymore, but this time I wasn't eating the food that I had coming to me and I really missed it. I tried to tell myself that I would just lose weight that much faster, but I know you don't want me to think like that—and anyway, I just felt lousy. And irritable. You could just feel the tension in the air. Then he sat there and ate a piece of strawberry shortcake. I could have screamed. I thought of ordering a piece to take home for my Reward Meal, but I would have looked like such a pig, ordering this rich dessert, charging it to him, and taking it home."

Elaine said that the business part of the lunch did not go well. She felt very tense and could not control it. She felt false and obviously ill at ease. The conversation was stilted.

"Finally it was time for him to go. He had another appointment, and I can't tell you how happy I was to get away. All I wanted to do was to be alone. I walked home deciding what to buy for my Reward Meal, and I must have stopped at four different stores. I bought more food than I could eat at ten meals."

We asked Elaine for some details and she continued. "First I stopped and got bagels, not two but an entire dozen. I reasoned that they give you a free bagel when you buy a dozen and at over seven dollars a dozen, I figured I deserved a free one. Besides, I figured, I would freeze any extras for future Reward Meals. I thought I would get some smoked salmon on the next block, but I ended up buying more food than they could fit into one shopping bag. I got lunch meats of every description, smoked turkey, and two kinds of cheeses. I crossed the street and splurged on gourmet chocolate-chip cookies and hit the supermarket for a pint of my favorite chocolate ice cream. I spent a fortune. I tried to tell myself that I was, in fact, still on my diet and that if I ate what I wanted within my hour limit that I was still following the diet.

"It was hard, though. How do you convince yourself that you're going to lose weight when you're eating like that? And the cost! I must have spent a hundred bucks. It's not that I can't afford it. It just seems so crazy to spend that much money on food.

"I had my Reward Meal within the hour, and when I look at it rationally I really didn't eat that much. But all that food! It just seems crazy. I mean, if anyone saw me buy like that they'd think I was nuts. I know it will last all week, maybe longer, and I really do enjoy the food and I know that I'm losing weight, but it just doesn't make sense. This can't be right. When you say we can eat what we want, you can't really mean for someone to be acting like this."

After she finished recounting her difficult day, we asked Elaine to tell us how she felt at that moment. "I feel like no matter how hard I try, I'm doing something wrong. Either I'm eating food that you say I should be eating but I know that I shouldn't, or I'm spending much too much money, or I'm buying like a nut or something. But whatever I do, I'm doing something wrong. I give up. I just can't do it right." Finally Elaine's tension dropped. She looked tired and vulnerable.

We decided to spend some time with Elaine and to walk through her day's frustrations with her. Her day had not started out well. An out-of-control waterfall in the toilet can upset anyone, but Elaine did not accommodate to the crisis by looking for alternative choices for her low-carbohydrate breakfast. We told her that as an alternative to sticking stubbornly to her plans for a homemade breakfast, she might have forgotten the bacon plan and enjoyed a bacon-and-egg breakfast at the airport while she waited for her friend's plane to arrive. "But I would have had to throw out the bacon in my refrigerator, and I just can't waste food. I couldn't just throw it out. And the food at the airport is so expensive. It seems crazy to throw out perfectly good food at home and pay an arm and a leg for it at the airport. That doesn't make sense."

We reminded Elaine that she ended up throwing out the burned bacon anyway and that given her current income, and the potential value of her airport appointment, she could have splurged on a breakfast for herself. She agreed reluctantly, saying that perhaps she was trying to do too many things at once.

Many of the people that we work with try so hard to do so many things that they end up being unable to do the very things that they want to do the most. We try to have our carbohydrate addicts see that treating their addiction has to be the highest priority on their list. Sometimes that may mean breaking some of the rules they were taught when they were young, rules like "Never throw away food" and "Don't 'waste' money." Sometimes the hidden rule that they are attempting to follow is to do everything perfectly: follow your diet perfectly; waste nothing; spend very little money; please everyone; handle every emergency to perfection. The greater the number of rules, the greater the frustration they experience, and the more likely that following a diet will be one of the goals that will fall to the wayside over time.

Elaine could not do everything. Or, at least, she could not do everything to perfection. Or if she did, she couldn't do it without paying a heavy toll of frustration and exhaustion.

Then we looked at the rest of her day.

Elaine arrived at the airport ten minutes prior to her friend's arrival but she was late because she had to park her car. She could have chosen to take a cab (easy to get given the location of her apartment), but she did not even consider the option because it would have cost her more. Elaine suggested that part of the cost of the cab would have qualified as a tax deduction. "But it would have been a waste to take a cab when my car was right outside."

We asked her to consider the wear and tear on her body and mind given the pressure she felt when she was trying to arrive on time to meet the plane. Elaine admitted that the financial cost was not worth the emotional pain but admitted that she found it difficult to spend the money on herself. "I don't know, it seems like such silly pampering. I should be able to handle it."

We told Elaine that many of the people that we work with have trouble spending money on themselves to buy peace of mind or an easier way to deal with daily frustrations, although many had, in the past, spent great amounts of money on food or on weight-loss programs to help them to take off the pounds.

Elaine was once again trying to do everything herself and trying to do it perfectly. Our years of experience have shown us that, in the end, something has to give, and for the carbohydrate addict, that can spell disaster. We explained that it was much better for Elaine to take some of the time pressure off herself before the demands pushed her to give up her commitment to her diet.

Elaine was sticking to her program but it was not the pleasant experience so many of the people we work with report. Elaine seemed to be in conflict at almost every point in her day. She was trying very hard but clearly she was not reaping the full rewards of her hard work. Still she was losing weight. Within her first three weeks she had lost six of the twenty-two pounds she wanted to lose. Her carbohydrate hunger was no longer a problem and she found that the desire to cheat, which had almost always been present in past diets, was simply gone. Her energy level was higher than she ever remembered but still she felt ambivalent and frazzled.

We continued through her day. With the frustration of a late arrival, Elaine had given up in trying to get her low-carbohydrate breakfast. This was understandable considering the demands of not-throwing-away-food-nor-spending-money rules that she had added to her time and dieting requirements.

Elaine's demands on herself resulted in a state of hunger that would have been hard for anyone to control, but much to her credit, she held on until she arrived at the restaurant for lunch. Here was her chance to have a delicious and satisfying low-carbohydrate meal, but again, in keeping with her demands on herself, Elaine didn't get the meal she wanted because she was afraid that her friend would spend too much money treating her to the meal.

This is a common concern for many of the people we work with. Most people have trouble spending other people's money freely. Often they don't get what they want if someone else is paying. We recommend either of two approaches: either tell the person clearly and repeatedly that you would rather pay for yourself and that that will truly make you happier—or close your eyes, bite the bullet, and order exactly what you want. In any case, we never recommend that you accommodate your meal to fit someone else's pocketbook, or rather, your perception of someone else's ability or willingness to pay.

Your eating needs must come first. Sometimes you can't take care of others and yourself at the same time. If friends really want to treat you, let them.

Order what you want and what you need.

It was understandable that Elaine's tension spilled over into the rest of the afternoon. She was fighting so many battles that she must have been emotionally exhausted. But again she rose to the occasion and, as per our request, on her own once again bought the food that she wanted for her Reward Meal.

As so many people experience, however, old voices emerged, and with every purchase Elaine blamed and criticized herself. We told her that it was not the food purchases that were problematic for her but rather the thoughts that would not allow her to enjoy the food that she had coming as her Reward Meal.

The food she bought would serve to provide her with a week's worth of delicious Reward Meals and several Low-Carbohydrate Meals as well. The food was satisfying. "Maybe that's the problem," she confided. "Maybe I just have trouble believing I can live like this and lose weight. I see it happening. I just can't believe it. Somehow I feel as if I'm going to be punished."

We have seen this over and over. Dieters like Elaine, who have deprived themselves for so long, have trouble accepting that they can, in fact, enjoy guilt-free eating. They fear making mistakes, and have trouble accepting the reality that they can make choices that will make it easier for them to stay on their diets and to take care of themselves as well.

Elaine's perfectionism was a difficult burden for her to bear, and we tried to show her how it was complicating her handling of her addiction.

"You can't serve five masters," we told her. There are times when the demands will tell you to do opposite things. "Eat your low-carbohydrate breakfast," one voice says. "Don't waste food. Eat the bacon," says another. "You're late. You can't take the time to cook now. Grab something that's not on the diet, just this once," demands a third. To whom do you listen?

With our guidance, Elaine examined the demands that she placed on herself. Her need to be perfect, her need to not make mistakes, was taking its toll, psychologically and physically. She had reached her limit and we helped her to admit it.

Over the months that followed, Elaine fought many battles with her perfectionism. Each success was a triumph.

"It's getting easier. When in doubt I have only one obligation, to treat my addiction. If I have to spend a few dollars on myself or not meet some deadline or fail to keep a promise in order to take care of myself, to buy the food I need or take time to prepare it, then that's what I do. Things were really getting out of control. Now there's some sanity in my life. I'm in control. That's better than anything."

A WEEKEND OF PARTIES

One by one the members of the Wednesday Carbohydrate Addict's Group filed in. Each carried a low-carbohydrate lunch and a weight chart.

Fern G. slid into her chair directly opposite us and started talking even before the others got to their chairs. "I had a great weekend. It was a challenge," she began.

Everyone turned to listen. Fran is a gentle, relatively unassertive woman who usually spoke after everyone else in the group had had a chance to talk about their week. But she was unable to restrain herself.

"It was the most incredible weekend." Fran had talked about her weekend plans at last Wednesday's group. She had a weekend she described as "wall-to-wall eating" coming up. We had helped her to plan the strategies that, along with her Reward Meals and her reduced cravings, would help her to stick to her diet plan, but now we waited to hear how she had done.

"Okay. First there was Friday night. That was the pre-bridal party." Some of us had never heard of this kind of party but no one wanted to interrupt.

"I had my Reward Meal and basically there was no problem. I was fine but by the time the dessert came, I was over my hour."

"I knew it was going to happen, but I was prepared. I decided that I could take the dessert home if I wanted to and have it with tomorrow night's [Reward] dinner, but when it came, it just wasn't appealing, so I had no trouble giving it up. Also, I knew that if I really wanted it, I could have asked the waiter to bring it sooner, or I could have brought a goodie for myself in case dinner dragged on, but it just didn't seem that important. That's part of the beauty of this diet. I just don't crave sweets the way I used to. Besides, I knew I could always have it tomorrow.

"Then came the party for my husband's friend's new baby. That was Saturday morning. I knew that they were having a catered breakfast buffet and I would have no trouble getting low-carbohydrate foods. They had scrambled eggs and a chef who made omelets. I had a cheese omelet, and bacon and sausage. I had a delicious cup of coffee with milk and I felt wonderful. Also, I knew that I had another party that night and that I could have anything I wanted then. It didn't hurt to remember that I was wearing a dress that night that I couldn't have fit into a month before."

Fran never made it to the bachelorette party that night. She didn't tell us why but she said that her husband left early in the evening for the groom's bachelor party. She didn't leave her friends' house until ten o'clock that evening. "By now," she said, "I was really hungry. I knew I could have gone home and not eaten anything. I could have skipped my Reward Meal and gone directly to bed. But I really wanted to have my dinner and I knew what you said about not skipping meals to lose weight faster. So I stopped on the way home and got exactly what I wanted. I was really craving fried chicken, just wings, so I got some coleslaw and a whole bucket of extra-crispy wings just for myself. I could only finish half of it but I totally enjoyed myself. We had some ice-cream cake in the freezer but I really only wanted some watermelon. It was cool and delicious, and I went to sleep in total bliss."

Sunday was the wedding ceremony and dinner. "They were having a smorgasbord followed by the dinner. I knew that I was going to have one part of the meal as my Low-Carbohydrate Meal and one as my Reward Meal. You said that as long as I waited at least an hour and a half or so between the two meals, that would be fine. There was no problem. The smorgasbord was at about six and they served the dinner at nine but we didn't actually start eating until just about ten. I wasn't sure which meal to have as my Reward Meal. I figured if they had something worthwhile I would have the smorgasbord as my Reward Meal. I usually enjoy the smorgasbord more than the meal. If they had those little hot dogs, I was going to have my Reward Meal then.

"There was nothing thrilling in the smorgasboard. I had cheese and olives and celery and some pepper steak. I checked with the caterer, and told him that I couldn't have sugar, and asked what was in the sauce. Only soy sauce and some spices, he said, no corn starch, so I had some of that.

"Best of all, I looked great and I felt terrific. When we went into dinner I knew that I could have anything I wanted as long as I watched the time [stayed within the one-hour time limit]. I held off on eating the roll and salad until they served the main meal because I wanted to make sure that my hour wasn't up before they served dessert. I had a drink with dinner. I had club soda during the smorgasbord.

Then came the meal. It wasn't that great of a meal but it was okay. While I was waiting for them to cut the cake, I had cookies and coffee. They put cookies on each of the tables but I was holding out for the Viennese table. Anyway, it turned out that they didn't have a Viennese table, only the wedding cake. So I had some of that and by then it was 10:55."

Fran handed us her weight chart. She had lost a pound and a half that week. "You tell me how many other people at that wedding lost weight this week," she said with satisfaction.

"It's funny," she said. "Food is so much less of a focus. Now the focus is on planning. But you know," she confided, smiling, "these were friends of my husband. I'm more pleased that I succeeded in staying on my diet than I was with the wedding."

PART III

LIVING THE GOOD LIFE

CHAPTER

9

Strategies for Success

Sometimes you have to fight for what you want. Every long-term dieter knows that unexpected temptations can undo the best-laid plans for weight loss or maintenance.

If you're like most people, you probably have found that challenges to your dieting plans appear suddenly and unexpectedly. Often the enemy appears just at the moment that your diet seems nicely under control. The nature of potential enemies is endlessly varied: people, places, situations, stresses, even your very own thoughts can be temptations.

Almost anything—*if you let it*—can bring your weight loss to a sudden and permanent halt. If you're going to win the weight-loss war, you've got to fight off each and every opponent that you face.

This diet arms you very well for your dietary battles. Unlike diets that simply say "Don't cheat" or "You *must* stay on this program," we offer you real help in order to conquer the inevitable challenges that will come your way.

Choosing the Carbohydrate Addict's Diet was your first strategy for success, one that you have already taken if you've reached this point in this book. If followed carefully, the diet deals with your carbohydrate addiction and enables you to conquer your single greatest enemy, the underlying physical disorder that makes you crave carbohydrates.

The second strategy at your disposal is your Reward Meal. It constitutes a promise, one that you make to yourself and that you can cash in on each and every day. "If I can make it through to my Reward Meal," the promise affirms, "I can eat anything I want. I don't have to wait for two weeks or a month or until I reach my weight-loss goal before I can eat the foods that give me pleasure."

At your Reward Meal, you can eat what you want, in the quantities you want. You can eat them today, and tomorrow, and every day after that. *Any* food you desire is *never* more than a day away.

With your addiction under control and your daily pleasure assured, you will find your battle is much easier. That's where other key strategies come in; they will help you deal with different challenges.

Recall that according to the Carbohydrate Addict's Diet guidelines, there will be twenty-three hours out of every day in which you should not eat carbohydrates and, except at mealtimes, that you are not to snack on any food, carbohydrate or otherwise. Old and new enemies will pop up at odd times, tempting you to try this and or that snack, to join the people around you in enjoying foods at forbidden times, to sneak a serving of something ("Just to tide me over," you may hear that inner voice advising you), or to prolong your Reward Meal past the sixty-minute limit.

Don't do it. And don't decide that you can go off this diet and get back on later. It's a mistake to think of your diet as a temporary eating plan—doing so is one reason why so few diets succeed in producing long-term weight loss. They aren't workable for more than a brief period. In contrast, it's essential to think about the Carbohydrate Addict's Diet as a permanent change in your eating habits.

This chapter has been written to help you in resisting the enemies that may tempt you to eat. These simple strategies have worked for many of our dieters. Although some of them will probably work for you, others may not apply. Use those strategies that are appropriate for your habits and your lifestyle; discard those that don't work or don't fit.

Don't hesitate to modify them. Make them suit your needs, your challenges, and your lifestyle. Just remember that you must follow the three basic rules of the diet—always, without exception.

This is *your* fight. As you seek your goal of weight loss and weight-loss maintenance, you must be willing to fight for what you want.

We will supply you with plans to help you, as they have helped many others. You must be willing to put them to use to help you win the fight to lose weight and keep it off.

Beware the Enemy

Your spouse, your friends, your children, the receptionist at work, the nurse at your doctor's office—any of these people or others may seem to be on your side. But they can be diet enemies in disguise. They may actually think that they are helping you as you strive to lose weight, but even their best intentions can sometimes produce disaster.

Identifying well-intentioned friends and family as the enemy may seem harsh but we have found that, time and again, our dieters run into difficulty because they are too understanding—they give up what is important to them for the sake of others.

We've found that many dieters are too selfless. They put themselves last and hope that somehow they will be compensated. Trying a mid-afternoon piece of Aunt Ida's cake ("I couldn't very well say no, she'd made it especially for me!") may mean that the price will be another dietary failure. Our files are filled beyond bursting with stories of dieters who, in the past, have allowed themselves to fall into this predictable pattern.

Many dieters want to accommodate the people around them. They want to be giving, to be kind, to be selfless. The desire to please others outweighs the dieter's own needs. Person after person, demand after demand, is given a higher priority than the dieter's desire to lose weight. Too often, this means such dieters find themselves more and more unhappy—and gaining pound after pound.

There is a simple lesson here: *anybody* who wants you to put your diet guidelines and needs aside, even temporarily, has to be regarded as an *enemy*; perhaps not an enemy to you, but to your success.

You can still like them or love them, and they can still care deeply for you.

You don't have to stop seeing them or stop being nice to them or caring about their feelings.

You just have to remember that you cannot let their feelings, desires, or demands stand between you and successful weight loss or weight-loss maintenance.

When your co-workers offer to share their midafternoon snack with you, recognize them as wolves in sheep's clothing. That box of donuts that the boss brings tomorrow morning as a gesture of thanks for your work today? It's really Pandora's box, just waiting for you to unleash countless dietary demons.

That piece of birthday cake—even if it's from a surprise cake just for you—can always go home wrapped in a napkin. You can express your thanks at that moment; if you like you can explain that you will save it for your Reward Meal. Blame your diet, or explain that you have a physical disorder. People understand that. Then you can eat it later with your Reward Meal and tell the cake baker how good it was tomorrow.

That way, no one is hurt. And you don't allow your friends and family to betray you unwittingly and you have not betrayed yourself.

Stand firm. You hold the controls.

KNOW YOUR ENEMIES!

Watch out for friends, co-workers, and family members who fit these profiles:

THE (SEEMING) SUPPORTERS

- Seeming supporters will tell you that they want to help, that they approve of your goal of losing weight. But then they turn around and bring you gifts of food.
- They tease you about your weight, telling you that they tease you because they care.
- They tell you that dieting is just a matter of willpower—then proceed to urge you to eat.

THE SKEPTICS

- The skeptics may tell you that your weight is "in your genes" and that there's nothing you can do about it.
- They'll tell you that your diet will never work or that you're losing weight too slowly. Or that you're losing weight too fast.
- Then they tell you that you looked better before you lost the weight.

THE DOUBLE-CROSSERS

• Double-crossers listen and nod when you talk about your diet—and then they make you feel self-conscious about everything you eat.

• They tell you that you would lose weight if you *really* wanted to.

• They eat in front of you, or leave food around where you are forced to see it.

THE NAY-SAYERS

• Nay-sayers pull no punches; they just straight out try to convince you to give up your diet.

• Nay-sayers don't help you in any way—their lack of interest or support can lead to feelings of anger, hurt, or, for many, a loss of confidence in your diet choice.

• They refuse to believe that you have an addiction.

Do you recognize any of your enemies here?

Don't Let Doubters Deflect You

Some people are supportive from the start. Family members may help shop and prepare appropriate meals to help you; some friends or co-workers are understanding from the start and want to learn about carbohydrate addiction.

More often, however, people will, knowingly or unknowingly, attempt to sabotage your attempt to control your addiction. The interference may be from ignorance; the person may feel threatened or competitive; the causes are numerous.

Some of the people that we have worked with have dealt with the hurtful words and doubting challenges very well. Others have found it tiresome or difficult to deal with the interferences and have let it stand between them and their dieting success.

In order to help you to understand that you are not unique and that the objections that you hear can be answered, we have assembled the most commonly reported challenges. Remember that most people who care will gradually change, abandoning their sabotaging stance and assuming a more supportive position as long as you continue with your commitment to the diet.

Challenge Number 1: "I've heard it all before. You've tried everything. What makes you think this diet will be different?"

It's true, most of us have tried other ways of losing weight. But now we understand the process of carbohydrate addiction and understand that we are different.

We can also see that, to friends and family, our initial enthusiasm looks much the same as that which they have seen in the past. Some people have found it's best not to try to defend or to explain, whereas others have been able to enlist support from friends and family by making an explanation. It's your call—but if a preliminary attempt to explain falls on deaf ears, you may find it best to stop explaining and devote your energy to working at your diet instead.

*Challenge Number 2: "If you eat that much, you'll **gain** weight!" or "If you eat that much food, you'll never **lose** weight!"*

Given how most diets work, such reactions are hardly surprising. But these comments reflect the old weight-loss rules, rules that have repeatedly failed you and other dieters.

Be patient with these doubters—they may be trying to give you advice that they think will be helpful. Explain, if you can, that you have a physical disorder. But at least tell them that you just want to give the diet a chance to work.

Challenge Number 3: "It's only water weight. It won't keep coming off."

This is a typical reaction to early weight-loss success. People are shocked that you've lost weight while eating so generous a Reward Meal every day. And people don't like to hear what they don't expect and can't seem to understand. They will often try to make reality fit their rules rather than try to understand new ones.

Give it time. Don't let their doubting get to you. They will have to accept that water weight isn't the answer after a few weeks have passed and your weight loss has continued.

Challenge Number 4: "That diet doesn't make sense. It can't be good for you."

You know better: you understand the mechanism and know that you can fit virtually any dietary or health recommendation into the parameters of the diet. Tell the skeptics that in each day's menu you include a well-balanced assortment of all four food groups. Remember that losing weight and maintaining that weight loss is one of the best things you can do for your health.

If cholesterol is a concern, consult your physician. You can still follow the Carbohydrate Addict's Diet while watching your intake of saturated fat, and still meet the recommendations of the American Heart Association (see page 190).

Challenge Number 5: "You can afford a little of this. After all, you're doing so well! And a little bit won't hurt!"

Watch out for this reaction. It may be meant as a friendly gesture, but can spell disaster to your diet.

The person who makes this remark fails to understand that you have an addiction problem. Remember: small quantities of carbohydrates, outside of the designated hour, will almost surely cause an addictive reaction.

Educate your family and friends if you like. Or give yourself the right to say simply, "No thanks. I really don't want any now."

HINTS ON EATING OUT

Eating a Reward Meal at a restaurant can be a lot of fun, though you must keep in mind that the duration of your meal is to be no more than sixty minutes. The Low-Carbohydrate Meals may seem to present more of a challenge, but they can be a delicious change as well.

Eating out at most restaurants is wonderfully easy on the Carbohydrate Addict's Diet if you know your choices and you stick to them.

Here is just a sampling of the foods you might order at a restaurant for a Low-Carbohydrate Meal:

- For breakfast, you can have eggs and bacon or sausage (but don't forget, no toast or potatoes are allowed).
- At lunchtime, how about a salad? A chef's salad, a spinach salad, or Caesar or Greek salad. With dressing. Tuna and chicken salad are fine, too, but be sure to ask whether sugar or breading as a filler have been added (they often are). Ask, too, before ordering coleslaw or cucumber salad—sugar is often added in their preparation.
- You may also try a cheeseburger (remember, skip the roll), or a piece of fish or chicken, or even roast beef. Add a large salad, a pickle, some green beans, or even a *diet* gelatin (if available).
- Have coffee or tea with a little cream, once a day; a diet soda, or club soda.

Enjoy your meal: luxuriate as you sit down, relax, and enjoy someone else having done the work.

For your Reward Meal hour enjoy any well-balanced choice and top it off with your favorite dessert.

Watch Out for Other Pitfalls

There it is: the open bag of potato chips your son left beside the sofa. You've asked him three times to stop doing that.

Places, situations, stresses, even thoughts can threaten your success, just as people can. And for the carbohydrate addict, the threats are everywhere. Whether you're at home, at work, in the shopping mall, or walking past the candy machine at the gas station. The dangers are never far away.

Your experience is the best guide as to what the greatest risks are to *you*. You may be quite conscious of what triggered cheating episodes in the past. Perhaps it's pizza, or another favorite food. The mere mention of a particular kind of cookie or ice cream may make your mouth water.

The following challenges are among those most commonly reported to us:

Places: Establishments that stock candy, ice cream, snack foods, or pizza are at the top of the list. These foods, rich in carbohydrates, are classic temptations for the carbohydrate addict. Food stores in general may entice you, but specialty shops are the downfall of many dieters.

The "just-one-cookie" philosophy is deadly: beware the bakery, cookie stand, or coffee shop. The produce or fruit seller offers another danger, selling fruits rich in the simple sugar, fructose. On some city streets, the pretzel wagon and ice cream vendor offer additional temptations to the carbohydrate addict.

Situations: Your boss hands you a letter to be typed, five minutes before your lunch break. It's an imposition, one that makes you cranky and irritated. Perhaps it's an excuse, too, to break the rules and eat what you know you are not supposed to eat.

If you shop and cook for your family, you may find the temptation to cheat constant and overwhelming. Special strategies and planning in the pages that follow will help you to cope successfully.

Going on vacation is a treat for all of us but, unfortunately, time off from work or away from home usually means a whole new range of temptations. Countless dieters have found themselves abandoning their good habits in the face of the chance to try new foods or reexperience favorite ones. Do these rationales sound familiar? "It's only once a year . . ." or "Vacations are different . . ."

Parties and celebrations of all kinds can be hazardous to your diet. Ironically, the greatest temptations to the carbohydrate addict often aren't the traditional feasts. Thanksgiving dinner, for example, can be the Reward Meal for the day, so it may present no particular danger to the discipline of the diet. But extended parties of many kinds—at the office, to celebrate a special holiday—may present foods and drinks to trap the most disciplined dieter.

Stresses: Simple fatigue may make you crave a pick-me-up snack. Worry, too, causes many people to feed themselves—almost unconsciously—food they ordinarily take care to avoid. Stress, in the form of pressure, frustration, overwork, or repressed anger can have the same effect.

Loneliness, boredom, a fear of failure, the trapped sensation that comes from unwanted events, even pain and illness—all these common stresses can provoke the dieter to break the regimen that, on another day, seemed so easy.

Thoughts: Our ability to think elevates us above lower animals. That also means, however, that there are times when we run amuck. And we talk ourselves into things.

For the dieter, that can mean little voices saying things like:

"I've been so good, I *deserve* this."

or:

"Well, I've already lost twenty-five pounds, so what's one snack?"

or:

"Since I've only lost eight pounds after all this, what do I care about one little cheat? It can't make any real difference, can it?"

or:

"It's *my* vacation."

or:

"I was so good in not eating *that*, so a little of *this* is really insignificant."

How about:

"But on other diets . . ." or "Everyone else can . . ." or any of the hundreds of other little rationalizations we are capable of making to ourselves.

Then there's the voice that says, "This little bite won't hurt." That is your addiction talking.

Under any circumstance, this thought is dangerous. It's based on the old dietary wisdom that only total daily calorie count matters—and it disregards the idea that you may have an addiction to carbohydrates that can be triggered by a small amount of the addictive substance.

If you find yourself tempted by these little voices, face up to the challenge. If the thoughts are persistent, you may be eating carbohydrates more frequently than once a day, perhaps without knowing it. Examine your food selections to be sure.

People, places, situations, stresses, and thoughts: All of these can betray you, undermine your will, and sabotage your diet. None of these challenges can be taken lightly. We will help you to try to anticipate them, and to be ready to fight for what you want.

A VACATION VARIATION: MARK'S STORY

Mark's was a success story: he'd come to us down in the dumps, overweight, and recently divorced. We helped him to lose forty pounds, and he had begun to put his life and confidence back together, though he buried himself in his work.

More than a year later, he came back to see us. "I want to arrange for a vacation—if I don't take my vacation time by the end of the year, I'm going to lose it. I'm not afraid that I'm going to gain the weight back any minute like I used to be, but I'm not sure how to handle eating on vacation."

Then he made an important admission. "I have to admit, there's a part of me that would love to give up the diet during my vacation."

We advised him not to abandon the diet: it was working well for him, and he had told us he didn't mind being on the diet at all. "It's no problem. I don't think twice about it and you know I love my Reward Meals." We helped Mark work the Carbohydrate Addict's Diet into his vacation plans. It wouldn't be hard. "Just tell the hotel or restaurant or airline that you have a physical disorder and need to plan your meals," we advised him.

We didn't tell Mark any more than that. But, when he came back a week later, he had a round-trip airline ticket in hand and an itinerary for his trip. More important, he had total confidence that the trip (and the diet) were going to work out beautifully.

"The diet doesn't really present a problem. I called the hotel. They have a buffet brunch on weekends so I can have a low-carbohydrate breakfast. During the week I can have bacon and eggs, even a cheese and fresh vegetable platter. A low-carbohydrate lunch is really never a problem.

"But for my Reward Dinner, I plan on attacking a new restaurant every night. I'm really looking forward to it."

Even the air trip proved to be no problem. When he told the airline of his special dietary needs, they offered him a large shrimp cocktail platter for no additional cost. "It will make a *perfect* low-carbohydrate lunch," Mark boasted.

It should come as no surprise that Mark's trip was a complete success. His energy level was high, and he enjoyed himself totally.

He even met a companion he enjoyed—*and* lost two pounds while he was away.

"Can you believe it? I lost weight on vacation!"

"SIXTY MINUTES": MELANIE'S STORY

Melanie would have been pretty at almost any weight. Her makeup and wardrobe were meticulous, her face was open and sweet. But she was carrying fifty or sixty extra pounds—and she didn't *feel* pretty.

She was concerned about her weight and her eating. She took our test, and she appeared to be a severe carbohydrate addict. She didn't want to talk much about her dieting failures of the past (they were, apparently, numerous). She did tell us that she had found it easier to fast and eat no food at all than to eat those "itty-bitty unsatisfying diet meals that everyone says you have to get used to."

Melanie took to the Carbohydrate Addict's Diet as if it were designed for her and her alone. Over the next three months, she lost weight consistently, and reported feeling wonderful. At one point her rate of weight loss rose to three pounds a week, and we recommended Plan A along with increased portions at her Low-Carbohydrate Meals.

But then, after twelve weeks, her weight loss suddenly halted. Though she moved to Plan B, Plan C, and Plan D, her weight did not budge. At week fifteen, it was still unchanged. At seventeen weeks, the scale registered only a questionable one-half pound weight loss.

We asked Melanie if something had changed. She swore she was eating the same amounts of the same kinds of foods she had been eating all along. We assumed she had hit a weight-loss plateau, not uncommon in many other weight-loss programs but rarer in the Carbohydrate Addict's Diet.

At nineteen weeks, Melanie's weight was still constant, so we asked her to keep an eating diary of the foods she was consuming. In order to get a complete picture of her eating experience, we asked her to record what she ate, where she ate, with whom she ate, whether she was experiencing any physical or emotional discomforts, and when she started and finished each meal.

Her diary provided us the key to her problem. Melanie had fallen into the habit of extending her Reward Meal; sometimes she nearly doubled the sixty-minute time limit. Although she didn't appear to be eating great quantities of food during the dinner, by postponing dessert or otherwise extending the meal her level of insulin output appeared to be greatly increased. This seemed to cause her weight loss to stop and, worse yet, she reported her hunger cravings were returning.

She started observing her Reward Meal time limit once more and lost two pounds the following week.

Melanie's weight continued to drop and she learned to make adjustments in her lifestyle to keep within her Reward Meal hour. She told us in advance of her worries about the Christmas dinner she was having—she knew it would be a great temptation to exceed the sixty-minute limit. But she came through, setting aside some pre-dinner canapes and hors d'oeuvres; she kept busy during the soup course by carving the turkey. Then she joined her friends for a pleasurable hour of guilt-free eating. And she lost two pounds that week, like the one before and the one after.

At times, Melanie found her weight loss slowed, but she moved closer and closer to her goal. She continued to observe her one-hour Reward Meal limit strictly and, at one year, reached her goal of a sixty-pound weight loss. Melanie put it beautifully: "Sixty pounds and sixty minutes—two important numbers to me."

MAKING A LIST, CHECKING IT TWICE

Dieting isn't like a boxing match where one knockout punch makes you the winner. Instead, you will be forced to take on one opponent after another. And there isn't a referee on hand to keep things fair.

In order to prepare yourself for the fight, assemble a list of what you know to be trouble spots. Be sure not to overlook any of the following:

PEOPLE

- Make a list of your enemies. Who are they and what do they do to foil your attempts to lose weight?

PLACES

• Are there specific stops in your daily, weekly, or monthly routine that have led to cheating in the past?

SITUATIONS

• How about circumstances? Do you find temptation lurks most often at happy hour on Fridays? Or when you go out with friends? Do gatherings with your family present you with special problems?

STRESSES

• Can you predict pressures that might set off your cravings? The little disagreements or frustrations at work? The inevitable rebelliousness of your teenage child? The pressures of a hectic schedule?

THOUGHTS

• Are there patterns of doubt you've observed with past diets? How have you convinced yourself that cheating is okay or even good for you?

In the pages that follow, we'll talk about developing individual strategies to deal with these diet-threatening daily occurrences. The attacks will come, be assured of that.

But they will be a great deal easier to deal with and conquer if you're prepared for them.

Planning Your Strategy

Using your past dietary slips, cheatings, and failures to good advantage—*that's* what successful dietary strategies are about.

Perhaps each of the difficulties that you have experienced in the past felt, at the time, like a defeat. All your good work went out the window. But the wealth of information that you, as an experienced dieter, have accumulated from those experiences can now be put to advantageous use.

Every enemy that undid your resolve in the past can help prepare you now for better results. For most of us, it's a matter of *knowing* ourselves (not *blaming* ourselves) and knowing how we react to specific circumstances.

Perhaps, like many dieters, you have had the experience of discovering that someone else ate the food that you had planned to eat for your meal. Maybe it was what you had planned to eat for lunch, and you found yourself suddenly without the proper food. You discover it's gone, and it makes you angry.

"Who did this?" you demand of the empty refrigerator. Then a little voice deep down inside of you says, "Don't get mad, get even." Or you shrug your shoulders and decide that you can't win this one, so you eat whatever you want (or whatever is available) for lunch. And in the process, you abandon the diet altogether. Or perhaps you eat very little or nothing at all and feel hungry, deprived, and cheated.

Nothing good comes of that, of course. You haven't taught the person who took your food anything and, as you've already learned, he or she will probably do it again. Worst of all, you exchanged your anger at someone else for anger at yourself, which only makes going back to the diet even harder. Or worse, you feel victimized.

That's a common self-destructive pattern—which occurs when people feel frustrated, ignored, or powerless. It's one of the thousands of reasons why it's important to have strategies for success.

FALLING OFF THE WAGON

"I began to take the diet for granted," Angela told us.

"I can't explain it. When I first came to the Carbohydrate Addict's Center I was totally out of control. A few weeks on the diet and I felt invincible. Then I started messing with the guidelines. I felt like nothing could hurt me. You know, I wasn't hungry, I wasn't tired, and I was losing weight. I felt like I could do anything. I forgot that it was the diet itself, the guidelines that I had been following, that were making me feel so good.

"First I started to extend my Reward Meal. I'd run back for an extra bite of cake or a cookie. At my cousin's wedding I extended it to about an hour and a half. After that, I stopped even looking at the time. I stopped reading labels when I bought food for my Low-Carbohydrate Meals. It was no surprise to find that at the same time my weight loss stopped and my hunger returned, full blown. Once again I was hungry before lunch and tired in the afternoon. I hadn't felt like that in weeks. I was losing it and I knew it. You know there's a saying I've heard you use, 'If it works, don't fix it.' I really see what you mean. It was working and I started to mess with it.

"But then I got it together. I just decided to stop messing with a good thing. I can't explain it, I just knew this was the right diet for me and I didn't want to live with hunger and tiredness anymore. I went back on the diet perfectly. My Reward Meal is now absolutely no longer than one hour. I don't buy any food for my Low-Carbohydrate Meals unless I'm sure that it's low in carbohydrates. If I'm not sure, I don't buy it. In restaurants, I'm really careful, and now I ask for information about the ingredients in food.

"I feel terrific. I'm losing weight again, just like before. The hunger is gone and I have more energy than my daughter. I am so glad that I turned it around. I could have blown it, but I just couldn't stand being out of control again. I've learned my lesson. I don't ever want to do that again."

Beth's Story

Beth T. and her husband loved going to the movies. They went often. As much as she enjoyed the movies, however, Beth found movies presented a persistent challenge to her diet.

While Beth was always fighting to control her weight, her husband was one of the lucky ones who seemed to be able to eat whatever he wished without gaining any weight. One of his favorite places to indulge his appetite happened to be at the movie theater, and he invariably bought two boxes of candy when he and Beth went to a show.

We encouraged Beth to use her experience to help her in following the diet. When we asked her about events in her life that had undone her attempts to lose weight in the past, she told us about her husband's candy. She also told us that she had found that although she was able to avoid eating any of the candy in the movies, the sounds and smells of her husband eating his sweets—the crackling of the wrapper, the chewing of the candy, and the rest—seemed to haunt her. Almost invariably, she said, a day or two would pass and she'd find the recollection of the candy irresistible. She'd find herself with candy bar in hand (and mouth), cheating.

Beth told us that her husband was supportive of her diet: "He never offers me candy anymore." So we suggested that she ask him to refrain from snacking at the theater. Then she admitted that she had already asked him to, several times, but that he felt that it was his right to enjoy some movie-time goodies.

It was Beth who devised the strategy. Instead of trying to force her husband to skip his candy, she took control of her own life. She offered her husband a choice. "If you watch the movie without eating candy, I will sit next to you during the entire show. If you eat candy next to me at the movies, I will move to another part of the theater until you have finished. This isn't meant as an ultimatum or a threat. I just need to avoid exposing myself to something that will fuel my addiction."

The result was that her husband ate his candy, and she moved to another part of the theater until he was done.

You may think her husband was inconsiderate or uncooperative, but Beth didn't. She knew that he loved her, but that he thought that she could control herself if she really wanted to. Beth said that she realized that she didn't want to be concerned with changing his behavior—*his* weight was fine. Instead, Beth focused on changing *her* behavior. When she presented her husband with a choice, she presented *herself* with a choice, too. After their next movie outing, Beth reported that she experienced a wonderful feeling of control and freedom. She realized she would never again have to sit and suffer in silence while the crunching and smells overwhelmed her.

When dieting, many people make the mistake of trying to force themselves and other people to act in certain ways. Threats are often used. Ultimatums are presented that offer no escape. *Do it, or else!*

Beth's way is better: she gave her husband a choice, and he made his selection. Then Beth made hers.

Take Control

Beth placed no blame—we had warned her that blame is an enemy, too, when you're trying to take control of your eating.

Blame and threats are dead ends, the weapons of the truly desperate. Avoid the one-way danger of blaming or threatening others. Instead, let your friends, family, and co-workers know that they are free to do what they want, but that you, too, must do what is best for you.

Inform the other person of what you will do to meet your goal of weight loss and weight-loss maintenance. Then live up to it. If you find yourself weakening, go to the bathroom. Being alone for a moment can give you the strength to resist temptation.

Taking control means that your friends and family will eventually realize that you mean what you say. *They* will come to expect that you will do whatever is necessary in order to lose weight and maintain that weight loss. *You* will experience a sense of self-respect that you may never have experienced before.

Think It Through

Taking control also means that you must work through the alternatives that you offer people before you offer them. If you advise a member of your family that snack foods left in the living room will be thrown out, then you must be willing to live up to your promise.

You must not only make your choices, you must anticipate consequences. You are fighting for your own happiness and success. That bears repeating. *You are fighting for your own happiness and success.* Don't work from other people's ideas of what is acceptable and what is not. Make choices that are acceptable to you and that will enable you to be successful.

Giving in won't make you feel better. Making choices to please others may win their approval for a time. But the chances are if your own needs are not met, then the self-blame and frustration you feel will far exceed the approval others may give you.

If you make choices that help you to be successful, you won't need to be so concerned about what other people think.

The process of devising strategies—of presenting choices and anticipating outcomes—isn't complicated, but it's a new way of thinking. Here are some examples.

Sample Strategy Number 1: Terminating the Teasing

The problem: Many dieters report that otherwise supportive friends, co-workers, and family tease them. Needling about overweight is often seen by the insensitive teasers as being "all in good fun" or even affectionate.

"We only tease you because we care about you," is one common justification.

The strategy: Don't put up with it. Don't yell or get upset, but show the teaser it just won't work with you.

Tell your family and friends that if they refrain from teasing you, you will enjoy spending time with them even more. On the other hand, they should be told that you will leave or go to another room if they begin to tease you. Don't explain or defend yourself. It is not a decision that they have to approve. This is what you want.

Your focus should not be on anger. This strategy involves setting the stage, clarifying for yourself and others the choices and the potential outcomes. The choice is theirs: one behavior will lead you to respond one way, another behavior will produce the other response. You have a preselected path to follow without anger or apology.

In either case, you get what you want: no teasing.

Sample Strategy Number 2: Favorite Food Trouble

The problem: You've told your family that you're on a diet and explained how it works. Or you've explained that you seem to have a physical disorder. Your loved ones seem supportive, but they bring a favorite food of yours into the house after you have asked them not to. They say they know that you like it.

The strategy: If the food contains carbohydrates, save it for your Reward Meal. Explain why: "I want to lose weight, and this is how I'm doing it. It's important to me."

If you want to avoid the food altogether, explain your decision honestly and candidly to the person who brought it for you. Without anger or apology, explain that though you know he or she brought it to make you happy, this food isn't the way to do it.

Then tell the person that, in the future, you'll have to give it away. That way, if he or she decides to bring it again, then that person has made the choice and knows what your response will be.

Don't get into the pattern of repeating yourself again and again. If you've given them fair warning, the rest is up to them.

Sample Strategy Number 3: Relative Temptation

The problem: Your spouse or child buys food for him- or herself. He or she eats it in front of you, triggering a craving for that food in you.

The strategy: First try sitting down with family members and openly discussing the problem. Explain that you have an addiction, and offer an alternative behavior. "I don't want to have to sit and listen to you munch your snack while I'm balancing the checkbook, so please eat that in the kitchen." Don't defend your choices. You are doing what is necessary to take care of yourself.

An alternative strategy to relative temptation is to buy some of the treat for yourself, then put it away to enjoy during your Reward Meal. Or announce that all opened goodies left around the house become your property and won't be returned, or they will be thrown away.

An understanding may be reached about not having the food in the house, but often this kind of support isn't forthcoming. More often, family members believe that they have a right to eat what they want, without depriving themselves because you have a problem. So you'll have to be strong.

Sample Strategy Number 4: Too Good to Pass Up

The problem: You're at a party and your favorite cake is being served. Or you're walking by a new bakery and you see a wonderful dessert in the window. Or some other eating temptation suddenly, unexpectedly, presents itself.

The strategy: This strategy is simple: save the treat for your Reward Meal. When the cake is served, take a generous portion for yourself, then pack it up and take it home. Buy that wonderful dessert—but take it home.

This is a good strategy for dealing with an old, yet recurring problem. You no longer have to give up something you want or pass it by. Just pack it up for later.

Choices and Outcomes

You know your habits best. Taking control means offering yourself some choices.

If you have discovered you cannot study or work in the kitchen without finding yourself in front of the refrigerator, find another place to study, one where you are not constantly reminded of food.

In the same way, if you have found you can't cook dinner without snacking on the food, then don't begin preparing food until immediately before the meal hour. Plan rapid, easy-to-prepare meals so that the nibbling that you find unavoidable during preparation can be kept within the sixty minutes allowed for the Reward Meal. Then you can nibble but not break the guidelines of the diet. Or freeze several meals and microwave them. Or eat out.

Some of the choices and outcomes you consider will probably surprise you; some will amuse you. Some you think you might like to express will scare you.

Think each one through. Our dieters express a new feeling of freedom and renewed hope as they take control of their eating and their weight. They report that once the choices and potential outcomes have been established in their minds, many temptations suddenly seem to lose their power.

DEALING WITH THE DANGERS

Earlier in this chapter, we advised you to make a list of the people, circumstances, stresses, and patterns of thinking that have led you to cheat in the past.

Now you must devise a strategy for each in order that it will not stand in your way to permanent weight loss. Essential to each strategy are these points:

ANTICIPATING TEMPTATION

- Consider each entry on that list (you haven't missed any important ones, have you?). Imagine (or recall) each circumstance in detail. Who are the players? What is the setting? How does the plot unfold?

• Try to enact the little drama in your head, focusing on the one that could lead to the break with the diet.

CONSIDERING THE *CHOICES*

• You are the playwright: how would you write the scene differently to alter the outcome?

• Remember, your goal is to take control. Therefore, you must devise *choices* for yourself and others. In the given situation, you need to be able to alter the circumstances so that you can remain or be able to walk away, without jeopardizing your diet. In addressing the enemies of your weight loss, you must give yourself options that will help to deal with the challenges that threaten your success.

ARRANGING THE *OUTCOMES*

• Don't feel you have to corner the culprit. It isn't necessary to force yourself or anyone else into a specific behavior. Offer choices to yourself and others. All choices should lead to acceptable outcomes.

• You need to devise choices that will meet your goals. If other people are involved, they must be informed of the choices and outcomes.

Once you have your plan in place, sit back and relax. You are prepared.

CHAPTER

10

Individualizing the Diet

In the preceding chapter, we examined potential enemies, the kinds of people, places, events, and daily pressures that can suddenly cause you to lose your commitment to your diet.

We talked about strategies you can use: the *anticipation* of the problem; how you must devise *choices* for yourself or others who can create challenges to your diet; and how you need to plan the *outcome* of each situation, providing alternatives for yourself and others.

With your strategies in hand, you are way ahead of dieters who try to decide upon a course of action at the moment of temptation. But now let's battle-test the strategies.

The challenge is approaching: perhaps it's Aunt Jean who's brought that carrot cake you love. Maybe it's the open bag of cookies on the kitchen shelf. The coffee cart at work, perhaps?

Whatever it is, here are some guidelines.

Plan the flight, then fly the plan. Once you have your plan, stay with it. Don't start to question your plan just as you put it into effect. Tell Aunt Jean you can't eat it now. Lay out the choices before you (and before Aunt Jean).

You planned for this challenge with your outcome alternatives. You thought them through at a time when you could think clearly, when you were not being tempted. Now your job is to stick to your battle plan.

If you want to rethink the plan, do it tomorrow. Get through the challenge at hand, learn from the experience, and improve your range of choices and outcomes for the next time. For now, stay with your plan.

Keep it simple. Some of our dieters have found themselves drawing lines of definition around what they can and cannot do in response to a threat to their diet.

One dieter reported she couldn't throw away open bags of junk food her children left around the house. Another said she couldn't just walk away from someone making a remark about her weight.

Such refusals are quite threatening to your success. The original choices these dieters made—to toss out the food, to ignore the mocking remarks—were calculated to produce a satisfactory outcome. But by compromising themselves, these dieters set the stage for losing control.

Failures to perform as you promised yourself mean you end up directing your anger at yourself. As the rules multiply ("I can't toss out that expensive candy, but I can throw out the popcorn"), maintaining your commitment gets harder. The simple fact is that the more qualifiers you add to every rule, the closer you get to letting your impulse eating take control again.

You cannot fight yourself and your enemies at the same time.

Act with determination. Don't hesitate in carrying out your plan. The first time you find yourself nibbling while you're reading the paper at the kitchen table, spit it out and move to another chair or another room. Don't hesitate. Act immediately. He (or she) who hesitates is lost in the dieting game.

Take no prisoners. A prisoner is an enemy that you don't want to, or are afraid to, destroy.

Many people keep such prisoners around. They are friends that tell you, "That diet won't work." Or that box of expensive chocolates: it sits there in the cabinet, threatening to transform itself from an allowable Reward Dinner treat into a midday cheat.

Get rid of all prisoners. Give your friend a choice; better yet, give your friend the candy and banish them both from your house.

Never volunteer. Many of the dieters that we've helped allowed themselves to fall into a dangerous pattern. They have trouble saying *no*.

They're just too nice. They try to do too much; they're too understanding. They try to help out, especially if they can rationalize to themselves that there's no harm in doing so.

Yet such praiseworthy helpfulness also produces a dangerous state of mind in which the helpful person begins to feel that it's sinful or selfish to take care of himself or herself as a first priority. And therein lies a clear and present danger to every dieter.

Take the stance that every army recruit learns to adopt at basic training—never volunteer.

If you are asked to do things that may make it more difficult for you to take care of yourself, say that this is not a good time. Or say that you need to think it over. Or that you must check your appointment book.

Take care of yourself first. You aren't going to be much good to anyone else if you are angry, frustrated, and defeated. Not to mention unhealthy.

Beware the narrow focus. No doubt you will encounter many enemies along the way. Take special care that you don't fix upon a particular person or circumstance to the exclusion of others.

Keep your strategies in perspective. If you find yourself involved in a power play, step back a moment. Your goal isn't to defeat this particular enemy, it's to ensure your own success.

Let's say that you are confronting the challenge of a pushy person or a spouse who refuses to help. Remember that your goal is to get what you need and not to get them to act as they should. There may be other ways to get what you want without their cooperation or help.

Your purpose is to succeed at losing weight and to maintain that weight loss. Don't allow yourself to be dominated by fighting one particular battle that overshadows other concerns. Keep your broader goals in mind. You must focus your energies on what will help you to lose weight and keep it off. That's a full-time job.

Short-Term Strategies

In helping dieters at the Carbohydrate Addict's Center, we have found that certain patterns recur. Not everyone loses weight at the same rate. The challenges are different for every dieter, yet there are some common themes that we hear, time and again.

Some of the most common are described in the following pages. Accompanying each are strategies for dealing with the problems.

Dieter's Dilemma Number 1: "I'm Not Losing Any Weight"

First, a reminder: don't compare two daily weights and conclude that you aren't losing weight. The only way to determine your weight-loss rate is to compare *average* weights from one week to the next.

If your weight has, in fact, remained the same and you have been strictly following the guidelines to the Carbohydrate Addict's Diet for three weeks or more, your body is probably adjusting. It may be slowing your metabolism in order to conserve energy.

This often happens after a quick weight-loss or liquid-fasting diet, but is less common in the Carbohydrate Addict's Diet. Thus, the effect may be left over from repeated dieting. Fast-dieting regimens that did not offer you enough food energy may make you prone to weight-loss plateaus caused by your body's more efficient use of the calories (we called them efficiency plateaus). Weight-loss plateaus are the body's response to what it perceives as a starvation situation. Too-rapid weight loss in the past, a pattern of yo-yo dieting, or, in some individuals, an inherited tendency can lead to this failure to lose weight in the earliest phase of the Carbohydrate Addict's Diet.

Don't despair, however. The Carbohydrate Addict's Diet will combat such efficiency plateaus and help a slowed metabolism. Through the use of Reward Meals, your metabolic processes will perceive that the situation is not one of starvation, your metabolism will adjust, and you will begin to lose weight. Follow the appropriate plan—probably Plan C or Plan D—and soon your weight should start dropping.

And be sure you are drinking your six or more glasses of water or other noncaloric liquids each day.

Hold on. There have been a handful of instances in our experience where a plateau lasted for a month or more, but that's rare. Even a week more may seem like an eternity right now, but you can do it. Those who break the diet at this point invariably regret doing so, often realizing they were just about to begin to lose weight.

Remember that this is a lifelong program. Give it a chance to correct the many times that you insulted your body with past diets. Don't forget that as you wait for your weight loss to resume, you are not being deprived of the food you enjoy. Each day you are eating all that you want at your Reward Meal.

Enjoy your Reward Meal, stay within the guidelines. Weight loss will follow.

Dieter's Dilemma Number 2: "I've Stopped Losing Weight"

The diet was proceeding nicely. You were happy with your progress. Then something changed.

You haven't cheated or changed your eating, but the weight loss stopped. Perhaps you even put back on a pound or two. You feel fine, with good energy levels, and you don't feel too hungry, but you are concerned, even frustrated.

What's the explanation?

Once again, you have hit what we call an efficiency plateau (see Dieter's Dilemma No. 1). Your body is conserving energy. It is using the calories you are taking in more efficiently, producing the pause in the weight-loss progression.

The good news is that efficiency plateaus are usually only temporary. Your metabolism is showing signs of having slowed, often because of previous failed diets. This efficiency plateau is common among dieters who have lost weight too rapidly in a recent diet or who admit to patterns of yo-yo dieting. There may be a genetic explanation, too, in that some people inherit a tendency to hold on to weight.

Some of our dieters have long and difficult dieting histories. As a result, their bodies have become super-efficient. They have found that it helps to minimize or even to skip one of the Low-Carbohydrate Meals on occasion. If you want to help your body break through an efficiency plateau, you can choose to skip a Low-Carbohydrate Meal now and then.

If you do so, however, be sure to *never* skip your Reward Meal. That is essential, providing you with both nutrition and pleasure.

You might also consider minimizing rather than skipping a Low-Carbohydrate Meal, eating lesser quantities of the same foods. A reminder: make sure you are eating all of your Reward Meal at one sitting within the sixty-minute limit. Don't leave the table and come back later to finish the meal; don't hold off on dessert for another time. When the eating light is lit, eat what you want—then stop eating.

You can shop for foods you want to eat at your Reward Meal any time during the day. You can even cook them during any of the other twenty-three hours of the day. But don't even taste them *except* during the designated hour of your Reward Meal.

Make certain that your Reward Meal is well rounded and balanced. All four food groups should be included.

Make sure you drink at least six to eight glasses of water or other noncaloric liquid each day.

If you wish, have one cup of coffee or tea during the day. You can have a bit of milk in it but no sugar except during your Reward Meal. Although you may have all the coffee with milk you want during your Reward Meal, be sure to have no more than one cup of coffee with milk at a time other than your Reward Meal. Be sure to complete that cup of coffee and milk within 15 minutes. You may have black coffee at any time.

Make sure that none of your low-carbohydrate foods contain hidden carbohydrates, because even a little can mean insulin release, which spells diet disaster. One of our dieters discovered sugar was an ingredient of processed cheddar food spread. She removed it from her daily Low-Carbohydrate Meal and began to lose weight again.

Most important, however, is to maintain your confidence. Hang in there: very few of the people with whom we have worked have ever stayed at the efficiency plateau longer than a few weeks.

It may seem like a lifetime of waiting while you're there, but you can get through it. Your body will gradually readjust, and following Plan C or D will help you to begin to lose weight again. Just check your adherence to the guidelines and hold on. This is not a fast weight-loss program—it is designed to treat your carbohydrate addiction. Give it time.

Dieter's Dilemma Number 3: "I'm Putting Weight Back On"

First of all, be honest with yourself: if you're not following the guidelines, you know it.

Cut it out. Go back to living by the diet—it'll produce the results you want.

If you aren't consciously cheating, double-check your low-carbohydrate meals for hidden carbohydrates. One of our dieters discovered that tuna salad at his favorite restaurant had bread crumbs in it, a forbidden carbohydrate, and it triggered his addiction.

Our experience has been that once the hidden carbohydrate has been eliminated, weight loss resumes. At the end of the next two-week period, you will probably find you have lost the weight you had temporarily gained. Most likely, you will find that you have lost more than you gained.

Stay or get active. If you are not active, it's harder to lose weight.

Check your sixty-minute Reward Meal time limit—it's essential to the success of the diet. Follow Plan C or Plan D until you start losing again, and make sure you are eating your salads before every Reward Meal.

Making the Commitment: Donna's Story

Even before we met her, we had some sense of Donna: she'd already canceled and rescheduled three appointments at the Center.

When she did arrive, she raced in, packages and briefcase in hand, a scarf half-tied around her neck. She was late, harried, and looked like she was ready to collapse. She did, sort of, into a comfortable chair. We asked why she had come to see us.

"My life is out of control," was her reply. "I don't mean part of it, I don't mean just my weight, my whole life. I know you can't solve all of my problems at once, but I have to start something and if I could just lose some weight and keep it off, I would feel like I was getting somewhere."

The rest of her story came out in a rush. She and her husband were a bit strapped for money; they fought about it often. She didn't have a career. She worked at jobs she could pick up, usually in sales, but in recent weeks had only been making $120 for a twenty-five-hour work week.

"I have no real job skills and I'm so heavy that it's affecting my health," she concluded. "I'm forty and I feel like it's all over."

She admitted to being eighty pounds overweight, but said her doctor estimated she was more like a hundred pounds over her ideal weight. When we gave her the Carbohydrate Addict's Test, she tested as having a moderate addiction, but the results were somewhat ambiguous because she had bounced back and forth between yes and no on many questions.

We told her about the diet at length. We made a special point of talking about emotional and stress-related triggers that led to eating and how the diet could help control them. The Carbohydrate Addict's Diet can't solve all your problems, we cautioned, but perhaps it can help with your weight.

Donna listened politely but, unfortunately, she seemed unable to focus on our words. She told us her schedule was too uncertain for her to make an appointment for the following week. She said she'd call to make one. She never did.

We saw Donna on the street some months later. She seemed heavier still, and, again, in a disorganized rush. She told us that she had thought of coming to consult us, but "just couldn't get it together." That was two years ago.

We have not seen her since. Donna had many commitments, and her commitment to her weight loss did not come first.

Dieter's Dilemma Number 4: "I've Reached My Target Weight, and My Weight Loss Has Stopped. What Do I Do Now?"

After you have reached your goal weight and that weight is holding, there's no need for change.

If you are like most long-term users of the Carbohydrate Addict's Diet, you feel content. You don't crave fattening foods; your intake of carbohydrates has become more reasonable—the craving and bingeing episodes are a thing of the past.

The program has helped you establish an eating program that suits your biological needs. Make sure that it meets your wishes as well: don't skimp on the foods you want during your Reward Meal. You'll only feel deprived later—and avoiding a sense of deprivation is crucial to long-term dietary success.

Your input and output of energy are balanced. By this time, the effects of past dieting behavior have been counterbalanced by the diet. There is a comfortable constancy about the diet—its regimen and its results serve to reassure.

Don't get careless. Weight maintenance requires that you continue to watch the food that you eat, each and every day. The plan works for you, but you must also work the plan.

Live by the guidelines: only one hour a day is set aside for carbohydrate consumption. Don't give in to a momentary impulse to taste this or that food outside of the prescribed limits. Save the treat for the Reward Meal. Just a little cheating *can* hurt you.

Weigh yourself every single day. Write it down. Average it every week. This is essential to your continued success.

In time, you may begin to lose weight as your metabolism normalizes even more. If you lose a pound or two more than you desire, move to the appropriate plan as detailed in the Carbohydrate Addict's Diet Guide (page 86).

If you gained a pound or two, don't panic. Don't switch to other weight-loss programs. Don't try fasting. As you continue on the Carbohydrate Addict's Diet, you will see that there is a normal process of adjustment in your weight patterns. Check the Diet Guide (page 86) every week to make sure that you are following the best plan for *you*.

Remember that the human body isn't a machine that runs at a never-changing rate. It moves into weight-loss and weight-gain periods for reasons that are both complicated and poorly understood. What we do know, however, is that it is dangerous to allow a minor gain in weight to cause you to radically change your eating: stay with the program and work it.

Give your body a chance to reach a balance. Remember, this is a lifetime program, and therefore, there are inevitable ups and downs.

Seasons may cause weight fluctuations, with gains in the fall and winter and losses in the spring and summer. The best approach is to relax, give it time, stick to the guidelines, weigh yourself daily, record and average the weight, and enjoy yourself.

Dieter's Dilemma Number 5: "I'm Losing Too Much Weight"

Yes, it happens: your goal weight comes and goes, and more pounds drop off. Not every dieter experiences this, but many do.

Or you're not at your goal weight but you're losing more than one-half to two pounds a week.

What should you do?

First of all, be honest with yourself: are you following the guidelines precisely? We've had more than a few dieters who want to lose weight quickly and don't follow the rules, skipping meals or exaggerating the limitations. Follow the guidelines, and don't make up rules of your own. Check the Diet Guide (page 86) every week and follow the plan that's recommended for your weight-loss rate and weight-loss needs.

Dieter's Dilemma Number 6: "I've Fallen Off the Wagon"

You were doing beautifully—losing weight and not feeling hungry—and you figured that just a little bit of carbohydrate-rich food eaten at a time other than your Reward Meal wouldn't hurt you. Or you thought that adding ten or fifteen minutes to your Reward Meal hour wouldn't really do any harm. After all, you might have reasoned, you were doing so well that you could afford it.

Or you had come to a standstill in your weight and you started to become discouraged. You might have told yourself that since you weren't losing anyway, it really didn't matter if you didn't follow the guidelines exactly. How much worse could it be? You weren't losing anyway. And now you see the results.

Chances are you are having one or more of these three experiences:

- You may again be feeling hunger or carbohydrate cravings.
- You may have gained some of your weight back or stopped losing weight.
- You may feel tired, unmotivated, worried, and/or irritable. You may have trouble getting yourself to do your work.

Most of the people we have worked with say that these experiences help to remind them of the hunger, tiredness, and feelings of being out of control that they experienced before they began the Carbohydrate Addict's Diet.

If you have broken your diet guidelines and you are experiencing hunger, tiredness, and/or weight gain, or if you are feeling irritable, worried, or out of control, it is quite likely that you are now ready to return to the safety, pleasure, and control that you experienced on your diet. But how do you go back on the diet? First, don't hesitate. Immediately re-enter the program.

- If the break in your diet was a single incident (or two) or lasted for no more than one day, go back to the plan you had been following before the break. At the end of each week re-evaluate your plan by consulting the Carbohydrate Addict's Diet Guide (page 86).

- If your break lasted for two or more days, or if it occurred on three or more instances, go back to the Entry Plan. No matter which plan you were following before these breaks in the program, go back to the Entry Plan. Follow the Entry Plan for two weeks, and record your weight daily. At the end of two weeks, the Diet Guide (page 86) will help you to select the plan that is best suited to your individual needs.

Some people think they should return to the plan they were following when they had their break. This is true *only* if the break was an unusual occurrence or lasted for a very short time. Longer breaks in the diet may change the way your body will respond to the diet. For *longer diet breaks* you are most likely to regain your success by re-entering the program and following the Entry Plan.

Most important, stop thinking about the past. Deal with the present and the future. Remember, this is your diet. It will work for you. It was designed for you and it adapts to your needs. If you have skipped through this book, read it from the start. Don't skip around. **This book is your guide to treating your carbohydrate addiction. Know what it says.** Read it carefully. Don't just read a bit here and a bit there. Spend your time learning about your addiction and, please, stop blaming yourself.

THE LOW-CARBOHYDRATE SNACK

There are two sets of circumstances in which you want to slow your weight loss: (1) when you have reached your goal weight but are continuing to lose weight, or (2) when your weekly rate of weight loss is greater than about 1 percent of your body weight (i.e., about one pound for each 100 pounds you weigh).

In either of these situations, you may wish to add a Low-Carbohydrate Snack to your eating program.

★ ***Food Selection:*** Foods for this snack should be chosen from the same low-carbohydrate foods that make up your Low-Carbohydrate Meals.

★ *Serving Size:* Servings should be approximately half of the average servings specified for Low-Carbohydrate Meals, or equal to:

- 3 to 4 ounces of meat, fish, or poultry; or
- 1 to 1½ ounces of cheese; or
- 1 egg; and
- 1 cup of vegetables with a pat of butter or margarine, or salad with a small amount of dressing.

★ *Snacking Schedule:* You can eat your once-a-day Low-Carbohydrate Snack at any time of day. Most dieters, however, report that midafternoon or evening is preferable.

Eat your snack as a mini-meal. Don't eat it on the run; sit down and enjoy it.

Never add carbohydrate-rich foods such as fruits, fruit juices, breads, pasta, snack foods, or sweets to your snacks. *Never*.

Fight the Good Fight

You're ready for the opposition you will face. You have worked out strategies to deal with any enemies you might encounter.

You have armed yourself with a diet plan that will use your own body to help you to reduce your addictive response to carbohydrates. Yet you are allowed to eat without restraint once every day.

You now have what you need to take control of your eating, your weight, and your life. Don't obsess about what will happen tomorrow or a month from now—take the diet one day at a time. Remember that for more than 80 percent of the carbohydrate addicts who have come to us at the Carbohydrate Addict's Center, the Carbohydrate Addict's Diet has proved to be a permanent weight-loss solution.

You will find it can succeed for you, too.

CHAPTER

11

Waking Up Thin

As a child and, later, as a young woman, Rachael used to have a single dream. It ran over and over in her mind.

"I dreamed that I would wake up one morning as a normal, thin person. This morning—as I write this—and every morning for the last seven years, I've had my dream come true.

"I wake up knowing that when I walk past a group of children I don't need to fear their cruel taunts.

"I'm no longer afraid to speak up for myself in a store or a theater line. Children don't call me names like 'pig' and 'fat slob' anymore in front of countless strangers. At three hundred pounds, I cringed at the verbal abuses of others, feeling that I was to blame for my condition.

"When I walk by store windows, I still pause, struck by the reflection I see there. My husband, Richard, smiles when he sees me do it, knowing that I'm still getting used to my thin reflection looking back at me.

"In the seven years since my weight loss, I have come to expect that a size six will fit. I don't have to be worried about getting stuck in chairs anymore. Physical exhaustion isn't the inevitable result of an active day. I move freely and unselfconsciously. For the first time in my life, I feel and look sexy.

"Every day I wake up renewed, alive, and grateful. The simple act of dressing, of slipping on stylish clothes, of seeing my new self in the mirror is a miracle.

"I cannot imagine that I will ever take these wonders for granted."

PART IV

LOW-CARBOHYDRATE MEAL PLANS AND RECIPES

CHAPTER

12

Low-Carbohydrate Sample Meal Plans

The following sample Meal Plans have been assembled to guide you in selecting foods for your Low-Carbohydrate Meals in order to meet the guidelines of the Carbohydrate Addict's Diet. You will find recipes for many of the dishes identified here in the recipe section that follows.

We have not specified menus for your Reward Meal (which, for consistency, we have designated as dinner in these menus). That's because you can eat *anything* during your Reward Meals, literally *any* low- and high-carbohydrate food you desire. And for those meals you may consult any cookbook in creation. It's up to you. But please, keep them nourishing and well-balanced.

These menus for the Low-Carbohydrate Meals are by no means all-inclusive. You may mix and match between them, and develop your own low-carbohydrate dishes to suit your tastes, cooking talents, and desires. You have only to keep in mind the basic rules of the diet.

Incorporating Health and Diet Recommendations into the Carbohydrate Addict's Diet

The Surgeon General of the United States has issued his Report on Nutrition and Health.

The U.S. Department of Agriculture and the Department of Health and Human Services have prepared a Report on Dietary Guidelines for Americans.

The American Heart Association Diet offers an Eating Plan for Healthy Americans.

Each of these reports has been designed to offer dietary recommendations to aid in the prevention of one or more of the following: cardiovascular diseases, cancer, diabetes, obesity, osteoporosis, chronic liver disease, chronic kidney disease.

These recommendations—and, in particular, *low-fat and/or low-cholesterol* dietary choices—are easily incorporated into, and are completely compatible with, the Carbohydrate Addict's Diet. Suggestions for incorporating these guidelines into the Carbohydrate Addict's Diet follow.

Please note that only your doctor can determine which dietary recommendations are appropriate for you. Before incorporating any dietary guidelines into your eating regimen, you should consult your physician.

The Low-Carbohydrate Meal Plans that follow are based on two Low-Carbohydrate Meals and one Reward Meal per day. If your plan includes a salad (Plan C or Plan D), a Low-Carbohydrate Snack (Plan A), or only one Low-Carbohydrate Meal per day, adjust your meal plan accordingly.

Day One

BREAKFAST

Carbohydrate Addict's French Toast* (page 202)

Cappuccino Slush (page 249), tea, coffee, or diet soda

LUNCH

Baked Fish with Lemon and Herbs (page 212)
Steamed cauliflower or spinach with butter or low-cholesterol margarine
Carbohydrate Addict's Bread* (page 200)
Coffee, tea, or diet soda

DINNER

Your Reward Meal:
in short, you get to eat anything you want.

Day Two

BREAKFAST

Carbohydrate Addict's Light and Airy Muffins* (page 201)
Cappuccino (page 249), tea, coffee, or diet soda

LUNCH

Baked Herb-Marinated Chicken (page 208)
Tossed Green Salad (page 239) with dressing of your choice (pages 241 and 242)
Lemon Heaven (page 248)
Iced tea (sugarless), iced coffee, or diet soda

DINNER

Time for another Reward Meal. But don't forget—you must complete it within sixty minutes.

* This is a specially designed low-carbohydrate recipe. Regular varieties of this food are too high in carbohydrates to consume during Low-Carbohydrate Meals. Therefore, during Low-Carbohydrate Meals, *do not* substitute regular varieties of this food in place of this recipe.

Day Three

BREAKFAST

Onion-Cheese Omelet (page 223)
Sausage links (or no-cholesterol sausage substitute)
Tea or coffee

LUNCH

Tuna Salad (page 226)
Tossed Green Salad (page 239) with oil and vinegar as dressing
Iced tea with lemon (sugarless), coffee, or diet soda

DINNER

Your Reward Meal can include anything, even carbohydrate-rich foods like breads and pasta, rice, beans, potatoes, and fruits.

Day Four

BREAKFAST

Scrambled eggs (or no-cholesterol egg substitute)
Low-Fat Pork Sausage (page 220) or no-cholesterol substitute
Sliced cucumber
Coffee, tea, or diet soda

LUNCH

Chicken Salad (page 226)
Brie or cheddar cheese
Finger salad (celery, green or red pepper strips, radishes, green beans) with Spicy Creamy Dip or Dressing (page 199)
Coffee, tea, or diet soda

DINNER

Balance your diet at your Reward Meal, selecting delicious foods from each of the four basic food groups.

Day Five

BREAKFAST

Carbohydrate Addict's Pancakes* (page 203)
Spicy Hot Sausage (page 221), or low-cholesterol substitute
Tea or coffee

LUNCH

Chef's Salad (page 225) with dressing of your choice (pages 241 and 242)
Coffee, tea, or diet soda

DINNER

Along with the food you enjoy, you may have beer, wine, or spirits at your Reward Meal, but they must be consumed within the designated 60 minutes.

Day Six

BREAKFAST

Carbohydrate Addict's Cinnamon Bread* (page 201)
Tea or coffee

* This is a specially designed low-carbohydrate recipe. Regular varieties of this food are too high in carbohydrates to consume during Low-Carbohydrate Meals. Therefore, during Low-Carbohydrate Meals, *do not* substitute regular varieties of this food in place of this recipe.

LUNCH

Sliced turkey or turkey wings
Sliced cucumber, radishes, and olives
Dill pickle
Iced tea (sugarless) or diet soda

DINNER

How about a salad, meatballs and pasta, and a wonderful dessert as your Reward Meal? It's up to you.

Day Seven

BREAKFAST

Western Omelet (page 222)
Cappuccino (page 249), coffee, tea, or diet soda

LUNCH

Puffy Fish Fillets (page 213)
Vegetables Vinaigrette (page 233)
Carbohydrate Addict's Bread* (page 200)
Strawberry Slush (page 249), coffee, tea, or diet soda

DINNER

You can schedule your Reward Meal for *any* meal, not just dinner, but remember: eat carbohydrate-rich foods only once per day.

* This is a specially designed low-carbohydrate recipe. Regular varieties of this food are too high in carbohydrates to consume during Low-Carbohydrate Meals. Therefore, during Low-Carbohydrate Meals, *do not* substitute regular varieties of this food in place of this recipe.

Day Eight

BREAKFAST

Carbohydrate Addict's Cinnamon Coffee Cake* (page 243)
Coffee, tea, or diet soda

LUNCH

Cheese-Covered Mixed Vegetables (page 238)
Spinach Salad (page 239) with dressing of your choice (pages 241 and 242)
Carbohydrate Addict's Bread* (page 200)
Coffee, tea, or diet soda

DINNER

But try to keep to the same daily schedule. Vary your Reward Meal only on special occasions.

Day Nine

BREAKFAST

Scrambled eggs (or no-cholesterol egg substitute)
Bacon (or no-cholesterol bacon substitute)
Coffee, tea, or diet soda

LUNCH

Baked or broiled chicken
Tossed Green Salad (page 239) with dressing of your choice (pages 241 and 242)
Coffee, tea, or diet soda

* This is a specially designed low-carbohydrate recipe. Regular varieties of this food are too high in carbohydrates to consume during Low-Carbohydrate Meals. Therefore, during Low-Carbohydrate Meals, *do not* substitute regular varieties of this food in place of this recipe.

DINNER

If you nibble while you are preparing your Reward Meal, the clock starts then, and you must complete your meal within sixty minutes of your first bite.

Day Ten

BREAKFAST

Carbohydrate Addict's Blintzes* (page 247)
Coffee, tea, or diet soda

LUNCH

Lamb chops
Fresh green beans with Cool Summer Dip (page 198)
Coffee, tea, or diet soda

DINNER

Really, it's allowed. You can eat as much as you want. This is your Reward Meal, after all. Eat and enjoy.

Day Eleven

BREAKFAST

Salami and eggs (or low-cholesterol substitutes)
Coffee, tea, or diet soda

LUNCH

Fresh Seafood Salad (page 227)
Celery, green pepper strips, and cucumber slices with Creamy Herb Dressing (page 242)
Coffee, tea, or diet soda

* This is a specially designed low-carbohydrate recipe. Regular varieties of this food are too high in carbohydrates to consume during Low-Carbohydrate Meals. Therefore, during Low-Carbohydrate Meals, *do not* substitute regular varieties of this food in place of this recipe.

DINNER

Your Reward Meal is coming to you. Eat it without guilt.

Day Twelve

BREAKFAST

Cottage cheese (regular or low-fat)
Cool cucumber slices
Coffee or tea

LUNCH

Chicken Paprikash (page 210)
Celery stuffed with cream cheese (regular or low-fat variety)
Tossed Green Salad (page 239) with dressing of your choice (pages 241 and 242)
Coffee, tea, or diet soda

DINNER

Be creative with your Reward Meal. Go to an exotic ethnic restaurant. Buy a new cookbook and experiment. Have fun.

Day Thirteen

BREAKFAST

Ham and Cheese Omelet (page 223)
Coffee, tea, or diet soda

LUNCH

Hot dogs (regular or low-fat chicken variety)
Sauerkraut
Tossed Green Salad (page 239) with dressing of your choice (pages 241 and 242)
Iced tea (sugarless) or diet soda

DINNER

If you finish your Reward Meal in less than sixty minutes, don't go back and eat more. Eat all you want at one sitting.

Day Fourteen

BREAKFAST

Breakfast Soufflé* (page 224)
Cappuccino (page 249), coffee, tea, or diet soda

LUNCH

Spicy Shrimp with Mushrooms (page 217)
Steamed green beans with butter or low-cholesterol margarine
Coffee, tea, or diet soda

DINNER

Don't skimp on your Reward Meal in order to lose weight faster. The diet will work for you, if you work with it.

* This is a specially designed low-carbohydrate recipe. Regular varieties of this food are too high in carbohydrates to consume during Low-Carbohydrate Meals. Therefore, during Low-Carbohydrate Meals, *do not* substitute regular varieties of this food in place of this recipe.

CURRENT HEALTH AND DIET RECOMMENDATIONS†

Recommendation	*To Incorporate Recommendation into the Carbohydrate Addict's Diet*
1. Reduce consumption of fat (especially saturated fat) and cholesterol.	1. Choose low-fat cheeses and milk or low-cholesterol dairy and egg substitutes whenever possible. Low-fat, low-cholesterol margarine and cooking sprays may

† Condensed from The U.S. Surgeon General's *Report on Nutrition and Health*; The U.S. Department of Agriculture and the Department of Health and Human Services, *Report on Dietary Guidelines for Americans*; The American Heart Association Diet, *Eating Plan for Healthy Americans*.

CURRENT HEALTH AND DIET RECOMMENDATIONS (*continued*)

Recommendation	*To Incorporate Recommendation into the Carbohydrate Addict's Diet*
	be used in place of butter. Chicken, turkey, fish, veal, and lamb or very lean cuts of beef should replace fattier choices. Prepare low-fat, low-cholesterol bacon and sausage substitutes as well as low-cholesterol mayonnaise. Avoid tropical oils; choose olive or polyunsaturated vegetable oils.
2. Achieve and maintain a desirable body weight by choosing a dietary pattern in which energy (caloric) intake is consistent with energy expenditure.	2. The Carbohydrate Addict's Diet will help you to reach and maintain a desirable body weight by normalizing the way your body uses the calories that you consume. Keep your activity level high, and never, never eat high-carbohydrate foods at times other than during your Reward Meal.
3. Increase consumption of complex carbohydrates and *fiber* by choosing *whole-grain* foods and cereal products, vegetables, and fruits.	3, The Carbohydrate Addict's Diet is a diet high in fiber. Make sure to eat a salad and a variety of vegetables at your Low-Carbohydrate Meals and include salad, whole-grain foods, and plenty of fruits in your Reward Meal.
4. Reduce intake of sodium by choosing foods relatively low in sodium and by limiting the amount of salt added in food preparation and at the table.	4. At all meals you may choose low-salt variations of your favorite foods, such as low-salt cheese and other dairy products. And you may avoid salted and smoked products. If you wish, you may limit the amount of added salt to cooking and serving.
5. Those who are particularly vulnerable to dental cavities should limit their consumption and frequency of use of foods high in sugars.	5. The Carbohydrate Addict's Diet will automatically limit the frequency of your exposure to foods high in sugar to no more than once a day, during your Reward Meal. If you are vulnerable to dental cavities, then you might choose foods lower in sugar content during that meal.

CURRENT HEALTH AND DIET RECOMMENDATIONS (*continued*)

Recommendation	*To Incorporate Recommendation into the Carbohydrate Addict's Diet*
6. Women should increase consumption of foods high in calcium, including low-fat dairy products.	6. At Low-Carbohydrate Meals choose low-fat cheese, canned fish such as salmon and sardines (with bones), and mackerel. Spinach and greens (collard, mustard) as well as oysters and tofu are high in calcium and low in carbohydrates. During Reward Meals enjoy all the calcium-rich foods above as well as low-fat milk, broccoli, and almonds.
7. Women of childbearing age should consume foods that are good sources of iron.	7. Low-Carbohydrate Meals may include lean beef, lamb, chicken, turkey, green beans, and mushrooms. Reward Meals may include potatoes, popcorn, pasta, fruits, raisins, or rice.

CHAPTER

13

Low-Carbohydrate Recipes

Fundamental to the Carbohydrate Addict's Diet is the avoidance of carbohydrate-rich foods during all but the one hour each day that is devoted to the Reward Meal. No snacks are allowed between meals, but low-carbohydrate foods may be eaten at designated mealtimes, as detailed in the Diet Guide (page 86).

The recipes that follow are intended for consumption at the Low-Carbohydrate Meals. These are by no means the *only* dishes you can eat at your Low-Carbohydrate Meals, but are intended to help you plan your menu. (You might also wish to consult the sample menus on page 182.)

In planning your meals, if you are unsure as to whether a food is too high in carbohydrates, consult the low-carbohydrate food lists that begin on page 98.

Remember, your Low-Carbohydrate Meals are to consist of average portions of about four to six ounces of meat, fish, or poultry; or two to three ounces of cheese; and one and one-half to two cups of salad or vegetables with two to three tablespoons of salad dressing or a pat or two of butter or margarine. Low-carbohydrate foods may be broiled, boiled, sautéed, baked, poached, roasted, or even fried. However, no breading or batter can be used.

You may also have a low-carbohydrate dessert at any of your Low-

Carbohydrate Meals. (Remember to save fruits for your Reward Meal.)

The recipes are organized within sections for hors d'oeuvres (beginning on this page), breads and pastries (page 200), main courses (page 204), vegetables and salads (page 228), and desserts and beverages (page 243).

Where appropriate, we have inserted low-fat and low-cholesterol options into the recipe ingredients. This should allow you to adjust these recipes for a low-fat, low-cholesterol diet.

Note that many of the main courses specify yields to serve two or three people. If you are eating them alone, you may choose to prepare half the recipe or, if you prepare it all, refrigerate the unused portions for use next day.

You may elect to use a microwave for reheating them. Some of our dieters have reported that their offices or places of work have microwaves for employee use, and thus they prepare their delicious low-carbohydrate lunch entrées in this fashion.

Remember, these suggested recipes are provided for use in your low-carbohydrate meals. You are *not* confined to low-carbohydrate foods during your Reward Meal hour.

Low-Carbohydrate Hors d'Oeuvres

Salmon Canapés

Makes 10

1 ounce canned salmon, drained
1 ounce cream cheese or low-fat substitute, softened
1 teaspoon chopped fresh dill or parsley
1 cucumber
A few leaves of lettuce for lining plates (optional)
A few stalks of celery, radishes, and black and green olives for garnish (optional)

1. Combine the salmon, cream cheese, and dill. Chill for an hour or more.

2. Meanwhile, peel and slice the cucumber into 20 rounds. Blot the slices dry with paper toweling.
3. Spread the salmon mixture on half the cucumber slices and top with the remaining slices to make tiny "sandwiches."

If you wish, serve on a bed of lettuce surrounded by stalks of celery, radishes, and black and green olives.

Turkey and Cheese Cucumber Canapés

Makes 10

2 ounces thin-sliced turkey
2 ounces thin-sliced cheese, such as Swiss, Muenster, or cheddar
1 cucumber
Dijon mustard
A few lettuce leaves, for lining plates (optional)
A few tiny dill pickles (cornichons), and green and black olives for garnish (optional)

1. Cut the turkey and cheese into pieces that will fit neatly on a cucumber round.
2. Peel and slice each cucumber into 20 rounds. Blot the slices dry with paper toweling.
3. Spread a little bit of mustard onto half of the cucumber rounds. Put a piece or two of turkey and cheese onto half of the rounds.
4. Top with the remaining cucumber rounds.

If you wish, line a plate with the lettuce leaves, arrange the canapés on the leaves, and surround with radishes and olives.

Cream Cheese Celery Stuffers

These creamy mixtures are super-satisfying when stuffed in celery or wrapped in crisp lettuce leaves.

Makes about ½ cup

Celery Stuffer 1: Fish and Cucumber

1½ ounces cream cheese or low-fat substitute, softened
1½ teaspoons sour cream or low-fat sour cream substitute
1 ounce canned tuna, canned salmon, or anchovies
Garlic powder or ground black pepper to taste
2 tablespoons chopped cucumber
10 stalks celery or 5 crisp lettuce leaves

Mix the cream cheese and sour cream together well. Flake the tuna or salmon or chop the anchovies. Stir the fish into the mixture along with the garlic powder or pepper and the chopped cucumber. Stuff celery stalks with mixture or wrap mixture in crisp lettuce leaves.

Celery Stuffer 2: Italian Cheese and Herbs

This recipe makes enough for several meals or a party. If you like, cut the recipe in half.

Makes about ½ cup

1½ ounces cream cheese or low-fat substitute, softened
1½ teaspoons sour cream or low-cholesterol sour cream substitute
¼ cup grated Parmesan or Romano cheese
¼ teaspoon marjoram
¼ teaspoon oregano
Garlic powder or ground black pepper to taste
10 stalks celery or 5 crisp lettuce leaves

Combine all the ingredients except the lettuce or celery, mixing well. Stuff the celery stalks with the mixture or wrap it in crisp lettuce leaves.

Celery Stuffer 3: Cheddar and Mustard

This recipe makes canapés for several servings.

Makes about ½ cup

1½ ounces cream cheese or low-fat substitute, softened
¼ cup shredded cheddar cheese
1½ teaspoons sour cream or low-cholesterol sour-cream substitute
1 teaspoon Dijon mustard or prepared yellow mustard
10 stalks celery or 5 crisp lettuce leaves

Combine all ingredients except the celery or lettuce, mixing well. Stuff the celery stalks with the mixture or wrap it in the lettuce leaves.

Tofu Garlic Cheese

Serve this low-fat cheese as an hors d'oeuvre with sliced vegetable rounds such as summer squash, zucchini, and cucumber. It's also good when sliced and served as a main course at lunch on a bed of lettuce.

Makes 1¼ cups

- 1 cup mashed tofu
- ¼ cup chopped fresh basil, parsley, or thyme
- 4 cloves garlic
- 1 tablespoon plus 1½ teaspoons fresh lemon or lime juice
- 2 tablespoons plus 1½ teaspoons sour cream or low-cholesterol substitute
- 2 or 3 dashes Tabasco (optional)
- Ground black pepper to taste (optional)
- ¾ cup freshly grated Romano or Parmesan cheese

1. Wrap the tofu in a clean towel and squeeze to wring out excess moisture. Mash the tofu with a fork.
2. Combine the basil and garlic cloves in a blender or food processor. Process or blend briefly, until chopped moderately fine. Add the lemon juice, sour cream or substitute, Tabasco, and black pepper to taste, if using. Process briefly to blend.
3. Add the tofu and grated cheese to the mixture and blend until smooth. Pour the mixture into a bowl, cover, and chill for several hours.
4. Remove from the refrigerator, shape into a log about 6 inches long, wrap in plastic, and chill overnight.

Lox and Cream Cheese Dip

This dip is great stuffed in celery stalks or served with pepper strips, on raw summer squash or cucumber rounds, or with raw cauliflower florets.

Makes about ¾ cup

2 pieces lox or other smoked salmon, about 1 ounce
3 ounces cream cheese or low-fat substitute, softened
2 tablespoons mayonnaise, or low-cholesterol substitute

1. Shred the lox finely.
2. Combine the softened cream cheese and the mayonnaise, mixing well. Stir in the shredded lox and stuff into celery stalks or serve with raw vegetables.

You might also try spreading a lettuce leaf with a couple of teaspoons and rolling it up into a cylinder.

Tofu Mustard Sauce

This sauce makes a high-protein spicy dip for steamed or raw vegetables.

Makes about ½ cup

½ cup mashed tofu
6 tablespoons Dijon or prepared yellow mustard
6 tablespoons olive or polyunsaturated vegetable oil
3 tablespoons white wine vinegar
2 packets artificial sweetener

Combine all of the ingredients in a blender or food processor and mix until smooth.

Serve with steamed vegetables such as asparagus or green beans, or raw vegetables such as fennel, celery, mushroom caps, scallions, summer squash or zucchini, sliced turnips, or cucumbers.

Cool Summer Dip

Serve as a dip with crisp celery sticks, cucumber slices, green and red pepper strips, mushroom caps, and cauliflower florets. Toss with shredded cabbage for a fresh-tasting coleslaw.

Makes about ½ cup

½ cup sour cream or low-cholesterol substitute
2 teaspoons finely chopped fresh basil, or ½ teaspoon dried
¼ teaspoon garlic powder

Combine the ingredients, mixing well.

Mustard Horseradish Dip and Sauce

This dip is terrific served with vegetables, but it also makes a great sauce for broiled chicken, fish, or meat.

Makes 1 cup

½ cup sour cream or low-cholesterol substitute
½ cup Dijon mustard
2 teaspoons white horseradish or to taste

Combine the sour cream, mustard, and horseradish. Cover and chill.

Serve with steamed or raw vegetables such as green beans, asparagus spears, celery stalks, green or red pepper strips, and mushroom caps.

Spicy Creamy Dip or Dressing

This sauce is good as a dip for vegetables or poultry, or as a dressing for salad.

Makes about 1 cup

1 cup regular or low-fat cottage cheese
2 tablespoons regular or skim milk
1 tablespoon white horseradish
¼ teaspoon ground black pepper
3 dashes Tabasco

Combine the ingredients in a food processor, blender, or mixer and beat until smooth. Cover the mixture and chill.

Use as a dip with steamed vegetables, such as green beans and asparagus, or raw vegetables, such as mushroom caps, green or red pepper strips, sliced summer squash or zucchini, cucumber, or fennel.

Fragrant Herb Dipping Sauce

Use this dip for pieces of chicken or raw vegetables. When thinned with water, it can also be used as a dressing for a green salad.

Makes about 1 cup

½ cup mayonnaise
¼ cup sour cream or low-cholesterol substitute
2 tablespoons fresh lemon juice
2 tablespoons chopped fresh parsley
1 tablespoon chopped scallions
1 tablespoon finely chopped fresh tarragon or 1 teaspoon dried
1 tablespoon snipped fresh chives or 1 teaspoon dried
1 small clove garlic, chopped finely
1 anchovy fillet, finely chopped (optional)
Salt and ground black pepper to taste (optional)

1. Stir together the mayonnaise, sour cream, and lemon juice, mixing well. Stir in the parsley, scallions, tarragon, chives, garlic, and anchovy, if using. Mix well and season with salt and pepper to taste.
2. Cover and chill for several hours, if possible, to allow the flavors to develop.

Low-Carbohydrate Breads and Pastries

Carbohydrate Addict's Bread

This is an unusual but delicious substitute for high-carbohydrate breads. Serve it with butter or margarine, or low-carbohydrate preserves.

Makes 1 small loaf (about 4 × 7 inches)

Polyunsaturated vegetable oil, butter, or pan spray
3 eggs
½ teaspoon cream of tartar
¼ cup regular or low-fat cottage cheese
2 tablespoons soy flour*
1 package artificial sweetener

1. Preheat the oven to 300 degrees. Oil a small loaf pan with vegetable oil, butter, or pan spray.

2. Beat the egg whites with an electric mixer until frothy. Add the cream of tartar and beat until stiff peaks form, but the whites are still moist.

3. Combine the egg yolks, cottage cheese, soy flour, and sweetener and fold into the egg whites. Do not overmix.

4. Pour the mixture into the prepared pan and bake in the preheated oven for about 40 to 45 minutes, or until the loaf is lightly browned and springs back when touched with a finger.

VARIATIONS:

To make Cinnamon Bread, stir ½ teaspoon cinnamon into the soy flour before adding to the egg mixture.

To make a Savory Onion Bread, sauté ¼ cup finely diced onion in 1 tablespoon polyunsaturated vegetable oil, butter, or margarine. Cool and blot with paper toweling. Fold the onions into the egg mixture before it is turned out into the prepared bread pan.

Carbohydrate Addict's Light and Airy Muffins

This recipe will give you a fluffy muffin that tastes a little like a popover. Serve warm or cold with butter, margarine, cream cheese, or low-carbohydrate preserves.

Makes 14 muffins

½ tablespoon polyunsaturated vegetable oil
4 eggs
½ teaspoon cream of tartar
¼ cup regular or low-fat cottage cheese
2 tablespoons soy flour*
1 package artificial sweetener

* May be purchased at most health food stores.

1. Preheat the oven to 300 degrees. Coat muffin cups with a little vegetable oil (or use butter, margarine, or pan spray).

2. Separate the eggs very carefully, allowing no egg yolk to mix with the whites.

3. Beat the egg whites with an electric mixer until frothy. Add the cream of tartar and continue beating just until stiff peaks form.

4. Combine egg yokes, cottage cheese, soy flour, and sweetener. Fold this mixture carefully into the egg whites.

5. Fill each muffin cup ⅔ full of batter. Bake the muffins for about 30 minutes, until they are golden brown and spring back when touched with a finger.

VARIATION:

To make Spice Muffins, stir ½ teaspoon cinnamon, ¼ teaspoon ground ginger, and ⅛ teaspoon cloves into the soy flour before adding to the egg yolks.

Carbohydrate Addict's French Toast

Serves 1

1 egg
1 teaspoon cream
2 slices Carbohydrate Addict's Bread (page 200)

1. Beat the egg and cream together lightly in a bowl.

2. Oil a griddle or frying pan with up to a teaspoon of vegetable oil, margarine, butter, or pan spray, and heat until hot but not smoking.

3. Dip the slices of bread into the egg mixture, place in the pan, and cook on each side until browned.

Present this breakfast specialty warm with butter or margarine and Fruity Syrup (page 203), low-carbohydrate preserves, low-carbohydrate pancake syrup, or a sprinkling of cinnamon.

Carbohydrate Addict's Pancakes

Serve this treat with butter or margarine, and Fruity Syrup (below). Bacon, sausage, ham, or low-cholesterol breakfast meat substitutes make a good accompaniment.

Makes 4 to 6 3-inch pancakes

2 egg whites
½ teaspoon cream of tartar
1 egg yolk
1 cup regular or low-fat cottage cheese
1 tablespoon soy flour*
½ package artificial sweetener
Butter, margarine, or polyunsaturated vegetable oil for oiling the pan.

1. Beat the egg whites until frothy. Add the cream of tartar and beat just until stiff peaks form.
2. Combine the egg yolk, cottage cheese, soy flour, and sweetener. Fold the mixture gently into the egg whites.
3. Lightly oil a griddle or frying pan with up to a tablespoon of butter, margarine, or vegetable oil. Heat until hot but not smoking.
4. Pour the batter into 3-inch pancakes in the hot skillet. Cook until browned on one side, about 2 minutes, then turn and brown the other side.

Carbohydrate Addict's Fruity Syrup

This syrup is wonderful served over Pancakes (above) or French Toast (page 202).

Makes 1 cup

½ cup water
½ cup low-carbohydrate preserves (such as strawberry, raspberry, plum, blueberry, or marmalade)

Heat the water in a saucepan until simmering. Add the preserves, a tablespoon at a time, stirring constantly. Return the mixture to a simmer and cook for 2 to 3 minutes.

* May be purchased at most health food stores.

NOTE: Use any brand of low-calorie preserves containing no more than 4 grams of carbohydrate per average serving.

Carbohydrate Addict's Luncheon Crepes

To make a satisfying luncheon main course, fill these thin pancakes with Creamed Celery, Cauliflower, or Spinach (page 231), Creamed Mushrooms (page 237), or Cheese-Covered Mixed Vegetables (page 238).

Makes 4 crepes

2 eggs
¼ teaspoon cream of tartar
2 tablespoons small-curd regular or low-fat cottage cheese
1 tablespoon sour cream
Polyunsaturated vegetable oil or pan spray for oiling the pan

1. Separate the eggs carefully, allowing no yolk to mix with the whites. Beat the egg whites with the cream of tartar until stiff. Set aside.
2. Combine the cottage cheese, egg yolks, and sour cream, mixing well. Fold the mixture carefully into the egg whites.
3. Oil a nonstick griddle or frying pan with a little vegetable oil or pan spray. Heat the pan over moderate heat.
4. Pour the batter into 4-inch crepes using about 2 tablespoons of batter. Cook over moderate heat until the crepe sets and appears to be brown on the bottom. Turn and brown the other side.

Low-Carbohydrate Poultry, Fish, Meat, and Eggs

Broiled Chicken with Lime and Garlic

Makes an excellent light lunch served with a salad, or a heartier meal served with Cauliflower Pancakes (page 231) and Coleslaw (page 228).

Serves 4

4 thick chicken breast halves, skinned
Juice of ½ lime
¼ cup vegetable or chicken broth
1 clove fresh garlic

1. Adjust the broiling pan so the meat will cook 5 to 6 inches from the heat.
2. Place the chicken in a shallow baking pan. Pour the lime juice and the vegetable broth over the chicken, turning to coat the pieces well.
3. Peel and slice the garlic clove. Sprinkle the slices over the chicken pieces.
4. Broil the chicken for 15 to 20 minutes, until the juices run clear when the meat is pricked with a fork. Try not to overcook.

Serve on its own, or with a sauce such as Mustard Horseradish Dip and Sauce (page 199).

Crispy Chicken

Delicious either hot or cold. You might also double the recipe to have the basics on hand for several quick meals and salads.

Serves 2

4 pieces chicken
1 tablespoon sesame oil, olive oil, or polyunsaturated vegetable oil
1 tablespoon soy sauce
1 clove garlic, finely chopped
1 tablespoon finely chopped fresh ginger (optional)

1. Preheat the oven to 350 degrees.
2. Dry the chicken pieces with paper toweling.
3. Mix the oil, soy sauce, garlic, and ginger, if used, together in a bowl. Dip the chicken pieces in the mixture, stirring the sauce as you dip.
4. Place the chicken on a cookie sheet. Bake for 45 minutes or until the juices run clear when the meat is pierced with a fork.

Although the chicken is quite good on its own, it's also delicious served with Spicy Creamy Dip or Dressing (page 199).

Basic Broiled Chicken (with Several Sauces)

Plain broiled chicken is a good standby for a variety of meals. It's good hot with a sauce, and it's terrific cold. With an extra piece or two, you can even make a chicken salad for the following day.

Serves 2

2 chicken quarters (legs or breasts)
1 tablespoon polyunsaturated vegetable oil or butter
1 clove garlic, peeled and cut in half
1 teaspoon lemon juice
Salt and pepper to taste

1. Adjust the broiling pan so that the meat will cook 5 to 6 inches from the heat. Preheat the broiler.
2. Rinse the chicken and pat dry with paper toweling. Skin if you wish. Rub the oil or butter onto the skin or flesh of the chicken. Rub the garlic clove over the chicken pieces. Sprinkle with the lemon juice and with salt and pepper to taste.
3. Place the chicken, skin side down, in a shallow pan. Broil 5 to 6 inches from the heat for about 15 minutes. Baste occasionally with any juices that form in the bottom of the pan.
4. Turn the pieces and broil on the remaining side for an additional 15 to 20 minutes or until the juices run clear when the meat is pricked with a fork.

Serve the chicken on its own or with a sauce such as Hollandaise (recipe below), Mustard Horseradish Dip and Sauce (page 199), Spicy Creamy Dip or Dressing (page 199), or Fragrant Herb Dipping Sauce (page 200).

Hollandaise Sauce

This version of hollandaise sauce using the whole egg or no-cholesterol substitute instead of just the yolk is a classic accompaniment to plainly cooked poultry, fish, or vegetables.

Makes 1 cup

2 eggs, or the equivalent no-cholesterol egg substitute
2 tablespoons fresh lemon juice
Dash Tabasco or a pinch of ground red pepper
⅓ cup unsalted butter or margarine, melted and hot

Combine the eggs or egg substitute, lemon juice, and Tabasco in a blender, mixing briefly. Turn the setting to medium speed and add the hot butter or margarine a little at a time, until it is all incorporated. Remove from the blender immediately.

Hollandaise should be served at once, but may be held in the top of a double boiler over hot (not boiling) water for up to 10 minutes.

Baked Chicken with Sage and Parmesan Cheese

This dish can provide a spicy change of pace from plain baked chicken. It is delicious cold as well as hot, making it ideal to carry along for lunch.

Serves 2

2 chicken quarters
½ cup chicken broth
¼ teaspoon dried sage
Ground black pepper to taste
¼ cup freshly grated Parmesan or Romano cheese

1. Preheat the oven to 350 degrees.
2. Wash the chicken and place in a shallow baking pan. Pour the broth over the chicken and sprinkle with the sage and a little pepper. Cover the chicken with a lid or foil and bake for about 45 minutes.
3. Remove the cover and sprinkle the cheese over the chicken. Cook for an additional 15 minutes, or until the juices run clear when the meat is pierced with a fork.

Creamy Mushroom Chicken

This low-carbohydrate creamed chicken dish will nourish, warm, and satisfy you.

Serves 2

2 tablespoons olive oil or polyunsaturated vegetable oil
2 chicken breast halves, skinned
1 cup sliced fresh mushrooms
2 tablespoons finely chopped onion
1 clove garlic, finely chopped
2 cups sour cream or low-cholesterol substitute
2 tablespoons dried rosemary (crumbled) or dried basil
Black pepper to taste
1 cup vegetable or chicken bouillon

1. Heat the oil in a skillet until hot but not smoking.
2. Add the chicken breasts and cook, turning frequently, until browned on both sides and the juices run clear when the meat is pierced with a fork.
3. Remove the chicken from the skillet and set aside. Add the mushrooms, onion, and garlic to the pan and sauté until brown and the mushrooms give up their liquid and brown.
4. Return the chicken to the pan. Stir in the sour cream, the rosemary, and black pepper to taste.
5. Stir in the bouillon and simmer the mixture over very low heat for 3 to 4 minutes.

Baked Herb-Marinated Chicken

Equally tasty for turkey or chicken wings, and excellent with the Cucumbers with Sour Cream (page 232).

Serves 2 to 3

½ cup olive or polyunsaturated vegetable oil
¼ cup tarragon vinegar
1 teaspoon soy sauce
3 tablespoons chopped fresh parsley or 1 tablespoon dried
2 bay leaves
2 teaspoons dried basil or oregano
¼ teaspoon dried mustard
¼ teaspoon ground black pepper
3 to 4 pieces chicken, skinned

1. Combine all ingredients but the chicken in a glass bowl, stirring well to incorporate. Add the chicken and turn to coat the pieces well.

Cover the mixture or transfer everything to a heavy zippered plastic bag. Refrigerate overnight, turning the chicken or the bag occasionally.

2. Preheat the oven to 350 degrees.

3. Place the chicken in a baking pan and pour the marinade over.

4. Bake for about 45 minutes, turning once during cooking. Chicken is cooked when the juices run clear when the meat is pricked with a fork.

Garlic-and-Mustard-Marinated Chicken

The marinade for this chicken can be made in a food processor, in a blender, or by hand.

Serves 2 to 3

- 3 cloves garlic, finely chopped
- 2 tablespoons Dijon mustard
- ¼ cup red wine vinegar
- ¾ cup olive oil
- 3 or 4 pieces chicken

1. Combine the garlic, mustard, and vinegar in a jar with a lid. Add the olive oil and shake vigorously to combine well.

2. Skin the chicken and place the pieces in a bowl large enough to hold them comfortably. Pour the marinade over the chicken, and stir to coat the pieces well. Cover the bowl and chill overnight.

3. Preheat the oven to 350 degrees.

4. Place the chicken in a baking pan and pour the marinade over.

5. Bake for 45 minutes, turning once during cooking. When the meat is pricked with a fork and the juices run clear, the chicken is cooked.

Chicken Paprikash

Serves 3 to 4

2 tablespoons butter or margarine
2 tablespoons olive oil or polyunsaturated vegetable oil
1 to 2 tablespoons mild paprika
½ cup chopped onion
½ cup chopped green or red peppers
1 2½- to 3-pound chicken, cut into pieces
2 cups chicken stock, broth, or bouillon
1 teaspoon flour
1½ cups sour cream or low-cholesterol substitute

1. Melt the butter or margarine in a large heavy frying pan over moderate heat. Add the oil and paprika and heat until hot but not smoking. Add the onion and peppers and sauté for 2 minutes.
2. Move the onion and peppers to the sides of the pan and add the chicken pieces, skin side down. Cook for about 3 minutes, until the skin begins to brown.
3. Turn the pieces to brown the other side, cooking for about 3 minutes.
4. Stir in the chicken stock. Cover and simmer for 45 minutes to an hour, until the chicken is tender and the juices run clear when the meat is pierced with a fork. Transfer the chicken to a plate.
5. Stir the flour into the sour cream and slowly stir the mixture into the pan.
6. Cover the pan and simmer over low heat for 3 minutes. Stir, cover again, and simmer for an additional 2 minutes. Do not let the mixture boil.
7. Pour the cream mixture over the chicken.

Herb-Flavored Turkey Burgers

Serves 4 to 6

1½ pounds ground raw turkey
1 egg
3 tablespoons soy sauce
2 tablespoons dried marjoram or basil
1½ teaspoons garlic or onion powder
Black pepper to taste (optional)
4 to 6 slices tomato (optional)
4 to 6 lettuce leaves (optional)
4 to 6 slices dill pickle (optional)

1. Preheat the broiler.
2. Combine the turkey, egg, soy sauce, marjoram, garlic powder, and black pepper, if used, in a bowl. Form into four or six patties.
3. Broil the burgers until well done, about 10 minutes, turning once during cooking.

If you wish, top each burger with a slice of tomato. Serve on a lettuce leaf with a slice of dill pickle on the side.

VARIATIONS:

To make a Turkey Cheeseburger, top each burger with a slice of cheddar, Swiss, or low-fat cheese substitute.

As an alternative method of cooking, generously coat the inside of a frying pan with vegetable oil or spray. Heat the pan until hot but not smoking, add the burgers, and cook, turning once during cooking, until the juices run clear when the meat is pierced with a fork.

Baked Fish with Lemon and Herbs

Serves 4

4 firm-fleshed fish fillets, such as cod, perch, monk, or flounder, about 1½ pounds
2 tablespoons olive oil or polyunsaturated vegetable oil
¼ cup chopped celery
2 tablespoons chopped onion
1 tablespoon chopped fresh dill or basil, or 1 teaspoon dried
1 tablespoon chopped fresh parsley
1½ teaspoons grated lemon rind
2 tablespoons lemon juice
Black pepper to taste (optional)
Salt to taste (optional)

1. Preheat the oven to 350 degrees. Lightly oil a baking dish with olive oil or polyunsaturated vegetable oil.
2. Rinse the fish fillets and pat dry with paper toweling.
3. Heat the oil in a skillet over moderate heat. Add the celery and onion and sauté until soft, about 10 minutes. Stir in the basil, parsley, lemon rind, and lemon juice. Season with black pepper and salt to taste, if you wish.
4. Place the fish fillets in the oiled baking dish. Spread a portion of the herb-and-lemon mixture on each fillet. Bake for 30 to 40 minutes, until the fish is just opaque and flakes with a fork.

Baked Fish with Sour Cream

Serves 4

4 fish fillets, such as cod, perch, sole, flounder, or monk
1 teaspoon paprika
½ teaspoon ground black pepper
½ teaspoon salt
1 cup sour cream or low-cholesterol substitute

1. Preheat the oven to 350 degrees.
2. Rinse the fish and pat it dry with paper toweling.
3. Sprinkle each fillet with a little of the paprika, pepper, and salt.

4. Place the fish in a non-stick baking pan and cover with the sour cream.

5. Cover the pan and bake in the preheated oven for 20 to 30 minutes, or until the fish flakes with a fork.

Puffy Fish Fillets

Very tasty, hot or cold. Add a nice cool salad for a marvelous summer lunch.

Serves 2 to 3

2 tablespoons olive oil, melted butter, or margarine
2 fish fillets such as sole, cod, perch, flounder, or other white-meat fish, about ¾ pound total
1 egg white
⅛ teaspoon cream of tartar
¼ cup Tartar Sauce (page 214)
Black pepper to taste

1. Preheat the broiler. Oil a flameproof baking pan with a little olive oil, polyunsaturated vegetable oil, or pan spray.
2. Rinse the fish fillets and pat dry with paper toweling. Set aside.
3. Beat the egg white with the cream of tartar until stiff. Gently fold in the tartar sauce. Do not overmix. Set aside.
4. Place the fish fillets in the oiled baking pan. Brush with the oil, butter, or margarine and sprinkle with black pepper to taste.
5. Broil the fish for 4 to 5 minutes per side. The fish is done when it is just opaque and flakes with a fork.
6. Spread the egg white mixture over one side of each fillet and broil for 1 to 2 minutes, until the mixture puffs and turns golden brown.

Tartar Sauce

Makes about ¼ cup

¼ cup mayonnaise or low-cholesterol substitute
¼ teaspoon tarragon vinegar
½ teaspoon finely chopped fresh parsley
1 tablespoon finely chopped dill pickle

Combine the ingredients, mixing well.

Fish Soufflés

Serve this satisfying and luxurious luncheon dish with Hollandaise Sauce (page 206).

3 servings

1 egg
½ pound white-meat fish, such as cod, sole, or flounder
2 teaspoons butter
1 teaspoon soy flour*
½ cup plus 2 tablespoons heavy cream
¼ teaspoon salt
Pinch ground white pepper
1 tablespoon snipped fresh chives

1. Preheat the oven to 350 degrees.
2. Oil 3 custard cups or ramekins with olive oil, polyunsaturated vegetable oil, or pan spray.
3. Carefully separate the egg and set aside.
4. Chop the fish finely in a food processor or blender.
5. Heat the butter in a medium-sized saucepan over moderate heat. When melted, stir in the soy flour and then 2 tablespoons of the cream. Remove the pan from the heat and stir in the egg yolk. Stir in the salt and the white pepper before stirring in the fish. Set the mixture aside to cool.
6. Whip the egg white until stiff peaks just form. Whip the ½ cup cream until stiff peaks just form. Fold the egg white and whipped cream into the fish mixture.

* May be purchased at most health food stores.

7. Fill a baking pan with about an inch of hot water.

8. Pour the mixture into the prepared cups. Place the cups in the prepared baking pan. Place the pan in the oven and bake for about 20 minutes, or until the individual mousses are set.

Salmon Steaks with Lemon Sauce

Serves 2

½ cup chopped celery
3 tablespoons olive oil or polyunsaturated vegetable oil
2 tablespoons fresh lemon juice
1 teaspoon grated fresh lemon or orange rind
2 tablespoons finely chopped fresh basil or dill
2 fresh salmon steaks, about ½ pound each

1. Preheat the oven to 325 degrees.

2. Combine the celery, oil, lemon juice, lemon rind, and basil in a frying pan. Sauté over moderate heat for 2 minutes. The celery should remain crisp.

3. Place the salmon steaks in a shallow baking pan. Pour the celery mixture over the fish. Cover the dish with aluminum foil and bake for 20 to 30 minutes. The fish is done when it is opaque and flakes with a fork.

Poached Salmon Steaks with Fresh Herbs

This dish is subtle and satisfying, yet low in fat. In addition, it takes only minutes to prepare.

Serves 2

1 cup chicken broth
½ cup water
½ teaspoon chopped fresh dill
¼ teaspoon dill seed
1 bay leaf
2 salmon steaks, about ½ pound each
Fresh dill and lemon slices for garnish

1. Combine the chicken broth, water, fresh dill, dill seed, and bay leaf in a saucepan large enough to hold the salmon in a single layer. (The mixture should cover the fish. If not, add water to barely cover.) Remove the salmon and heat the mixture to a boil.

2. Add the salmon and heat again. The moment the mixture begins to boil, reduce the heat to a gentle simmer and cook for an additional 4 to 5 minutes, or until the fish flakes easily with a fork.

Present the salmon on plates, garnished with fresh dill and lemon slices. Serve this with Hollandaise Sauce (page 206) or Cheesed Cauliflower (page 228).

Baked Trout with Bacon

Serve this classic English dish with a green salad or Coleslaw (page 228).

Serves 2

4 slices lean bacon
2 small fresh rainbow trout, cleaned, about 1 to 1½ pounds total
1 tablespoon chopped fresh parsley or dill
¼ teaspoon salt (optional)
⅛ teaspoon black pepper

1. Preheat the oven to 375 degrees.
2. Line a baking pan with the bacon slices.
3. Lay the fish open side down on the bacon. Sprinkle with half of the parsley or dill and the salt and pepper.
4. Cover the dish tightly with foil. Bake for 20 to 25 minutes in the preheated oven, or until the fish flakes easily with a fork.

Serve the fish on warm plates and sprinkle with the remaining parsley or dill.

Spicy Shrimp with Mushrooms

Delicious either warm or cold. Make two portions if you wish, one for now and one for tomorrow. Serve with a crisp green salad or, for a special treat, use as a filling for the Luncheon Crepes (page 204).

Serves 2

8 ounces medium-size shrimp
3 tablespoons olive oil
½ cup chopped celery
½ cup chopped fresh mushrooms
2 to 3 dashes Tabasco
Salt to taste

1. Shell and devein the shrimp.
2. Heat the olive oil in a skillet over high heat until hot but not burned. Add the celery and sauté for about 3 minutes.
3. Reduce the heat to moderate. Add the shrimp and sauté until the shrimp turn pink, about 5 minutes. Stir in the mushrooms, increase the heat, and sauté for 2 minutes. Add the Tabasco and salt to taste.

Grilled Shrimp with Indian Spices

Serves 2

8 ounces large shrimp
2 tablespoons butter or margarine
½ teaspoon ground turmeric
¼ teaspoon ground ginger
¼ teaspoon ground cumin
¼ teaspoon ground coriander
¼ teaspoon salt
Juice of ½ lemon

1. Place the broiling pan about 3 inches from the flame. Preheat the broiler.
2. Shell and devein the shrimp.
3. Melt the butter in a small skillet and add the turmeric, ginger, cumin, coriander, salt, and lemon juice.

4. Place the shrimp in a shallow flameproof pan. The shrimp should be in one layer. Brush the warm butter mixture over the shrimp.

5. Place the pan under the broiler, and cook for 4 minutes. Turn and cook an additional 2 to 4 minutes, until the shrimp are golden brown and just cooked through.

Pepper Steak

Add an ounce or two of American cheese for a Philadelphia-style cheese-steak sandwich—without the bread, of course.

Serves 2

½ pound beef, such as London broil or sirloin, trimmed of all fat and sliced thin
2 tablespoons olive oil
3 tablespoons chopped onion
1 clove garlic, finely chopped
2 green or red peppers, seeded and sliced
½ cup sliced fresh mushrooms
1 tablespoon soy sauce

1. Pat the meat dry with paper toweling.

2. Heat the oil in a wok or frying pan. Add the onion and sauté over moderate heat until golden brown, about 10 minutes. Add the garlic and peppers and sauté for an additional 3 minutes.

3. Add the beef and cook, stirring constantly, until the meat browns.

4. Stir in the mushrooms and sauté for an additional 2 minutes. Season with the soy sauce and cook for another minute, stirring constantly.

Japanese-Style Marinated Steak

Serve this broiled steak dish with a large green salad to make a satisfying meal.

Serves 2

¾ pound sirloin steak, trimmed of fat
2 tablespoons soy sauce
1 clove garlic, finely chopped
½ teaspoon finely chopped fresh ginger
½ packet artificial sweetener

1. Slice the steak into strips and then into pieces 1½ to 2 inches long. Place the meat in a bowl.

2. Combine the remaining ingredients, mixing well. Pour the mixture over the meat and cover. Marinate the meat for about an hour, turning several times to coat the meat with sauce.

3. Preheat the broiler.

4. Place the meat in a single layer on a rack in a broiling pan. Broil the meat about 3 inches from the heat for about 5 minutes. Brush with marinade, turn, brush with sauce again, and cook for an additional 3 to 5 minutes, until the meat is cooked to your liking.

Lamb Kebabs

Serves 2

3 tablespoons fresh lemon juice
2 tablespoons olive oil
1 teaspoon soy sauce, optional
¼ teaspoon dried oregano
¼ teaspoon dried thyme
1 clove garlic, finely chopped
¾ pound cubed lean lamb
¼ green pepper, cored, seeded, and cut into 1-inch pieces

1. Combine all the ingredients but the lamb and green pepper in a bowl, mixing well to combine. Add the lamb, turning to coat well. Cover, chill, and allow to marinate for several hours or overnight, turning the meat occasionally.

2. Preheat a broiler or grill.

3. Thread the meat onto skewers separating each piece of meat with a piece of pepper.

4. Broil or grill the lamb for about 3 minutes per side, turning on each side to cook.

Cheese-Stuffed Meatballs

Wonderful with Coleslaw (page 228) and a crisp green salad. These meatballs are also easy to pack up and take to work for lunch (keep in mind, however, that, as with all meats, they must be kept refrigerated).

Serves 2 to 3

1 tablespoon olive oil or polyunsaturated vegetable oil
2 tablespoons diced onion
8 ounces lean ground beef or turkey
1 tablespoon soy sauce
¼ teaspoon dried sage
4 ounces cheddar or Swiss cheese, or low-fat substitute, cut into 8 cubes

1. Preheat the oven to 325 degrees.
2. Oil a shallow baking pan with a little olive oil, polyunsaturated vegetable oil, or pan spray.
3. Heat the oil in a frying pan over moderate heat until hot but not smoking. Add the onion and sauté until golden brown, about 10 minutes.
4. Combine the onion, beef, soy sauce, and sage. Divide the mixture into eight portions. Take a chunk of cheese and cover with one portion of the mixture to form a meatball shape. Repeat to form a total of eight meatballs.
5. Place the meatballs in the oiled pan and bake for 30 minutes.

VARIATION: You can also fry the meatballs in a frying pan, using 2 tablespoons of oil.

Low-Fat Pork Sausage

Make it mild or make it hot—but enjoy it without high-carbohydrate or high-fat worries.

Makes 20 to 24 patties

2 pounds lean pork, trimmed of all exterior fat, finely ground
1 tablespoon dried sage
1 teaspoon soy sauce
½ teaspoon ground black pepper
½ teaspoon dried basil
½ teaspoon ground cloves
½ teaspoon ground nutmeg
1 tablespoon vegetable oil for frying

1. Combine all ingredients except the oil and mix well. Divide the mixture into 20 to 24 portions and shape each one into a patty about 1½ inches in diameter.
2. Oil a frying pan well with vegetable oil or use pan spray. Place over moderate heat until hot but not smoking. Cook as many of the patties as needed until well done.
3. Turn once during cooking to brown each side.
4. Freeze the remaining patties for future use.

Variation: To make extra low-fat sausage, use ground turkey mixed with an egg instead of the pork.

Spicy Hot Sausage

Makes 20 to 24 patties

2 pounds lean pork, trimmed of all fat, finely ground
1 teaspoon soy sauce
1½ teaspoons dried sage
1 teaspoon onion powder or dried onion flakes
½ teaspoon garlic powder
½ teaspoon dried basil
½ teaspoon ground cloves
½ teaspoon ground black pepper
½ teaspoon cayenne pepper or 3 dashes Tabasco

1. Combine all ingredients except the oil, mixing well. Divide the mixture into 20 to 24 portions. Form each portion into a patty about 1½ inches in diameter.
2. Oil a frying pan well with vegetable oil or use pan spray. Heat until hot but not smoking over moderate heat.

3. Cook as many of the patties as needed in the heated frying pan until well done.
4. Turn once during cooking to brown each side.
5. Freeze the remaining patties for future use.

VARIATION: To make extra low-fat sausage, substitute turkey mixed with a single egg for the pork.

Western Omelet

Serves 2

2 tablespoons unsalted butter or margarine
2 tablespoons diced green pepper
2 tablespoons diced onion
2 tablespoons diced tomato
¼ cup diced ham or low-fat turkey ham
1 tablespoon chopped fresh chives or parsley (optional)
3 eggs, or the equivalent in no-cholesterol egg substitute
1 tablespoon milk
Black pepper to taste (optional)
1 ounce cheddar, Muenster, or low-fat cheese substitute, thinly sliced

1. Heat the butter or margarine in an omelet pan or frying pan.
2. Add the green pepper and onion and sauté over moderate heat until the pepper softens and the onion turns golden brown, about 7 minutes.
3. Stir in the tomato and ham. Add the parsley or chives, if using.
4. Increase the heat to high and cook the mixture for 1 minute.
5. Remove the mixture from the pan, leaving a little of the butter or oil.
6. Combine the eggs, milk, and black pepper, if using, and beat lightly. Pour the mixture into the omelet pan. Cook over moderate heat until the edges begin to bubble. Pull the edges toward the middle, allowing the egg mixture to run underneath.
7. When the eggs are beginning to set, place the meat and vegetable mixture and the cheese on one half of the omelet. Using a spatula, flip the other side of the omelet over. Flip the whole omelet over to seal the edges and slide the omelet out of the pan onto a plate. Cut in half to serve.

Onion-Cheese Omelet

This dish is great served hot with Low-Fat Pork Sausage (page 220), bacon, or low-cholesterol breakfast-meat substitute.

Serves 2

3 eggs, or the equivalent of no-cholesterol egg substitute
2 tablespoons milk
2 tablespoons unsalted butter or margarine, or pan spray
2 tablespoons diced onion
1 ounce cheddar, Gruyère, or Muenster cheese, thinly sliced

1. Combine the eggs and milk and beat lightly.
2. Heat the butter in an omelet pan or frying pan. Add the onion and sauté over moderate heat until golden brown, about 5 minutes.
3. Pour the egg mixture into the pan. Cook over moderate heat until the edges begin to bubble. Pull the edges toward the middle, allowing the egg mixture to run underneath.
4. When the eggs are beginning to set, place the cheese on one half of the omelet. With a spatula, fold the other half of the omelet over. Flip the whole omelet over to seal the edges and slide the omelet out of the pan onto a plate. Cut in half to serve.

Variation: To make a Meat and Cheese Omelet, substitute ham, turkey ham, sausage, bacon, or low-cholesterol breakfast-meat substitute for the onion.

Cheese Flan

Yes, you can have quiche, or at least the crustless variety known as a flan. Make it ahead for breakfast or carry a slice with you for lunch. For an exceptional French-style meal, add sliced cold cucumbers in light sour cream.

Makes 6 servings

1 tablespoon butter or polyunsaturated vegetable oil, or pan spray
1½ cups heavy or light cream
1 cup grated Swiss, Gruyère, Parmesan, or cheddar cheese
2 teaspoons finely chopped onion or onion flakes
¼ teaspoon salt
¼ teaspoon paprika (optional)
4 eggs

1. Preheat the oven to 325 degrees. Butter a pie dish with a little butter, vegetable oil, or pan spray.

2. Pour the cream into a saucepan and heat until scalded (little bubbles will form around the edges). Reduce the heat to low and stir in the cheese. When the cheese is melted, stir in the onion, salt, and paprika, if using.

3. Remove the pan from the heat and let cool briefly. Beat each egg into the mixture separately, beating until thoroughly mixed after each addition.

4. Pour the mixture into the prepared pan and bake for about 45 minutes in the preheated oven. The custard should be set and firm.

VARIATIONS:

To make the dish like a crustless quiche Lorraine, add 4 strips of crumbled cooked bacon to the mixture in the pie pan.

To make an Asparagus Flan, parboil about 4 ounces of asparagus spears. Slice into lengths about 1 inch long and add to the flan mixture in the pie pan.

To make Ham Flan, slice 2 ounces of ham and add to the mixture in the pie pan.

To make Spinach Flan, stir ½ cup cooked spinach into the custard mixture before pouring into the prepared pie pan.

Breakfast Soufflé

This breakfast dish is great served by itself or with bacon, ham, or sausage (or low-cholesterol breakfast meat substitute).

Serves 2

2 egg whites
½ teaspoon cream of tartar
1 cup regular or low-fat cottage cheese
1 egg yolk
½ package artificial sweetener

1. Preheat the oven to 300 degrees. Butter a 9-inch round cake pan with a little butter, vegetable oil, or pan spray.
2. Beat the egg whites until frothy with an electric mixer. Add the cream of tartar and beat just until stiff peaks form. Combine the cottage cheese, egg yolk, and sweetener, mixing well. Fold gently into the egg whites, being careful not to mix too thoroughly.
3. Pour the soufflé mixture into the buttered cake pan and bake in the preheated oven for 25 to 30 minutes.
4. Turn the broiler up and brown the soufflé under the broiler for 2 to 3 minutes, watching carefully to make sure it doesn't burn.

Chef's Salad

The chef's salad, a filling and satisfying meal in itself, can be a staple for your low-carbohydrate lunches.

Serves 2

1½ cups romaine, Boston lettuce, endive, or spinach leaves
½ cup julienned cooked chicken or ½ cup julienned cooked turkey
½ cup julienned ham or low-cholesterol substitute
½ cup julienned hard cheese such as cheddar, Swiss, Gruyère, Muenster, Gouda, or Edam
½ can anchovies, drained
Lettuce leaves, for lining plate
2 hard-boiled eggs, halved
Radishes and green or black olives for garnish

1. Toss together the lettuce, chicken, ham, cheese, and anchovies.
2. Line a plate or bowl with lettuce leaves. Add the salad and the hard-boiled eggs. Decorate with the radishes and olives. Chill.

Serve with salad dressing to taste (pages 241 and 242).

Chicken, Turkey, or Tuna Salad

Serves 1

1 cup diced chicken or turkey, or ½ cup tuna packed in water, drained
1 cup diced celery
2 tablespoons mayonnaise or low-cholesterol substitute
2 tablespoons dried parsley
1 teaspoon chopped green olives to taste (optional)
1 teaspoon dried dill (optional)
Tabasco to taste (optional)
2 tablespoons chopped scallion
Lettuce leaves, for lining plate (optional)

1. Combine all the ingredients except the lettuce and mix well. Chill until serving time.
2. Line a plate with lettuce leaves, if you like, and pile the salad on them.

Deviled Ham and Tuna Salad

Serves 2

2 ounces lean ham, finely chopped
½ cup tuna packed in water, drained
1 hard-boiled egg, chopped
2 tablespoons mayonnaise or low-cholesterol substitute
2 teaspoons chopped dill pickle
1 teaspoon chopped scallions
1 teaspoon lemon juice
Lettuce leaves, for lining plate (optional)

1. Combine all the ingredients except the lettuce in a bowl, mixing well. Chill until serving time.
2. Line a plate with lettuce leaves, if you like, pile the salad on, and serve.

Fresh Seafood Salad with Dill Vinaigrette

The seafood in this recipe are particularly easy and fast to cook in a microwave oven, making this a truly quick dish to prepare.

Serves 3

Vinaigrette Dressing:

3 tablespoons olive oil
1 tablespoon fresh lemon juice
2 teaspoons chopped fresh dill
1 teaspoon Dijon mustard
Ground pepper to taste

Salad:

8 ounces medium-size fresh shrimp
4 ounces sea scallops
4 ounces salmon or other fresh firm-fleshed fish, cut into 1-inch chunks
¼ cup coarsely chopped cucumber
¼ cup sliced celery or fennel
2 tablespoons chopped scallions
Lettuce leaves, for lining plate (optional)

1. Combine the vinaigrette ingredients in a jar with a lid. Shake well to combine.
2. Peel and devein the shrimp.
3. To cook the seafood in a microwave, place the shrimp and scallops in a shallow glass dish. Cover with plastic wrap and cook on High for about 2 minutes. Repeat the procedure with the fish, cooking for about 2 minutes.
4. To cook the shellfish conventionally, bring a pot of water to a boil. Add the shrimp and scallops, turn off the heat, and let set for 1 minute, or until the shrimp and scallops are opaque. Drain the water.

To cook the fish conventionally, place the fish in a steamer over about an inch of water. Cover and cook for about 5 minutes, or until the fish flakes with a fork.

5. Place all the prepared seafood in a bowl. Add the cucumber, celery, and scallions. Pour the vinaigrette dressing over and toss lightly but thoroughly. Cover and chill for at least an hour to allow the flavors to develop before serving.
6. Line a plate with lettuce leaves, if you like, and arrange the salad in the center.

Low-Carbohydrate Vegetables and Salads

Coleslaw

This low-carbohydrate coleslaw rivals all others in taste. It's a good side dish for both cold and hot lunches.

Serves 2

½ cup sour cream or low-cholesterol substitute
2 tablespoons water
1 teaspoon cider vinegar
1 cup shredded cabbage
½ teaspoon celery seed
Artificial sweetener to taste
1 teaspoon dried basil or crumbled dried rosemary (optional)

Combine the sour cream and water. Add the vinegar, stirring well. Toss with the cabbage. Stir in the celery seed and sweetener to taste. Season with the basil, if you wish.

Cheesed Cauliflower

This combination blends together beautifully and tastes great.

Serves 3 to 4

1 small head cauliflower, cut into florets
3 tablespoons mayonnaise or low-cholesterol substitute
2 ounces shredded sharp cheddar cheese
Black pepper to taste

1. Fill a saucepan with ¼ inch water. Add the cauliflower and cover. Bring to a boil and cook for 5 minutes.
2. Turn off the heat. Drain any remaining water from the pan. Cover the cauliflower with the mayonnaise and sprinkle with the cheese. Cover and let sit for 5 minutes.
3. Season to taste with black pepper. Serve immediately.

Baked Cabbage

This dish makes a good complement for sliced ham or beef and is wonderful with our Japanese-Style Marinated Steak (page 218).

Serves 2

1½ cups shredded cabbage
¼ cup heavy cream
½ package artificial sweetener
¼ teaspoon salt
¼ teaspoon paprika
3 tablespoons grated Parmesan cheese

1. Preheat the oven to 325 degrees. Butter a small baking dish with the butter.
2. Place the cabbage in the prepared baking dish.
3. Combine the cream, sweetener, salt, and paprika. Pour over the cabbage, and stir lightly to mix.
4. Cover the dish and bake for about 45 minutes.
5. Remove the dish from the oven and heat the broiler.
6. Sprinkle the cheese over the top of the cabbage and broil for 2 or 3 minutes, until the cheese melts.

Sautéed Cabbage

Sautéed cabbage is luscious and filling when served with a mixed green salad. It's also full of vitamins and calcium. This dish is also good (and lighter) served simply sautéed without the addition of sour cream.

Serves 2

1 tablespoon olive oil or polyunsaturated vegetable oil
2½ cups shredded cabbage
½ teaspoon finely chopped garlic or pinch garlic powder
¼ teaspoon salt
Pinch ground black or white pepper
½ cup sour cream or low-cholesterol substitute

1. Preheat the oven to 375 degrees. Lightly oil a baking dish.
2. Heat the remaining tablespoon of oil in a skillet. Add the cab-

bage, garlic, salt, and pepper and sauté lightly over moderate heat for 3 to 4 minutes.

3. Transfer the cabbage mixture to the prepared baking dish. Pour the sour cream over the mixture. Bake for about 15 minutes.

Cauliflower Soufflés

These make a wonderful addition to a lunch or dinner of fish, meat, or salad.

Makes 10 individual soufflés

1 tablespoon olive oil or polyunsaturated vegetable oil
3 tablespoons grated onion
2 cups cauliflower florets
2 eggs
1 teaspoon baking powder
1 tablespoon flour
1 teaspoon salt
Dijon mustard, to serve on the side

1. Preheat the oven to 325 degrees.
2. Grease 10 muffin cups with a little polyunsaturated vegetable oil or pan spray or line with paper liners.
3. Heat the tablespoon of oil in a frying pan. Add the onion and sauté until lightly browned, about 5 minutes. Blot dry with paper toweling.
4. Combine the onion, cauliflower, eggs, baking powder, flour, and salt in a food processor or blender. Pour the mixture into the prepared muffin pans, filling each cup ⅔ full.
5. Bake the soufflés for 20 minutes, until puffed and lightly browned.

NOTE: To mix the soufflé by hand or using a mixer, chop the cauliflower fine. Beat the eggs before adding the other ingredients.

Serve with Dijon-style mustard on the side.

Cauliflower Pancakes

The secret to this recipe is to let the pancake brown completely on one side before you turn it. Serve with mustard, sour cream, or low-cholesterol sour cream substitute.

Makes eight 2-inch pancakes

- 1 cup cauliflower florets
- 1 egg
- 1 tablespoon grated onion
- ½ teaspoon baking powder
- 1½ teaspoons soy flour*
- ½ teaspoon salt

1. Chop the cauliflower very fine in a food processor or blender. Add the remaining ingredients, except for the oil, and process or blend briefly to mix.
2. Lightly oil a griddle or frying pan with vegetable oil or pan spray. Heat until hot but not smoking.
3. Form 2-inch pancakes using about 2 tablespoons of batter. Brown the pancakes well on each side before turning.

VARIATION: To make cheese pancakes, place a thin slice of cheddar, jalapeño, or American cheese on top of each hot pancake. Cover with a lid until the cheese melts.

Serve hot with mustard.

Creamed Celery, Cauliflower, or Spinach

This is a versatile dish, because it can be made from a variety of vegetables, including spinach, cauliflower, green beans or wax beans, or celery. You can also experiment with seasonings. If using spinach, try adding a little nutmeg; if using cauliflower, a little basil; if using beans, try a few chives.

Serves 1

* May be purchased at most health food stores.

1 teaspoon butter or margarine
2 tablespoons diced onion
½ cup sliced celery or cauliflower florets or 2 cups fresh spinach
¼ cup water
1 heaping tablespoon sour cream or low-cholesterol substitute
Black pepper to taste

1. Heat the butter in a frying pan. Add the onion and sauté until golden, about 5 minutes.
2. Add the celery and water. Cover the pan and steam for about 5 minutes.
3. Remove the cover, and if water remains, increase the heat to boil off the moisture.
4. When the water has evaporated, stir in the sour cream.
5. Season with pepper to taste.

NOTE: This dish may also be made using frozen spinach or cauliflower. If using frozen spinach, use ½ cup.

Cucumbers with Sour Cream

Serve this dish with Puffy Fish Fillets (page 213) or almost any other fish or chicken dish.

Serves 2

1 medium-size cucumber
¼ cup sour cream or low-cholesterol substitute
1 teaspoon finely chopped scallions
2 teaspoons cider vinegar or white wine vinegar
Ground black pepper to taste
Pinch salt (optional)

1. Peel the cucumber and slice thinly. Place in a bowl and set aside.
2. Combine the remaining ingredients, mixing well. Pour the mixture over the cucumbers and toss lightly to mix.

Vegetables Vinaigrette

This vinaigrette sauce is wonderful used on a variety of vegetables and is even great as a salad dressing. The vegetables used here are raw, but lightly cooked green beans or asparagus will work well, too.

Serves 3 to 4

Vinaigrette:

½ cup olive oil or polyunsaturated vegetable oil
2 tablespoons lemon juice
1½ teaspoons sesame oil
1 tablespoon dried basil
1 tablespoon dried oregano
1 tablespoon soy sauce
Dash of black pepper

Vegetables:

½ cup cauliflower florets
½ cup sliced cucumber
½ cup pitted green or black olives
½ cup sliced fresh mushrooms
½ cup sliced green or red pepper
½ cup sliced celery

Combine the vinaigrette ingredients, shaking to mix well. Combine the vegetables, pour the dressing over them, and refrigerate overnight.

Green Beans with Garlic and Lemon

This is a favorite of ours. We make it in advance and eat it several times during the week. The flavor seems to get even better after a day or two.

4 servings

1½ pounds green beans
¼ cup olive oil or polyunsaturated vegetable oil
½ clove garlic, finely chopped
2 tablespoons lemon juice
¼ teaspoon salt (optional)

Top and tail the beans. Place them in a steamer over about an inch of water. Steam for 10 to 15 minutes, or until just tender. Remove the steamer from the pan and drain the water. Add the olive oil and the garlic to the beans and heat until hot. Add the lemon juice and salt, stirring to mix thoroughly. Heat the mixture through. Serve hot or cold.

Green Beans and Sautéed Mushrooms

To make this dish part of a quick-fix meal, cook the green beans in advance until just barely tender. Plunge into cold water and reserve, chilled, until needed. The dish makes a good accompaniment for fish, poultry, or meat.

Serves 4

¾ pound green beans
1 tablespoon butter or margarine
1 clove garlic, finely chopped, or ¼ teaspoon garlic powder
2 teaspoons chopped fresh basil or tarragon, or ½ teaspoon dried
¼ teaspoon salt (optional)
Few drops Tabasco (optional)
1 cup sliced mushrooms

1. Place the beans in a steamer over about an inch of water. Cover and cook for 10 to 15 minutes or until just tender.
2. Heat the butter in a saucepan. When melted, stir in the garlic, basil, salt, and Tabasco, if using. Cook, stirring, for a minute or two before adding the mushrooms. Continue cooking, over moderate heat, stirring occasionally for 4 to 5 minutes, or until the mushrooms just begin to release their liquid.
3. Add the beans and toss lightly to mix before serving.

NOTE: If using beans that have been partly cooked in advance, add them to the mushroom mixture while it is still cooking to heat through and finish cooking.

Sautéed Pepper Strips with Garlic

Serves 3 to 4

¼ cup olive oil or polyunsaturated vegetable oil
¼ cup finely chopped scallions
1 clove garlic, finely chopped
3 green peppers, seeded and sliced into ¾-inch strips
¼ teaspoon salt, or to taste
Pinch ground black pepper, or to taste
Pinch ground red pepper (optional)

Heat the oil in a skillet over moderate heat. When hot, add the scallions and garlic. Cook, stirring constantly, for about 5 minutes. Add the peppers and sauté for about 10 minutes. Season with salt, pepper, and ground red pepper, if using, before serving.

Italian Pepper Salad

This is a hearty side dish that goes well with any beef dish. It also keeps well when made a day in advance.

Serves 4

2 green peppers
¼ cup olive oil or polyunsaturated vegetable oil
1 tablespoon red wine vinegar
Salt and ground black pepper to taste

1. Preheat the broiler.
2. Place the peppers on a broiling rack. Broil until the skins are charred, turning to char each side.
3. Rinse the charred peppers under cold water to cool and rub to remove the skins.
4. Core, seed, and remove the ribs of the peppers. Slice the peppers thin and place in a bowl.
5. Combine the olive oil, vinegar, and salt and pepper to taste. Pour over the peppers, and leave to marinate for at least 30 minutes before serving.

Radish Salad

Radish Salad is another dish that can be made ahead and served with several meals. It makes a delicious peppery accompaniment to chicken dishes of all kinds, especially our Baked Chicken with Sage and Parmesan Cheese (page 207).

4 servings

2 cups sliced radishes
½ cup cider vinegar or white wine vinegar
½ teaspoon salt
3 tablespoons olive oil or polyunsaturated vegetable oil
2 tablespoons coarsely chopped capers
1 small pickled chili pepper, seeded and chopped (optional)

Combine the radishes, vinegar, and salt and leave to marinate for several hours. Drain the liquid and combine the drained radishes with the olive oil, capers, and chili pepper, if using. Serve at room temperature or chilled.

Italian-Style Marinated Vegetables

A wonderful recipe that can be prepared ahead and that will provide side dishes for several lunches.

Serves 2 to 3

½ cup olive oil, extra-virgin if possible
¼ cup chopped fresh basil or 1 tablespoon dried
2 tablespoons chopped fresh marjoram or 1 teaspoon dried
1 clove garlic, finely chopped
Ground black pepper to taste
½ cup raw sliced celery
½ cup raw quartered mushrooms
½ cup raw red or green pepper strips
½ cup raw cauliflower florets
¼ cup green or black olives

Combine the olive oil, basil, marjoram, garlic, and pepper, shaking or stirring well. Combine the remaining ingredients in a bowl, pour the dressing over them, and toss to coat well. Cover and refrigerate overnight to allow the flavors to blend and seep into the vegetables.

Creamed Mushrooms

This side dish makes a simple lunch very special.

Serves 2 to 3

2 tablespoons olive oil or polyunsaturated vegetable oil
2 cups sliced mushrooms
1 clove garlic, chopped fine
¼ teaspoon paprika
1 cup sour cream or low-cholesterol substitute

Heat the oil in a frying pan. Add the mushrooms and garlic. Sauté over moderate heat until the mushrooms release their liquid, about 10 minutes. Add the paprika. Turn off heat and let the mixture cool until warm. Stir in the sour cream and serve immediately.

Stuffed Mushrooms

Serves 3 to 4

½ pound large mushrooms
½ pound ground raw turkey, chicken, veal, lamb, or beef
2 teaspoons olive oil or polyunsaturated vegetable oil
1 clove garlic, chopped fine
½ teaspoon dried basil
½ teaspoon white horseradish
½ teaspoon soy sauce
Black pepper to taste

1. Preheat the oven to 350 degrees. Oil a cookie sheet well with the vegetable oil or pan spray.
2. Remove the mushroom stems and chop finely. Combine with the ground turkey.
3. Heat the 2 teaspoons of oil in a frying pan and add the mushroom-and-meat mixture and the garlic. Cook over moderate heat until the meat is thoroughly browned. Cool the mixture.
4. Combine the meat-and-mushroom mixture with the basil, horseradish, soy sauce, and black pepper. Stuff the mushroom caps with the mixture.
5. Place the stuffed mushroom caps, stuffing side up, on the oiled cookie sheet. Bake for 18 minutes.

Cheese-Covered Mixed Vegetables

A protein-rich, wholesome dish that can be served as a side dish for meat, fish, or poultry, or as a main course at lunch when combined with a salad. Garnish with freshly ground pepper if you like. It can be made with any combination of the following vegetables or with a single vegetable.

Serves 2

2 cups total of a mixture of fresh sliced summer squash or zucchini, sliced mushrooms, sliced celery, cauliflower florets or sliced asparagus spears, green or red pepper strips, or sliced cabbage
2 ounces regular or low-fat cheese such as cheddar or Gruyère, thinly sliced

Place the cauliflower and cabbage, if using, in a steamer over 1 inch of water, cover, and cook for 5 minutes. Add the other vegetables and cook until all are just barely tender. Transfer the hot vegetables to a bowl and top with the thin slices of cheese. Cover until melted.

Chinese-Style Stir-Fried Vegetables

A quick-cook stir-fry that can be made in minutes. For a really quick cook, cut up the vegetables in advance, cover tightly, and keep chilled.

Serves 3

2 tablespoons sesame oil, olive oil, or polyunsaturated vegetable oil
1 clove garlic, finely chopped, or ½ teaspoon garlic powder
3 cups total fresh sliced summer squash or zucchini, sliced mushrooms, sliced celery, small cauliflower florets, sliced green beans, green or red pepper strips, sliced cabbage, sliced radishes, or sliced scallions
½ cup bamboo shoots
2 tablespoons soy sauce

Heat the oil in a wok or large frying pan. Add the vegetables and the garlic, and quickly stir-fry them until just barely tender. Stir in the soy sauce and serve.

Tossed Green Salad

A satisfying tossed green salad can be made from a variety of vegetables. You can make a salad based solely on greens, such as varieties of lettuce or spinach, or you can add raw vegetables of your choice. The following combinations should serve as a guide. You don't have to use every vegetable, and you may substitute other favorites from among those acceptable (page 101).

Serves 2

2 cups torn leaves of romaine, Boston, endive, Cos, or iceberg lettuce, or spinach
½ cup sliced cucumbers
½ cup sliced celery
¼ cup sliced fresh mushrooms
2 tablespoons alfalfa or bean sprouts
½ tomato, quartered, or 6 cherry tomatoes
3 radishes, sliced
2 scallions, sliced

Toss all the ingredients together in a big bowl. Just before serving, toss again with Blue Cheese Dressing, Tofu-Garlic Salad Dressing, Spicy Creamy Dip or Dressing (page 199), the dressing used in the recipe for Vegetables Vinaigrette (page 233), or the dressing of your choice.

Spinach Salad

Serve this satisfying salad with Spicy Creamy Dip or Dressing (page 199) or with Blue Cheese Dressing (page 241) for a wholesome, light lunch.

Serves 2

½ pound raw spinach
1 clove garlic, halved
2 teaspoons lemon juice
2 tablespoons olive oil
3 tablespoons crumbled crisply cooked bacon
3 tablespoons thinly sliced scallions
1 hard-boiled egg, cut into wedges
½ ripe tomato, cut into wedges

1. Wash the spinach thoroughly, changing the water several times. Drain the spinach and remove the tough stems. Wrap the leaves in a damp towel and chill.

2. Rub the inside of a salad bowl with the cut surface of the garlic clove. Coat the inside of the bowl with the lemon juice and the olive oil.

3. When the spinach is chilled, tear it into bite-sized pieces and place in the prepared bowl. Add the bacon and scallion and toss well.

4. Arrange the egg and tomato wedges around the edge of the salad and serve.

Caesar Salad

This is a favorite of ours. We enjoy it as a light main course at luncheon or as a side salad to chicken or fish dishes at dinnertime.

Serves 3

4 cups torn leaves of Romaine, Bibb, Cos, or leaf lettuce
1 egg
Salt, for sprinkling the bowl
1 clove garlic, peeled and sliced in half
½ teaspoon dry mustard
1½ teaspoons lemon juice
Few drops Tabasco
2 tablespoons olive oil
2 teaspoons Parmesan cheese
3 anchovies, drained

1. Chill the lettuce leaves.

2. Place the egg in a small saucepan, cover with water, and heat. When the water begins to simmer, cook the egg for 1 to 1½ minutes. Drain and set aside.

3. Sprinkle a little salt in the bottom of a wooden salad bowl. Rub the garlic clove around the inside of the bowl. Add the mustard, lemon juice, and Tabasco and stir to combine and dissolve the salt. Whisk in the olive oil, stirring briskly to blend the ingredients.

4. Add the lettuce to the bowl. Sprinkle with the Parmesan cheese and add the anchovies. Break the egg over the salad, and toss the mixture gently but thoroughly to combine the egg, the dressing that has settled to the bottom, and the lettuce, cheese, and anchovies.

Greek Salad

This attractive salad can be served as a main course or as an appetizer to your luncheon entrée. An appropriate finish to the meal would be a glass of Cappuccino (page 249) or a cup of espresso or tea.

Serves 2

4 cups torn leaves of crisp lettuce such as romaine or iceberg
2 tablespoons olive oil
2 teaspoons lemon juice or red wine vinegar
1 tablespoon finely chopped fresh oregano or 1 teaspoon dried
Salt and pepper to taste (optional)
4 ounces feta cheese
1 medium-size cucumber
½ small green pepper, cored, seeded, and sliced
4 ounces black and green Greek olives

1. Place the lettuce leaves on a platter or plate. Drizzle about half the olive oil and lemon juice over the leaves. Sprinkle with about half of the oregano and add salt and pepper to taste.
2. Crumble the feta cheese into small chunks. Sprinkle these over the lettuce.
3. Slice the cucumber (you need not peel it, but wash it carefully to remove any wax). Arrange the cucumber slices around the edge and in the center of the plate. Arrange the pepper slices in an attractive pattern around the cucumbers. Finally, arrange the olives in the center and around the edge of the platter.
4. Drizzle the remaining olive oil and lemon juice over the salad and sprinkle with the remaining oregano.

Blue Cheese Dressing

Serve ice-cold over crisp salad, as a dip for vegetables, or as a dressing for chicken or shrimp salad.

Makes about 1¾ cups

1 cup regular or low-fat cottage cheese
1½ to 2 ounces blue cheese
¼ teaspoon ground black pepper
1 garlic clove finely chopped or 1 teaspoon garlic powder
½ cup sour cream or low-cholesterol substitute

Combine the cottage cheese, blue cheese, pepper, and garlic in a food processor, blender, or in a mixer, and blend at high speed until creamy. Fold in the sour cream. Cover the dressing and chill.

Serve cold over crisp salad.

Creamy Herb Dressing

Serve this herb dressing over a green salad, or combine it with shredded cabbage to make coleslaw.

Makes about ½ cup

¼ cup cottage cheese, regular or low-fat
¼ cup sour cream or low-cholesterol substitute
½ teaspoon Dijon mustard
1 tablespoon chopped fresh basil or ½ teaspoon dried
1 tablespoon chopped fresh marjoram or ½ teaspoon dried
Salt and ground black pepper to taste (optional)

Combine the cottage cheese, sour cream, and mustard in a food processor or blender. Process until smooth. Add the basil and marjoram and mix briefly. Season with salt and pepper to taste. This dressing can be kept, chilled, for several hours or even a day or two.

Tofu-Garlic Salad Dressing

Makes about 1 cup

6 tablespoons tofu
6 tablespoons olive oil or polyunsaturated vegetable oil
½ cup white wine vinegar
6 cloves garlic, finely chopped
1 tablespoon lemon juice
Ground black pepper to taste

Mash the tofu with a fork. Blend in the remaining ingredients. Shake or stir well before serving over salad.

Low-Carbohydrate Desserts and Beverages

Carbohydrate Addict's Cinnamon Coffee Cake

Makes a 9-inch round cake

4 large eggs
½ teaspoon cream of tartar
2 tablespoons soy flour*
2 packages artificial sweetener
1 teaspoon ground cinnamon
3 tablespoons heavy cream or no-cholesterol nondairy liquid creamer
2 tablespoons butter or margarine, softened

1. Preheat the oven to 300 degrees. Coat a 9-inch round cake pan with a little vegetable oil or pan spray.
2. Carefully separate the egg yolks and whites. Beat the whites with the cream of tartar until stiff peaks form.
3. Mix the yolks in a separate bowl along with the soy flour, the sweetener, ½ teaspoon of the cinnamon, and the cream. Fold the yolk mixture gently into the egg whites. Do not mix them thoroughly.
4. Pour the batter into the prepared pan, filling it ⅔ full. Bake for 20 to 25 minutes, until the center springs back when touched.
5. Cool the cake in its pan on a rack until warm. Spread with the butter and sprinkle with the remaining cinnamon.

Carbohydrate Addict's No-Cook Cheesecake Cupcakes

Makes 18 to 24 cupcakes

1 package unflavored gelatin
1 cup boiling water
2 8-ounce packages cream cheese, Neufchâtel, or low-fat imitation cream cheese, softened
1 teaspoon vanilla extract
10 packages artificial sweetener (equal to ½ cup sugar)

* May be purchased at most health food stores.

1. Line 18 to 24 muffin cups with cupcake liners.
2. Dissolve the gelatin in the boiling water in a mixing bowl. Stir well.
3. Cut the cheese into small pieces and place in the dissolved gelatin. Add the vanilla and the sweetener and beat well with an electric mixer.
4. Pour the mixture into the prepared muffin cups. Chill until firm, about 2 hours.

VARIATIONS:

For Extra Creamy Cupcakes, add 1/4 cup regular or low-fat cottage cheese and 1/4 cup sour-cream substitute to the recipe above before beating. Makes an additional 8 to 10 cupcakes.

To make Fruit Cheesecakes, top each cupcake with a half teaspoon or so of low-carbohydrate preserves in the flavor of your choice. Strawberry, raspberry, and apricot are particularly good choices.

To make Lemon or Almond Cheesecakes, substitute 1/2 teaspoon lemon or almond extract for the vanilla.

Carbohydrate Addict's Sweet Tarts

A good, basic low-carbohydrate shell. Fill to the brim with cheesecake (see page 243) or any of the Pink Heaven desserts (page 248) or a low-carbohydrate Whipped Cream (page 246).

Makes 6 individual tart shells

Shells:

2 large eggs, separated
3/4 teaspoon cream of tartar
1/2 package artificial sweetener
3 tablespoons regular or low-fat cottage cheese

Filling:

No-Cook Cheesecake Cupcakes (page 243),
Pink Heaven dessert (page 248),
Lemon Heaven dessert (page 248),
Lavender or Golden Heaven dessert (page 248),

Chocolate Whip (page 247),
Coffee Whip (page 248),or
Mocha Whip (page 248)

1. Preheat the oven to 300 degrees. Coat six nonstick muffin cups with a little vegetable oil or pan spray.

2. Beat the egg whites with the cream of tartar and sweetener until stiff peaks form. Set aside.

3. Combine the egg yolks and cottage cheese. Fold gently into the egg white mixture, making sure not to mix too thoroughly.

4. Spoon the mixture into the oiled muffin cups. Form a shell by hollowing the center of each cup with a spoon and spreading the mixture up the sides.

5. Bake for 20 to 25 minutes, until the shells are puffed and golden brown.

6. Cool and fill with one of the desserts mentioned above, or spread with low-carbohydrate preserves and Whipped Cream (page 246).

Carbohydrate Addict's Napoleons

Makes 6 pastries

Pastry:

4 eggs
¼ teaspoon cream of tartar
1 teaspoon vanilla extract
3 packages artificial sweetener

Filling:

About ¼ cup strawberry or raspberry low-carbohydrate preserves
About ¼ cup Whipped Cream (page 246) or low-fat, artificially sweetened whipped topping

1. Preheat the oven to 350 degrees. Coat an 11 × 17-inch baking sheet with a little vegetable oil or pan spray.

2. Separate the eggs very carefully. Beat the egg whites with the cream of tartar in a mixing bowl, using an electric mixer, until stiff peaks form. Set aside.

3. Combine the egg yolks, vanilla extract, and sweetener, mixing well. Fold the mixture gently into the egg whites.

4. Turn the mixture out onto the baking sheet and smooth to the edges.

5. Bake the pastry for 20 minutes, until puffed and lightly browned.

6. Let the pastry cool in the pan and cut into 12 squares. Spread half of the squares with the preserves. Cover the preserves with one tablespoon Whipped Cream or low-fat whipped topping. Place the remaining halves of pastry on top of the whipped cream.

Whipped Cream

Lightly flavored real whipped cream (or its low-fat counterpart) is a versatile ingredient in a variety of desserts. We recommend it for filling the Napoleons (page 245) and Dessert Crepes (page 247), and for making various dessert Whips (pages 247 and 248). Flavor it with preserves and you can make a variety of desserts (page 248). Turn artificially sweetened fruit gelatin into a special dessert by topping any flavor with a spoonful of whipped cream.

Makes 1 cup

½ cup heavy cream, or low-fat artificially sweetened whipped topping
½ package artificial sweetener
1 teaspoon vanilla extract

1. Beat the cream using an electric mixer or an eggbeater until foamy. Add the sweetener and continue beating until soft peaks form. Stir in the vanilla extract. Chill.

2. If using low-fat artificially sweetened whipped topping, omit the artificial sweetener and stir the vanilla extract into the already whipped concoction.

VARIATIONS:

To make Almond-flavored cream, reduce the vanilla to ¼ teaspoon and add ¼ teaspoon almond extract.

To make Anise-flavored cream, reduce the vanilla extract to ¼ teaspoon and add ⅛ teaspoon anise extract.

To make Maple-flavored cream, substitute artificial maple flavoring for the vanilla extract.

To make Chocolate-flavored cream, sift 1 tablespoon unsweetened cocoa over the whipped cream and fold in gently.

Carbohydrate Addict's Dessert Crepes

Makes 4 to 6 crepes

3 egg whites
½ teaspoon cream of tartar
¼ cup small curd regular or low-fat cottage cheese
¼ teaspoon vanilla extract
½ package artificial sweetener
½ tablespoon vegetable oil, or pan spray

1. Beat the egg whites with the cream of tartar until stiff. Set aside.
2. Combine the cottage cheese, vanilla extract, and sweetener, mixing well. Fold carefully into the egg whites, without mixing too thoroughly.
3. Oil a nonstick griddle or frying pan with a little vegetable oil. Heat the pan over moderate heat.
4. Form 4-inch crepes by spooning about 2 tablespoons of batter into the pan and spreading mixture into a thin round. Cook over moderate heat until the crepe sets and appears to be brown on the bottom. Turn and brown the other side. Repeat with the remaining batter.

VARIATION: To make blintzes, spread a teaspoon of sour cream onto each crepe, and roll into a cylinder.

Chocolate Whip

2 servings

1 teaspoon chocolate extract
1 teaspoon vanilla extract
1 package artificial sweetener
1 cup Whipped Cream (page 246) or low-fat artificially sweetened whipped topping

Combine the chocolate extract, vanilla extract, and sweetener. Fold into the Whipped Cream or whipped topping. Chill.

VARIATIONS:

To make Coffee Whip, use 1 teaspoon low-calorie coffee-flavored syrup for the chocolate extract and ½ teaspoon vanilla extract. Serves 4.

To make Mocha Whip, combine Chocolate and Coffee Whips.

Pink Heaven

This satisfying light dessert and its variations are made simply by flavoring Whipped Cream or low-fat artificially sweetened whipped topping with various kinds of fruit preserves.

Serves 2

1 rounded tablespoon strawberry or raspberry low-carbohydrate preserves (see Note)
1 cup Whipped Cream (page 246) or low-fat artificially sweetened whipped topping
Artificial sweetener to taste (optional)

Gently stir the preserves into the Whipped Cream or whipped topping. Taste, and stir in sweetener, if necessary. Serve in pretty glass dishes.

VARIATIONS:

To make Lavender Heaven, use low-carbohydrate grape preserves.

To make Golden Heaven, use low-carbohydrate orange marmalade.

To make Lemon Heaven, stir the juice of ⅓ lemon and ½ package artificial sweetener (or to taste) into the cream.

NOTE: Low-carbohydrate preserves are any low-calorie preserves containing no more than 4 grams of carbohydrate per average serving.

Cappuccino

Serve with a Light and Airy Muffin or two (page 201) for a breakfast that is fast and hits the spot.

Serves 1

6 ounces hot strongly brewed coffee
2 heaping tablespoons Whipped Cream (page 246) or low-fat artificially sweetened whipped topping
Artificial sweetener to taste
Dash of ground cinnamon

Add sweetener to taste to either the coffee or the cream, or both, if you wish, stirring lightly. Top the coffee with the Whipped Cream or topping. Sprinkle with a little cinnamon.

Cappuccino Slush

A low-carbohydrate lifesaver on a hot day. But this is to be enjoyed *only* at your Low-Carbohydrate Meals, *not* in between.

Serves 1

6 ounces artificially sweetened coffee-flavored soda
½ cup cracked ice
2 tablespoons heavy cream or low-fat cream substitute
Dash of ground cinnamon
artificial sweetener to taste (optional)

Combine the soda, ice, cream, and cinnamon in a blender. Blend just until the mixture forms a slush. Add sweetener to taste, if desired.

VARIATIONS:

To make Fruit Slushes, use strawberry, raspberry, or cherry-flavored soda. Omit the cinnamon.

To make Chocolate Slush, use chocolate soda.

APPENDIXES

APPENDIX

I

THE FOOD TABLES

The food tables that follow cite the amount of carbohydrate to be found in a typical serving of most common foods. The organization is by food groups: beverages; dairy products; eggs; fats and oils; fish and shellfish; fruits and fruit juices; grains; legumes, nuts, and seeds; meat and meat products; mixed dishes and fast foods; poultry and poultry products; soups, sauces, and gravies; sugars and sweets; and vegetables and vegetable products.

These tables contain **both low-carbohydrate and carbohydrate-rich foods**. In general, low-carbohydrate foods are listed in Chapter 6. If a food is not found there, save it for your Reward Meal. By definition, low-carbohydrate foods contain fewer than 4 grams of carbohydrate per average serving (2 grams for condiments).

CARBOHYDRATE FOOD TABLE*

Food Item	*Portion*	*Carbohydrate Grams (Per Portion)*
Beverages:		
Beer, regular	12 fl. oz.	13
Beer, light	12 fl. oz.	5
Coffee	6 fl. oz.	0
Coffee, milk, and sugar	6 fl. oz.	14
Fruit punch drink	6 fl. oz.	22
Gin, rum, vodka, whiskey	1½ fl. oz.	0
Lemonade	6 fl. oz.	21
Soda, club	12 fl. oz.	0
Soda, cola, regular	12 fl. oz.	41
Soda, cola, diet	12 fl. oz.	0
Soda, flavored, regular	12 fl. oz.	32–46
Tea, unsweetened	8 fl. oz.	0
Tea, instant, sweetened	8 fl. oz.	22
Wine, dessert	3½ fl. oz.	8
Wine, red	3½ fl. oz.	3
Wine, white	3½ fl. oz.	3
Dairy Products:		
Cheese, bleu	1 oz.	1
Cheese, Camembert	1⅓ oz.	Trace
Cheese, cheddar	1 oz.	1
Cheese, feta	1 oz.	1
Cheese, mozzarella, whole milk	1 oz.	1
Cheese, mozzarella, skim milk	1 oz.	1
Cheese, Muenster	1 oz.	Trace
Cheese, pasturized process	1 oz.	1
Cheese, provolone	1 oz.	1
Cheese, ricotta, whole milk	1 cup	7
Cheese, ricotta, skim milk	1 cup	13
Cheese, Swiss	1 oz.	1
Cheese, American, past. process	1 oz.	0
Cocoa, nonfat, from powder	1 oz.	22
Cottage cheese, creamed	1 cup	6
Cottage cheese, dry	1 cup	3

* Information adapted from statistics cited in the USDA Human Nutrition Information Service Home and Garden Bulletin #72, *Nutritive Value of Foods*, 1981.

CARBOHYDRATE FOOD TABLE (*continued*)

Food Item	*Portion*	*Carbohydrate Grams (Per Portion)*
Dairy Products:		
Cottage cheese, low-fat	1 cup	8
Cottage cheese with fruit	1 cup	30
Cream, half & half	1 Tbsp.	1
Cream, heavy	1 Tbsp.	Trace
Cream, light	1 Tbsp.	1
Cream, sour	1 Tbsp.	1
Cream cheese	1 oz.	1
Cream, whipped, fresh	2 Tbsp.	Trace
Creamer, liquid frozen	1 Tbsp.	2
Creamer, powdered	1 tsp.	1
Ice cream, vanilla	4 fl. oz.	16
Ice cream, soft, custard	4 fl. oz.	18
Ice milk, vanilla	4 fl. oz.	15
Milk, whole	1 cup	11
Milk, skim	1 cup	12
Milk, chocolate, regular	1 cup	26
Milk, chocolate, low-fat	1 cup	26
Milk shake, chocolate	10 oz.	60
Milk shake, vanilla	10 oz.	50
Sherbet	4 fl. oz.	15
Yogurt, plain, whole milk	8 oz. cont.	11
Yogurt, plain, low-fat milk	8 oz. cont.	16
Yogurt, fruit, low-fat milk	8 oz. cont.	43
Eggs:		
Eggs, raw or cooked	2 eggs	2
Eggs, fried	2 eggs	2
Omelet, cheese	3 eggs, 2 oz.	6
Fats and Oils:		
Butter	1 Tbsp.	0
Margarine, regular, hard	1 Tbsp.	0
Margarine, imitation, soft	1 Tbsp.	0
Mayonnaise, regular	1 Tbsp.	0
Mayonnaise, imitation	1 Tbsp.	2
Oils: Corn, olive	1 Tbsp.	0

CARBOHYDRATE FOOD TABLE (*continued*)

Food Item	*Portion*	*Carbohydrate Grams (Per Portion)*
Fats and Oils:		
Oils: Peanut, safflower	1 Tbsp.	0
Oils: Soybean, sunflower	1 Tbsp.	0
Salad dressing, bl. cheese, reg.	1 Tbsp.	1
Salad dressing, French, reg.	1 Tbsp.	1
Salad dressing, French, diet	1 Tbsp.	2
Salad dressing, Italian, reg.	1 Tbsp.	1
Salad dressing, Italian, diet	1 Tbsp.	2
Salad dressing, Th. Island, reg.	1 Tbsp.	2
Salad dressing, Th. Island, diet	1 Tbsp.	2
Salad dressing, vinegar + oil	1 Tbsp.	0
Tartar sauce	1 Tbsp.	1
Vinegar and oil	1 Tbsp.	Trace
Fish and Shellfish:		
Clams, raw meat only	3 oz.	2
Clams, canned	3 oz.	2
Crabmeat, canned	1 cup	1
Fish sticks, frozen	4 sticks	16
Flounder or sole, baked	3 oz.	Trace
Haddock, broiled	3 oz.	Trace
Halibut, broiled	3 oz.	Trace
Halibut, breaded and fried	3 oz.	7
Herring, pickled	3 oz.	0
Oyster, raw meat only	½ cup	4
Oysters, breaded and fried	3 oz.	9
Salmon, canned, pink	3 oz.	0
Salmon, smoked	3 oz.	0
Sardines, in oil	3 oz.	0
Shrimp, boiled or broiled	3 oz.	1
Shrimp, fried	3 oz.	11
Trout, broiled	3 oz.	Trace
Tuna, oil pack	3 oz.	0
Tuna, water pack	3 oz.	0
Tuna salad	1 cup	19

CARBOHYDRATE FOOD TABLE (*continued*)

Food Item	***Portion***	***Carbohydrate Grams (Per Portion)***
Fruits and Fruit Juices:		
Apple	1 large	32
Applesauce, sweetened	1 cup	51
Applesauce, unsweetened	1 cup	28
Apricots, canned, heavy syrup	1 cup	55
Apricots, canned, juice pack	1 cup	31
Apricots, dried	1 cup	80
Avocado	1 avocado	12
Banana	1 banana	27
Blackberries, raw	1 cup	18
Blueberries, raw	1 cup	20
Blueberries, frozen, sweetened	1 cup	50
Cantaloupe	½ melon	22
Cherries, fresh	10 cherries	11
Cranberry juice cocktail, sweetened	1 cup	38
Cranberry sauce	¼ cup	27
Dates, whole	10 dates	61
Figs, dried	10 figs	122
Fruit cocktail, canned, heavy syrup	1 cup	48
Fruit cocktail, canned, juice pack	1 cup	29
Grapefruit, raw	½ fruit	10
Grapefruit, canned with syrup	1 cup	39
Grapefruit juice, canned, sweetened	1 cup	28
Grapefruit juice, canned, unsweetened	1 cup	22
Grape juice	1 cup	38
Grapes, seedless	20 grapes	18
Grapes, seeded	20 grapes	20
Honeydew	1/10 melon	12
Lemon juice	1 Tbsp.	1
Lemon juice	1 cup	21
Lime juice	1 Tbsp.	1
Lime juice	1 cup	22
Mangos	1 fruit	35

CARBOHYDRATE FOOD TABLE (*continued*)

Food Item	*Portion*	*Carbohydrate Grams (Per Portion)*
Fruits and Fruit Juices:		
Nectarines	1 fruit	16
Orange	1 orange	15
Orange juice	1 cup	26
Papaya	1 cup	17
Peaches, dried	1 cup	98
Peaches, fresh	1 fruit	10
Peaches, canned, heavy syrup	1 cup	51
Peaches, canned, juice pack	1 cup	29
Pears, raw	1 fruit	21–30
Pears, canned, heavy syrup	1 cup	52
Pears, canned, juice pack	1 cup	32
Pineapple, fresh	1 cup	19
Pineapple, canned, heavy syrup	1 cup	52
Pineapple, canned, juice pack	1 cup	39
Pineapple juice, unsweetened	1 cup	34
Plantains, cooked	1 cup	48
Plums, fresh	1 large	9
Plums, canned, heavy syrup	1 cup	60
Plums, canned, juice pack	1 cup	38
Prunes, dried	5 large	31
Prune juice	1 cup	45
Raisins	½ cup	58
Raspberries, raw	1 cup	14
Raspberries, frozen, sweetened	1 cup	65
Rhubarb, cooked, sweetened	1 cup	75
Strawberries, fresh	1 cup	10
Strawberries, frozen, sweetened	1 cup	66
Tangerines, raw	1 fruit	9
Watermelon	1 piece	35
Grain Products:		
Bagel, plain or water	1 bagel	38
Biscuits	1 biscuit	13
Breadcrumbs	1 cup	73
Bread, oatmeal	1 slice	12
Bread, mixed grain	1 slice	12

CARBOHYDRATE FOOD TABLE (*continued*)

Food Item	*Portion*	*Carbohydrate Grams (Per Portion)*
Grain Products:		
Bread, pita	1 pita	33
Bread, pumpernickel	1 slice	16
Bread, raisin	1 slice	13
Bread, wheat	1 slice	12
Bread, whole wheat	1 slice	13
Bread, white	1 slice	13
Stuffing	1 cup	50
Cereals:		
All-Bran	⅓ cup	21
Cheerios	1¼ cup	20
Cheerios, Honey Nut	¾ cup	23
Cap'n Crunch	¾ cup	23
Cornflakes	1¼ cup	24
40% Bran	⅔–¾ cup	22
Grits	1 cup	18–31
Grape Nuts Cereal	¼ cup	23
Oatmeal	1 cup	25
Shredded Wheat cereal	⅔ cup	23
Special K cereal	1⅓ cup	21
Sugar Frosted Flakes	¾ cup	26
Desserts:		
Cake, devil's food w/frost.	1 slice	40
Cake, devil's food w/frost.	1 cupcake	20
Cake, carrot w/cr. ch. frost.	1 slice	48
Fruitcake	1 slice	50
Cake, pound	1 slice	15
Cake, snack "Ding Dongs"	2 small cakes	17
Cake, cheese	1 slice	26
Cake, white w/white frost.	1 slice	42
Brownie w/nuts and frost.	1 brownie	16
Cookies, chocolate chip	4 cookies	28
Cookies, fig bars	4 cookies	42
Chips, corn	1 oz. pack	16

CARBOHYDRATE FOOD TABLE (*continued*)

Food Item	*Portion*	*Carbohydrate Grams (Per Portion)*
Desserts:		
Cookies, oatmeal w/raisins	4 cookies	36
Cookies, chocolate sandwich	4 cookies	29
Cookies, shortbread	4 sm. cookies	20
Cookies, sugar	4 cookies	31
Cookies, vanilla wafers	10 cookies	29
Crackers, cheese	10 crackers	6
Crackers, cheese w/p.butter	1 sandwich	5
Crackers, graham	2 crackers	11
Crackers, melba toast	1 piece	4
Crackers, saltine	4 crackers	9
Crackers, Wheat Thins	4 crackers	5
Croissant	1 croissant	27
Danish, round w/fruit	1 Danish	28
Doughnut, plain	1 doughnut	24
Doughnut, glazed	1 doughnut	26
English muffin, toasted	1 muffin	27
French toast	1 slice	17
Macaroni, firm stage	1 cup	39
Macaroni, tender stage	1 cup	32
Muffin, blueberry	1 muffin	22
Muffin, bran	1 muffin	24
Muffin, corn	1 muffin	21
Noodles, egg	1 cup	37
Pancakes	1 pancake	8
Pie crust	1 slice	13
Pie, apple	1 slice	60
Pie, blueberry	1 slice	55
Pie, cherry	1 slice	61
Pie, custard	1 slice	36
Pie, lemon meringue	1 slice	63
Pie, peach	1 slice	60
Pie, pecan	1 slice	71
Pie, pumpkin	1 slice	37
Popcorn, air popped	1 cup	6
Popcorn, popped in veg. oil	1 cup	6
Popcorn, sugar syrup coated	1 cup	30

CARBOHYDRATE FOOD TABLE (*continued*)

Food Item	*Portion*	*Carbohydrate Grams (Per Portion)*
Desserts:		
Pretzels, thin	10 pretzels	48
Rice, brown	1 cup	50
Rice, white	1 cup	50
Rolls, frankfurter + burger	1 roll	20
Rolls, hard	1 roll	30
Rolls, hoagie or submarine	1 roll	72
Rolls, dinner	1 roll	20
Spaghetti, al dente	1 cup	39
Spaghetti, tender stage	1 cup	32
Toaster pastries	1 pastry	38
Tortillas, corn	1 tortilla	13
Waffles	1 waffle	27
Legumes, Nuts, and Seeds:		
Almonds, whole	1 oz.	6
Cashews, dry roasted + salted	2 oz.	18
Cashews, roasted in oil + salt	1 oz.	16
Chickpeas	1 cup	45
Macadamia nuts, in oil + salted	2 oz.	8
Peanuts, roasted in oil + salted	2 oz.	10
Peanut butter	1 Tbsp.	3
Pistachio nuts, dried + shelled	2 oz.	14
Tofu (soy product)	1 piece	3
Meat and Meat Products:		
Bacon	3 slices	Trace
Beef, cooked, lean + fat	3 oz.	0
Beef, cooked, lean only	3 oz.	0
Beef, canned, corned	3 oz.	0
Beef, dried, chipped	2½ oz.	0
Bologna	2 slices	2
Frankfurter, meat	1 frank	1
Ham (no sugar added)	3 oz.	0
Hamburger patty, lean	3 oz.	0
Hamburger patty, regular	3 oz.	0
Lamb	2¾ oz.	0

CARBOHYDRATE FOOD TABLE (*continued*)

Food Item	*Portion*	*Carbohydrate Grams (Per Portion)*
Meat and Meat Products:		
Lamb, chops	3⅓ oz.	0
Liver, beef	3 oz.	7
Pork, bacon, regular	3 slices	Trace
Pork, bacon, Canadian style	2 slices	1
Pork, ham, luncheon meat	2 slices	2
Salami	2 slices	1
Sausages, brown-and-serve	1 link	0
Veal, braised or broiled	1 cutlet	0
Mixed Dishes:		
Chicken pot pie	1 piece	42
Chili con carne, canned	1 cup	31
Chop suey, home recipe	1 cup	13
Macaroni and cheese, canned	1 cup	26
Macaroni and cheese, homemade	1 cup	40
Spaghetti w/meatballs + sauce	1 cup	39
Mixed Dishes and Fast Foods:		
Cheeseburger	1 sandwich	28
Eng. muffin w/egg + cheese + bacon	1 sandwich	31
Fish sandwich w/cheese	1 sandwich	39
Hamburger sandwich	4½ oz.	20
Pizza w/cheese	1 slice	39
Roast beef sandwich	1 sandwich	34
Poultry and Poultry Products:		
Chicken, fried, batter-dipped	½ breast	13
Chicken, fried flour-dipped	½ breast	3
Chicken, roasted	½ breast	0
Chicken liver	1 piece	1
Chicken, frankfurter	1 frank	3
Chicken, roll	2 slices	1
Duck, roasted	½ duck	0
Turkey, roasted	3 pieces	0

CARBOHYDRATE FOOD TABLE (*continued*)

Food Item	*Portion*	*Carbohydrate Grams (Per Portion)*
Poultry and Poultry Products:		
Turkey, ham	2 slices	Trace
Turkey patty, breaded & fried	2¼ oz.	10
Soups, Sauces, and Gravies:		
Clam chowder, New Eng. w/milk	1 cup	17
Cream of chicken soup, w/milk	1 cup	15
Cream of mushroom soup, w/milk	1 cup	15
Tomato soup, with milk	1 cup	22
Tomato soup, with water	1 cup	17
Beef consomme	1 cup	0
Chicken noodle soup	1 cup	9
Minestrone soup	1 cup	11
Pea, green, soup	1 cup	27
Vegetable beef soup	1 cup	10
Vegetable soup, vegetarian	1 cup	12
Bouillon, chicken, veg., or beef	6 fl. oz.	1
Bouillon, onion	6 fl. oz.	4
Onion soup	6 fl. oz.	4
Cheese sauce	1 cup	23
Barbeque sauce, ready-to-serve	1 Tbsp.	2
Soy sauce	1 Tbsp.	2
Beef gravy, canned	1 cup	11
Chicken gravy, canned	1 cup	13
Mushroom gravy, canned	1 cup	13
Brown gravy, from mix	1 cup	14
Chicken gravy, from mix	1 cup	14
Sugars and Sweets:		
Caramels, plain or chocolate	1 oz.	22
Chocolate, milk, plain	1 oz.	16
Chocolate, milk, w/almonds	1 oz.	15
Chocolate, milk, w/peanuts	1 oz.	13
Chocolate, milk, w/rice cereal	1 oz.	18
Chocolate, semisweet	1 oz.	16
Chocolate, sweet, dark	1 oz.	16
Fondant, uncoated	1 oz.	27

CARBOHYDRATE FOOD TABLE (*continued*)

Food Item	*Portion*	*Carbohydrate Grams (Per Portion)*
Sugars and Sweets:		
Fudge, chocolate	1 oz.	21
Gumdrops	1 oz.	25
Hard candy	1 oz.	28
Jelly beans	1 oz.	26
Marshmallows	1 oz.	23
Gelatin dessert, from mix	½ cup	17
Honey	1 Tbsp.	17
Jams and preserves, reg.	1 Tbsp.	14
Jellies	1 Tbsp.	13
Popsicle	3 fl. oz. pop.	18
Pudding, chocolate, canned	5 oz.	30
Pudding, vanilla, canned	5 oz.	33
Pudding, choc. instant from mix	½ cup	27
Pudding, choc. cooked from mix	½ cup	25
Pudding, van. instant from mix	½ cup	27
Pudding, van. cooked from mix	½ cup	25
Pudding, choc. w/skim milk	½ cup	28
Pudding, rice, from mix	½ cup	27
Pudding, tapioca, from mix	½ cup	25
Sugar, brown	1 Tbsp.	13
Sugar, granulated	1 Tbsp.	12
Chocolate syrup, thin type	1 Tbsp.	11
Chocolate syrup, fudge type	1 Tbsp.	11
Syrup, maple and corn	1 Tbsp.	16
Vegetables:		
Alfalfa sprouts	1 cup	1
Artichoke	1 artichoke	12
Asparagus	4 spears	3
Bamboo shoots, canned	1 cup	4
Beans, lima	1 cup	32–35
Bean sprouts, raw	1 cup	6
Beans, black-eyed peas	1 cup	40
Beans, snap	1 cup	8
Beets, cooked	1 cup	11
Broccoli, raw or cooked	1 spear	10
Brussels sprouts	1 cup	13

CARBOHYDRATE FOOD TABLE (*continued*)

Food Item	*Portion*	*Carbohydrate Grams (Per Portion)*
Vegetables:		
Cabbage, raw	1 cup	4
Cabbage, Chinese, raw	1 cup	3
Cabbage, red, raw	1 cup	4
Carrots	1 carrot	7
Cauliflower	1 cup	5
Celery	1 stalk	1
Collards, raw	1 cup	5
Corn, fresh	1 ear	19
Cucumber	6 slices	1
Eggplant	1 cup	6
Endive	1 cup	2
Jerusalem artichoke	1 cup	26
Kohlrabi	1 cup	11
Lettuce	⅙ head	1–2
Mushrooms, raw	1 cup	3
Mustard greens	1 cup	3
Okra	8 pods	6
Onions, raw, chopped	1 cup	12
Parsley	10 sprigs	1
Parsnips, cooked	1 cup	30
Peas, edible pod, cooked, drained	1 cup	11
Peas, green, canned, drained	1 cup	21
Peas, green, frozen	1 cup	23
Peas, black-eyed	1 cup	42
Pepper, bell, sweet, raw	1 pepper	4
Pepper, chili, hot or sweet	1 pepper	4
Potato, baked	1 potato	34–38
Potato chips	10 chips	10
Potato salad with mayonnaise	1 cup	28
Potato, sweet	1 potato	28
Potatoes, f. fried, oven-heated	10 strips	17
Potatoes, f. fried in veg. oil	10 strips	20
Potatoes, hash brown, homemade	1 cup	35
Potatoes, hash brown, frozen	1 cup	44
Pumpkin	1 cup	12
Radishes	4	1

CARBOHYDRATE FOOD TABLE (*continued*)

Food Item	*Portion*	*Carbohydrate Grams (Per Portion)*
Vegetables:		
Sauerkraut	1 cup	10
Scallions	6	2
Spinach, cooked	1 cup	10
Squash, summer	1 cup	8
Squash, winter	1 cup	18
Tomatoes	1 tomato	5
Tomato juice	1 cup	10
Tomato paste	1 cup	49
Tomato puree	1 cup	25
Tomato sauce	1 cup	18
Turnips	1 cup	8
Turnip greens	1 cup	6
Vegetable juice cocktail, canned	1 cup	11
Vegetables, mixed, canned	1 cup	15
Vegetables, mixed, frozen	1 cup	24
Water chestnuts, canned	1 cup	17
Zucchini	1 cup	8
Miscellaneous Items:		
Catsup	1 Tbsp.	4
Cinnamon	1 tsp.	2
Curry powder	1 tsp.	1
Garlic powder	1 tsp.	2
Gelatin	1 envelope	0
Miso (soy product)	1 fl. oz.	8
Mustard powder	1 tsp.	Trace
Olives, all	4 olives	Trace
Onion powder	1 tsp.	2
Oregano	1 tsp.	1
Paprika	1 tsp.	1
Pepper, black	1 tsp.	1
Pickle, dill	1 medium	1
Pickle, fresh pack, sliced	2 slices	3
Pickle, sweet gherkins	1 pickle	5
Relish, chopped sweet	1 tbsp.	5
Salt	1 tsp.	0
Vinegar, cider	1 Tbsp.	1

APPENDIX

II

SELECTED BIBLIOGRAPHY

The following listing is only a representative selection of the immense body of scientific publications concerning carbohydrate addiction and related findings and research.

Ad Hoc Interdisciplinary Committee on Children and Weight (1984). *Children and Weight: A Changing Perspective*. December.

Altomonte, L., A. Zoli, G. Ghirlanda, R. Manna, and A. V. Greco (1988). *Pharmacology*. 36(2):106–11.

American Psychiatric Association (1987). *Diagnostic and Statistical Manual of Mental Disorders*. Third edition.

Assimacopoulos-Jeannet, F., and B. Jeanrenaud (1976). The hormonal and metabolic basis of experimental obesity. *Clin. Endocrinol. Metag.* 5:337–365.

Babb, T. G., E. R Buskirk, and J. L. Hodgson (1988). Exercise end-expiratory lung volumes in lean and moderately obese women. *Int. Journ. Obes.* 13:11–19.

Blundell, J. E. (1984). Serotonin and appetite. *Neuropharmacology.* 23:1537–51.

Blundell, J. E., and C. J. Latham (1982). Behavioural Pharmacology of Feeding. In T. Silverstone, ed., *Drugs and Appetite*. New York: Academic Press.

Booth, D. and T. Brookover (1966). Hunger elicited in the rat by a single injection of bovine crystalline insulin. *Physiol. Behav*. 3:439–46.

Booth, D. A. (1972). Modulation of the feeding response to peripheral insulin, 2-deoxyglucose or 3-0-methyl glucose injection. *Physiol. Behav.* 8:1069–76.

Brandes, J. (1977). Insulin-induced overeating in the rat. *Physiol. Behav.* 18:1095–1102.

Bray, G. A. (1981). The inheritance of corpulence. In L. A. Cioffi, E.P.T. James, and T. B. Van Itallie, eds., *The Body Weight Regulatory System: Normal and Disturbed Mechanisms.* New York: Raven Press.

Bray, G. A., and D. A. York (1979). Hypothalamic and genetic obesity in experimental animals: An autonomic and endocrine hypothesis. *Physiol. Rev.* 59:719–809.

Briese, E. and M. Quijada (1978). Sugar solutions taste better (positive alliesthesia) after insulin. *J. Physiol.* 285:20P–21P.

Brownell, K., and J. P. Forety, eds. (1986). *Handbook of Eating Disorders: Physiology, Psychology and Treatment.* New York: Basic Books.

Bryce, G. F., P. R. Johnson, A. C. Sullivan, and J. S. Stern (1977). Insulin and glucagon: plasma levels and pancreatic release in the genetically obese Zucker rat. *Horm. Metab. Res.* 9:366–70.

Campfeild, L. A., P. Brandon, and F. J. Smith (1985). On-line continuous measurement of blood glucose in meal initiation. *Brain Res. Sull.* 14:605–16.

Carruba, M. O., P. Mantegazza, P. Memo, C. Missale, M. Pizzi, and P. F. Spano. Peripheral and central mechanisms of action of serotoninergic anorectic drugs. In S. Nicolaîdis, ed., *Serotoninergic System, Feeding and Body Weight Regulation.* New York: Academic Press.

Contaldo, F. (1981). The development of obesity in genetically obese rodents. In L. A. Cioffi, E.P.T. James, and T. B. Van Itallie, eds., *The Body Weight Regulatory System: Normal and Disturbed Mechanisms.* New York: Raven Press.

Coulston, A. M., G. C. Liu, and G. M. Reaven (1983). Plasma glucose, insulin and lipid responses to high-carbohydrate low-fat diets in normal humans. *Metabolism.* 32(1):52–56.

Crepaldi, G., P. J. Lefebure, and D. J. Glaton (1983). *Diabetes, Obesity and Hyperlipidemias II.* New York: Academic Press.

Czech, M. P. (1977). Molecular basis of insulin action. *A. Rev. Biochem.* 46:359–384.

Darnell, J., H. Lodish, and D. Baltimore, (1986). *Molecular Cell Biology.* New York: Freeman.

De Kalbermatten, N., E. Ravussin, L. Maeder, C. Geser, E. Jequier, and J. P. Felber (1980). Comparison of glucose, fructose, sorbitol, and xylitol utilization in humans during insulin suppression. *Metabolism* 29:62–67.

Eaton, R. P., R. Oase, and D. S. Schade (1976). Altered insulin and glucagon secretion in treated genetic hyperlipemia: a mechanism of therapy? *Metabolism* 25(3):245–249.

Friedman, M. I. and J. Granneman (1983). Food intake and peripheral factors after recovery from insulin-induced hypoglycemia. *Am. J. Phys-* 244:R374–R382.

Fuh, M. M., S. M. Shieh, D. A. Wu, Y. D. Chen, and G. M. Reaven (1987). Abnormalities of carbohydrate and lipid metabolism in patients with hypertension. *Hypertension*, 147:1035–1038.

Garg, A., A. Bonanome, S. Grundy, Z. Zhang, and R. H. Unger (1988). Comparison of a high-carbohydrate diet with a high-monounsaturated-fat diet in patients with non-insulin-dependent diabetes mellitus. *New Eng. J. Med.* 319:829–34.

Garvey, W. T. (1989). Cellular and Molecular Pathogenesis of Insulin Resistance. In B. Draznin, S. Melmed, and D. LeRoith, eds., *Insulin Action*, vol. II. New York: Liss.

Geiselman, P. J. and D. Novi (1982). Sugar infusion can enhance feeding. *Science* 218:409–491.

Geiselman, P. J. (1985). Feeding patterns following normal ingestion and intragastric infusion of glucose, fructose, and galactose in the rabbit. *Nutr. Behav.* 2:175–188.

George, V., A. Tremblay, J. P. Despres, C. Leblanc, L. Perusse, and C. Bouchard (1989). Evidence for the existence of small eaters and large eaters similar fat-free mass and activity level. *Int. Journ. Obes.* 13(1):43–53.

Gormally, J. (1984). The obese binge eater: Diagnosis, etiology and clinical issues. In C. Hawkins, W. Fremouw, and P. Clement, eds., *The Binge-Purge Syndrome*. New York: Springer.

Goto, Y., R. G. Carpenter, M. Berelowitz, and L. A. Froham (1980). Effect of ventromedial hypothalamic lesions on the secretion of somatostatin, insulin, and glucagon by the perfused rat pancreas. *Metabolism* 29:986–990.

Harper, A. E. (1976). Protein and amino acids in the regulation of food intake. In D. Novin, W. Wyrwicka, and G. A. Bray, eds., *Hunger: Basic Mechanisms and Clinical Implications*. New York: Raven Press.

Hill, W., T. W. Castonguay, and G. H. Collier (1980). Taste of diet balancing? *Physiol. Behav.* 24:765–767.

Hoebel, B. G. (1984). Neurotransmitters in the control of feeding and its rewards: Monomines, opiates, and brain-gut peptides. In A. J. Stunkard and E. Stellar, eds., *Eating and Its Disorders*. Association for Research in Nervous and Mental Disease. vol. 62. New York: Raven Press.

Inselman, L. S., L. B. Padilla-Burgos, S. Teichberg, and H. Spencer (1988). Alveolar enlargement in obesity-induced hyperplastic lung growth. *Journ. Appl. Physiol.* 65(5):2291–2296.

Ionescu, E., J. F. Sauter, and B. Jeanrenaud (1985). Abnormal oral glucose tolerance in genetically obese *(fa/fa)* rats. *Am. J. Physiol.* 284.E500–E506.

Israel, A., J. Weinstein, and B. Prince (1985). Eating behaviors, eating style, and children's weight status: Failure to find an obese eating style. *Int. Journ. Eating Disorders.* 4:113–119.

Jeanrenaud, B. (1978). Hyperinsulinemia in obesity syndromes: Its metabolic consequences and possible etiology. *Metabolism,* 27:1881–1892.

Jeanrenaud, B. (1979). Insulin and obesity. *Diabetologia,* 17:133–138.

Jeanrenaud, B., S. Halimi, and G. van de Werve (1985). Neuroendocrine disorders seen as triggers of the triad: obesity-insulin resistance-abnormal glucose tolerance. *Diabetes Metab. Rev.* 1:261–291.

Jeanrenaud, B. (1985). An hypothesis of the aetiology of obesity: dysfunction of the central nervous system as a primary cause. *Diabetologia* 28: 502–513.

Kahn, C. R., D. M. Neville, Jr., and J. Roth (1973). Insulin receptor interaction in the obese hyperglycemic mouse. A model of insulin resistance. *J. Biol. Chem.* 248:244–250.

Kahn, C. R. (1978). Insulin resistance, insulin insensitivity, and insulin unresponsiveness: a necessary distinction. *Metab. Clin. Exp.* 27 (Suppl A):1893–1902.

Kanarek, R. B. and E. Hirsh (1977). Dietary-induced overeating in experimental animals. *Fed. Proc.* 36:154–158.

Kanarek, R., R. Marks-Kaufman, and B. Lipeles (1980). Increased carbohydrate intake as a function of insulin administration in rats. *Physiol. Behav.* 25:779–782.

Kanarek, R. B. and N. Orthen-Gambill (1982). Differential effects of sucrose, fructose, and glucose on carbohydrate-induced obesity in rats. *J. Nutr.* 112:1546–1554.

Keesey, R. E. and S. W. Corbett (1984). Metabolic defense of the body weight set-point. In A. J. Stunkard and E. Stellar, eds., *Eating and Its Disorders.* Association for Research in Nervous and Mental Disease, vol. 62. New York: Raven Press.

Kolterman, O. G., G. M. Reaven, and J. M. Olefsky (1976). Relationship between in vivo insulin resistance and decreased insulin receptors in obese man. *J. Clin. Endocrinol. Metab.* 48:487–494.

Kolterman, O. H., J. Insel, M. Seekow, and J. Olefsky (1983). Mechanism of insulin resistance in human obesity: Evidence for receptor and post-receptor defects. *J. Clin. Invest.* 65:1273.

Kreisberg, R. A., B. R. Boshell, J. DiPlacido, and R. J. Roddman (1967). Insulin secretion in obesity. *N. Engl. J. Med.* 276:314–319.

Kromhout, D. (1983). Energy and macronutrient intake in lean and obese middle-aged men (the Zutphen Study). *Am. J. Clin. Nutr.* 37:295–299.

Larue-Achagiotis, C. and J. Le Magnen (1985). Effects of long-term insulin on body weight and food intake: intravenous versus intraperitoneal foutes. *Appetite* 6:319–329.

Laube, H. and E. F. Pfeifer (1978). Insulin secretion and nutritional factors. In: H. M. Katzen and R. J. Mahler, eds., *Advances in Modern Nutrition: Diabetes, Obesity, and Vascular Disease*, vol. 2. New York: Wiley.

Lawrence, J. R., C. E. Gray, I. S. Grant, J. A. Ford, and W. B. McIntosh (1980). The insulin response to intravenous fructose in maturity-onset diabetes mellitus and normal subjects. *Diabetes* 29:736–741.

Leibel, R. L. (1984). *Obesity and Nutrient Metabolism.* Presented at the American Association for the Advancement of Science, May 26, 1984.

Leibowitz, S. F. and G. Shor-Posner (1986). Brain serotonin and eating behavior. In: S. Nicolaîdis, ed., *Serotoninergic System, Feeding and Body Weight Regulation.* New York: Academic Press.

Lennon, D., F. Nagle, F. Stratman, E. Shrago, and S. Dennis (1985). Diet and exercise training effects on resting metabolic rate. *Int. Journ. Obes.* 9:39–47.

Lotter, E. C. and S. C. Woods (1977). Somatostatin decreases food-intake. *Diabetes* 26:358.

Lovett, D. and D. Booth (1970). Four effects of exogenous insulin on food intake. *Quart. J. Exper. Psych.* 22:406–419.

Mader, S. S. (1985). *Inquiry into Life.* Brown: Dubuque, Iowa.

Maggio, C., M. Yang, and J. Vasselli (1984). Developmental aspects of macronutrient selection in genetically obese and lean rats. *Nutr. and Behav.* 2:95–110.

Maggio, C. A., M.R.C. Greenwood, and J. R. Vasselli (1983). The satiety effects of intragastric macronutrient infusions in fatty and lean Zucker rats. *Physiol. Behav.* 31:367–372.

Mahan, L. K. (1987). Family focused behavior approach to weight control in children. *Pediatric Clinics of North America.* 34(4):983–996.

Martin, R. J. and B. Jeanrenaud (1985). Growth hormone in obesity and diabetes: Inappropriate hypothalamic control of secretion. *Int. Journ. Obes.* 9(1):99–104.

Mayer, J., S. B. Andrus, D. J. Silides (1953). Effect of diethyldithiocarbamate and other agents on mice with obese-hyperglycemic syndrome. *Endocrinology* 53:572–581.

McLean, Baird I. and A. Howard (1969). The role of insulin in obesity *Obesity: Medical and Scientific Aspects.* Livingstone: Edinburgh.

Merkel, A. D., M. J. Wayner, F. B. Jolicoeur, and R. B. Mintz (1979). Effects of glucose and saccharine solutions on subsequent food consumption. *Physiol. Behav.* 23:791–793.

Mizes, J. S. (1985). Bulimia: A review of its symptomatology and treatment. *Adv. in Behav. Res. and Therapy.* 7:91–142.

Morgan, J. B., D. A. York, A Wasilewska, and J. Portman (1982). A study of the thermic responses to a meal and to a sympathomimetic drug (ephedrine) in relation to energy balance in man. *Br. J. Nutr.* 47:21–32.

Nuttall, F. Q., A. D. Mooradian, R. DeMarias, and S. Parker (1983). The glycemic effect of different meals approximately isocaloric and similar in protein, carbohydrate, and fat content as calculated using ADA exchange lists *Diabetes Care* 6:432–435.

Olefsky, J. M., G. M. Reaven, and J. W. Farquhar (1974). Effects of weight reduction on obesity: studies of carbohydrate and lipid metabolism. *J. Clin. Invest.* 53:64–76.

Olefsky, J. M. (1976). The insulin receptor: its role in insulin resistance of obesity and diabetes. *Diabetes* 25:1154–1165.

Olefsky, J. M. and O. G. Kolterman (1981). *Am. J. Med.* 70:151.

Perusse, L., C. Bouchard, C. Leblanc, and A. Tremblay (1984). Energy intake and physical fitness in children and adults of both sexes. *Nutr. Res.* 4:363–370.

Phinney, S. D., B. M. LaGrange, M. O'Connell, and E. Danforth, Jr. (1988). Effects of aerobic exercise on energy expenditure and nitrogen balance during very low calorie dieting. *Metabolism,* 37 (8):758–763.

Porte, D. and S. C. Woods (1981). Regulation of food-intake and body-weight by insulin. *Diavetologia* 20:274–280.

Raizada, M. K., M. I. Phillips, D. LeRoith (1987). *Insulin, Insulin-like Growth Factors, and Their Receptors in the Central Nervous System.* New York: Plenum Press.

Reaven, G. M., Y-Di. Chen, A. Golay, A.L.M. Swislocki, and J. B. Jaspan, (1987). Documentation of hyperglucagonemia throughout the day in non-obese and obese patients with non-insulin-dependent diabetes mellitus. *J. Clin. Endocrinol. Metab.* 64:106–110.

Reiser, S., A. S. Powell, C. Yang, and J. J. Canary (1987). An insulinogenic effect of oral fructose in humans during postprandial hyperglycemia. *Am. J. Clin. Nutr.* 45:580–587.

Rezek, M., V. Havlicek, and K. R. Hughes (1978). Paradoxical stimulation of food intake by larger loads of glucose, fructose, and mannose: evidence for a positive feedback effect. *Physiol. Behav.* 21:243–249.

Richter, C. P. (1942). Increased dextrose appetite of normal rats treated with insulin. *Am. J. Physiol.* 135:781–787.

Ritter, R. C. and O. K. Balch (1978). Feeding in response to insulin but not to 2-deoxy-D-glucose in the hamster. *Am. J. Physiol.* 234:20–E24.

Rodin, J., R. Reed, and L. Jamner (1988). Metabolic effects of fructose and glucose: Implications for food intake. *Amer. J. Clin. Nutr.* 47:683–689.

Rodin, J., J. Wack, E. Ferrannini, and R. DeFronzo (1985). Effect of Insulin and glucose on feeding behavior. *Metabolism* 34(9):826–831.

Rohner-Jeanrenaud, F. and B. Jeanrenaud (1980). Consequences of ventromedial hypothalamic lesions upon insulin and glucagon secretion by subsequently isolated perfused pancreas in the rat. *J. Clin. Invest.* 65:902–910.

Rohner-Jeanrenaud, F., A. C. Jeanrenaud Hochstasser, and B. Jeanrenaud (1983). Hyper-insulinemia of preobese and obese *fa/fa* rats is partly vagus nerve mediated. *Am. J. Physiol.* 244:E317–322.

Rose, G. A. and R. T. Williams (1961). Metabolic studies on large eaters and small eaters. *Br. J. Nutr.*, 151:1–9.

Rowland, N. and E. M. Stricker (1978). Differential effects of glucose and fructose infusions on insulin-induced feeding in rats. *Physiol. Behav.* 22:387–389.

Sahakian, B. J., M.E.J. Lean, T. W. Robbins, and W. P. James (1981). Salivation and insulin secretion in response to food in non-obese men and women. *Appetite* 2:209–216.

Silverstone, T. and M. Besser (1971). Insulin, blood sugar and hunger. *Postgrad. Med. J.* 47:427–429 (suppl.).

Silverstone, T. and E. Goodall (1986). Serotoninergic mechanisms in human feeding. In S. Nicolaîdis, ed., *Serotoninergic System, Feeding and Body Weight Regulation*. New York: Academic Press.

Simons, C., J. L. Schlienger, R. Sapin, and M. Imler (1986). Cephalic phase insulin secretion in relation to food presentation in normal overweight subjects. *Physiol. Behav.* 36:465–469.

Sims, E.A.H. (1979). Syndromes of Obesity. In L. J. De Groot, ed., *Endocrinology*, vol. 3. New York: Grune and Stratton.

Smith, G. P. and A. N. Epstein (1969). Increased feeding in response to decreased glucose utilization in the rat and monkey. *Am. J. Physiol.* 217:1083–1087.

Soll, A. H., C. R. Kahn, D. M. Neville, Jr., and J. Roth (1975). Insulin receptor deficiency in genetic and acquired obesity. *J. Clin. Invest.* 56:769.

Spitzer, L. and J. Rodin (1987). Differential effects of fructose and glucose on food intake. *Appetite* 8:135–145.

Starke, A.A.R., G. Erdhardt, M. Berger, and H. Zimmerman (1984). Elevated pancreatic glucagon in obesity. *Diabetes* 33:277–280.

Stunkard, A. J. (1980). *Obesity*. Philadelphia: Saunders.

Tappy, L., J. P. Randin, J. P. Felber, et al. (1986). Comparison of thermogenic effect of fructose and glucose in normal humans. *Am. J. Physiol.* 250:E718–E724.

Tepperman, J. and H. M. Tepperman (1987). Energy Balance. In: *Metabolic Endocrine Physiology*, 5th ed. Chicago and London: Year Book Medical Publishers.

Thompson, D. A. and R. D. Campbell (1977). Hunger in humans induced by 2-deoxy-D-glucose: glucoprivic control of taste preference and food intake. *Science* 198:1065–1068.

Vasselli, J. R. and A. Sclafani (1979). Hyperreactivity to aversive diets in rats produced by injection of insulin or tolbutamide but not by food deprivation. *Physiol. Behav.* 23:557–567.

Wardle, J. and H. Beinart (1981). Binge eating: A theoretical review. *Brit. J. Clin. Psych.* 20:97–109.

Welle, S. L., D. A. Thompson, R. G. Campbell, and V. Lilavivathana (1980). Increased hunger and thirst during glucoprivation in humans. *Physiol. Behav.* 25:397–403.

Werner, P. L. and J. P. Palmer (1978). Immunoreactive glucagon responses to oral glucose, insulin infusion and deprivation, and somatostatin in pancreatomized man. *Diabetes* 27:1005–1012.

Yamamura, H. I., S. J. Enna, and M. J. Kuhar (1985). *Neurotransmitter Receptor Binding*. New York: Raven Pres.

Zucker, L. M. and N. H. Antoniades (1972). Insulin and obesity in the Zucker genetically obese rat "fatty." *Endocrinology* 90:1320–1330.

INDEX

A

B

C

D

E

F

G

Q

R

S

T

YOUR WEIGHT CHART

Record your weight every day.

Compare only your weekly averages to see if you are losing weight. (To get your average for the week, add up all the weights in that week, and divide by the number of weighings.)

Week Beginning (date)	MON. (weight)	TUES. (weight)	WED. (weight)	THURS. (weight)	FRI. (weight)	SAT. (weight)	SUN. (weight)	Average Weight for Week

YOUR WEIGHT CHART

Record your weight every day.

Compare only your weekly averages to see if you are losing weight. (To get your average for the week, add up all the weights in that week, and divide by the number of weighings.)

Week Beginning (date)	MON. (weight)	TUES. (weight)	WED. (weight)	THURS. (weight)	FRI. (weight)	SAT. (weight)	SUN. (weight)	Average Weight for Week